ENVIRONMENTAL
POLITICS and POLICY

ENVIRONMENTAL POLITICS and POLICY

Walter A. Rosenbaum

University of Florida, Gainesville

A division of Congressional Quarterly Inc.
1414 22nd St., N.W., Washington, D.C. 20037

Printed in the United States of America

Library of Congress Cataloging in Publication Data

Rosenbaum, Walter A.
　　Environmental politics and policy.

　　Bibliography: p.
　　Includes index.
　　1. Environmental policy — United States.　　I. Title.
HC110.E5R665　1984 /9 8 5　　363.7'056'0973　　　　84-14205
ISBN 0-87187-306-0

Preface

This is a book about environmental politics in which environment and politics share equally. I have described for the reader the major political actors, institutions, and values that shape current U.S. environmental policies as well as the controversies that arise in translating those public policies into workable realities. To enliven the discussion I have included many illustrations. Most importantly, I have concentrated upon durable concepts and approaches, thereby providing the reader with insights that will be useful in interpreting future environmental issues.

The organization of the book reflects several themes old and new. First, I have grounded the analysis in the characteristics of the political system that determine most American public policies. Chapter 2 outlines the policy-making process and introduces the reader to fundamental aspects of U.S. government that are essential to understanding environmental policy. This approach seemed particularly useful to those using my earlier book on environmental policy, and I am pleased to preserve it. Second, I have emphasized implementation because so many environmental policies written in the 1970s have reached this crucial stage of policy development. I have provided in Chapters 4 through 8 a discussion of important substantive policy areas, including air pollution, water pollution, toxic and hazardous substances, energy issues, and the public lands.

A new environmental decade yields new themes. Chapter 3 analyzes the controversies that often occur when governmental institutions try to use scientific data essential to setting environmental standards or to resolve scientific disputes over the reliability of the data. Finding an acceptable scientific basis for environmental regulation has become an extremely difficult problem for policy makers. Finally, the Reagan administration merits major attention throughout the book. The environmental controversies spawned by Ronald Reagan and his legion of regulatory reformers raise fundamental and enduring questions about the basic concept of striving for environmental preservation through public agencies.

I am indebted to many people for the completion of this book. To my reviewers, Michael Kraft and Lettie McSpadden Wenner, who bear no responsibility for errors of fact and judgment herein, my thanks for conscientious and informative assistance. My editors Joanne Daniels and Nancy Lammers were consistently helpful and patient, paying especially close attention to factual details. My colleagues Mark Rushefsky and Albert Matheny acted as sympathetic listeners but also as valuable critics and research associates. To many other colleagues who encouraged me over the years to write this book, my appreciation.

Walter A. Rosenbaum
June 1984

Contents

As the 1970s began, Americans seemed to believe that the environment could be cleansed rather quickly.... After roughly a decade's experience ... it has become apparent that controlling pollution is neither easy nor cheap.

—President's Commission for a
National Agenda for the Eighties

'Neither Easy Nor Cheap': Environmental Policy in the 1980s

Late in May 1982 the administrator of the Environmental Protection Agency (EPA), Anne Burford, sent 31 state governors what she delicately described as a "courtesy letter." [1] It was sent, she explained, to eliminate a "surprise" that might otherwise occur when the governors discovered the EPA's intentions. Little more than a decade previously, the nation grandly proclaimed a new "Environmental Era" and committed itself to redressing more than a century's environmental abuse. Now the EPA and the states were apparently rushing toward a multimillion-dollar confrontation over the cost of that commitment. At stake was the Clean Air Act, centerpiece of the ambitious environmental program begun in the 1970s.

From State Plans to Sanctions

Each governor was warned that his or her state was partially or wholly failing to achieve within the required period the air quality standards mandated by the Clean Air Act of 1970. Unless each state could attain the standards by July 1, 1982—an impossibility—the EPA asserted it might impose sanctions: a prohibition on any new stationary source of air pollution and an impoundment of federal grants to highways and to pollution control and sewage treatment facilities.

The sanctions would be an economic shock to state and local economies across the United States. Half the regions failing to achieve the required air quality, the "nonattainment" regions, were located in the

1

nation's industrial heartland: California, Illinois, Louisiana, Michigan, New York, Ohio, and Pennsylvania. All the burgeoning Sun Belt states and most of the nation's major cities were also affected. New York was receiving at that time almost a billion dollars in highway and sewage treatment grants; Florida and California, respectively, were receiving $592 million and $875 million from the programs.[2] And the ban also would mean a virtual moratorium on new industrial and commercial development until air quality standards were attained.

Forcing State Regulation

The struggle beginning in May 1982 was rooted in a congressional gamble that shaped the character of most pollution legislation in the 1970s. Impatient with the glacial pace of state efforts to control air pollution, Congress wrote into the Clean Air Act of 1970 "action forcing" provisions intended to compel more aggressive state restoration of air quality.[3] Specifically, Congress placed in the act provisions intended to force each state to create rapidly a regulatory program for air pollution control, called a State Implementation Plan (SIP). It was a gamble that technical and governmental innovation could be forced by statutory mandate.

The Clean Air Act constituted the most complicated regulatory program ever enacted by Congress. The focus became the hundreds of "air quality airsheds" created by the act as the major administrative units. The act had required each state to produce a SIP demonstrating that it would attain all air pollution standards for airsheds within its boundaries by 1979. By 1977, however, it was apparent that few states would even have implementation plans by 1979.[4] So the Congress reluctantly extended the deadlines. States with nonattainment areas had to produce acceptable implementation plans by 1982 showing they would achieve air quality standards by 1987 for the nonattainment areas. Apparently formidable sanctions were added for failure to produce the 1982 plans. The statutory clock had been set ticking again. The deadline expired with the EPA's warning to the governors in May 1982 that their states had failed to produce the required SIPs.

'Don't Scream At Me.' The confrontation never occurred. EPA and the states were actually marching into an administrative morass where proponents of the Clean Air Act would struggle to enforce the law in a tangle of political squabbling, bureaucratic posturing, and legal wrangling. It was a lesson, frequently taught in the course of the Environmental Era, about the practical obstacles in turning congressional intentions into environmental realities.

EPA was an agency divided. The administrator, Anne Burford, disliked the sanctions she was expected to enforce. Like others in the Reagan administration, she came to Washington determined to give the nation "relief" from what were alleged to be excessive costs and cumbersome regulatory programs, among which she considered the Clean Air Act a prime example. Indeed, following President Ronald Reagan's lead, she had called for revisions of the Clean Air Act intended to relax the deadline for SIPs. Thus, the administrator seemed to be contradicting herself by warning governors they were violating the law while simultaneously broadcasting strong disapproval for the law. Indeed, the administrator hoped to pressure Congress into revising the act by threatening to enforce the sanctions—an action sure to alarm many legislators. As 1982 waned the administrator reminded her audiences that it was not her fault, but the law's, if sanctions were applied. "December 31st is coming and the law has not been changed," she chided a convention of state environmental officials. "We're going to enforce the law. When you all start screaming, don't scream at me. Scream at Congress, because they're the only ones who can do anything about it." [5]

Disputed Interpretations. Another issue enlivening the sanctions conflict was a problem often encountered in environmental legislation: the ambiguity of the law. There were differences of interpretation over when a state was actually liable for sanctions. There were internal arguments over how much of a SIP had to be acceptable. EPA had been left to decide how to interpret the sanction provisions. Yet whatever official position EPA eventually took, interests aggrieved at the interpretation would charge the agency had abused its authority. The trail of the sanctions controversy would be littered by legal briefs over the proper interpretation of every significant clause in the act related to sanctions. [6]

A Congressional Mauling

The sanctions issue also was swept into a virulent partisan battle long running between the majority Democrats in the House of Representatives and Republican Burford. The administrator had been the frequent target of strident criticism from House Democrats, especially those on committees with jurisdiction over the EPA, who accused her of subverting the

3

agency's programs and gutting its budget. This congressional hostility was abetted by environmental organizations that regarded Burford as the personification of the antienvironmentalism they sensed throughout the Reagan administration. The president of the National Audubon Society had dismissed her as "an environmental illiterate." She in turn commonly called her critics "environmental extremists." [7]

The revelation of the proposed EPA sanctions against the states prompted Democrats controlling five House subcommittees with oversight of EPA programs to hold an extraordinary joint session on July 22, 1982. Ostensibly intended to review the administrator's conduct of the agency, the hearings were turned into a media event, staged by the Democrats, where the administrator would be publicly rebuked for the Reagan administration's environmental record. During four hours on July 22, Burford defended herself before committee critics. Most other witnesses had been recruited from among the administrator's outspoken opponents. The tenor of their remarks was captured in the testimony of Sen. Patrick J. Leahy, D-Vt.: "Gorsuch [Burford] has so thoroughly mismanaged EPA's enforcement division that EPA's staff does not know what their job is or whether they dare to do it." [8]

Sanctions in Limbo

The statutory deadline for state submission of acceptable SIPs passed. What EPA now would do about the unacceptable SIPs was not clear. If it meant to impose sanctions, would they be enforced? And against which nonattainment areas? (The agency had carefully avoided a precise definition of which areas would be affected.)

While the issue lingered throughout the hot Washington summer, evidence began to suggest that it may have been difficult for some states to meet the SIP deadlines under any circumstances. EPA, for instance, may have failed to provide as many as 27 states with required guidance documents in sufficient time to meet the deadlines.[9] A variety of studies suggested that many cities then violating air quality standards would be unable to meet the standards even by the 1987 deadline set by Congress. Part of the problem appeared to be technical difficulties: Los Angeles, Houston, and New York, for instance, apparently lacked the necessary control technologies to meet ozone standards.[10] The cost of controls and public resistance also subverted compliance. Virtually every state had rejected mandatory inspection of automobiles to ensure emission control devices were working. Many motorists deliberately removed the devices to increase gas mileage. And many cities shrank from using zoning and other land use controls to keep polluting industries and activities from nonattainment regions lest economic growth be inhibited.

But in the summer of 1982 the ultimate ability of states to comply with the law was a moot issue. The EPA still had to decide what to do about sanctions.

On November 18, 1982, more than four months after the deadline for state compliance with the Clean Air Act had passed, EPA explained its intentions without clarifying much at all. It would begin enforcement against all nonattainment areas in January 1983. But some areas might be given an opportunity to prove they were actually complying with the law. And the agency was only giving notice that it might impose sanctions.

This was enough to draw the Senate into the fray. In December the influential leaders of the Senate Environment and Public Works Committee, where the Clean Air Act had been written and where its implementation was continually observed, wrote the administrator to dispute her interpretations of the sanction provisions in the act. EPA, they insisted, was not in fact compelled to issue the sanctions in January. The warning was clear: the EPA was inviting strong opposition from both congressional chambers if it proceeded with the sanctions.[11]

No sanctions were imposed in January 1983. No sanctions were imposed at all in 1983. Indeed it is unlikely that sanctions of the kind initially threatened by EPA ever will be applied to a nonattainment area.

One reason for EPA's inaction was a succession of administrative crises distracting the agency's leadership in late 1982 and early 1983 and plunging EPA into a series of heated confrontations with Congress. The administrator, acting upon orders from the president, had withheld documents requested by a House committee on grounds the material was a matter of "executive privilege." Before that dispute was settled, the administrator had been held in contempt of Congress—the highest executive branch official ever to be so charged—and shortly thereafter resigned from office. Additionally, several career professionals within the agency were charging before congressional committees that negligence and political manipulation were rampant throughout EPA programs. The administrator's resignation left behind an agency badly demoralized and disorganized, lacking the capacity to push aggressively for sanctions.

Officials within the agency and Congress came to realize, moreover, that administrative delays and technicalities would limit the actual

5

impact of the sanctions and postpone even their formal declaration for a long time.[12] For example, it appeared that a 1982 congressional enactment would make it almost impossible for EPA to cut off quickly federal highway grants to the nonattainment areas. Many state officials, in fact, already recognized that the sanctions were becoming a whip of reeds. It now seemed to numerous participants that the sanctions process might become interminable and that a more prudent course would be to seek informal administrative and political means of persuading the states to achieve the act's goals without depending upon the rapidly dwindling credibility of EPA sanctions. Yet informal methods would take more time; results would be flawed. Some nonattainment areas might never achieve the required air quality in this century. Possibly, a future EPA administrator might revive formal sanctions. In the meantime, the quest for air quality in nonattainment areas would proceed with no assurance of success.

While the end was indecisive, the struggle over sanctions throws into sharp relief many realities about environmental politics and policy that will be encountered repeatedly when other environmental laws are implemented—realities that might too easily be obscured if one focuses only upon the relatively few largely successful programs. The conflict over the Clean Air Act might variously be considered a primer of lessons learned from a decade's experience with environmental policy, a portrait of contemporary environmental politics, and a portent of future environmental trends. In short it sets several themes for this book.

Some Lessons About Environmental Reform

We stand on the farther shore of environmental reforms that swept the United States in the 1970s, the most innovative environmental era in a century. "It may well be," noted the Commission for a National Agenda for the Eighties, "that no other domestic policy challenge of recent times has been addressed as forcefully and quickly." [13] Its legacy is a multitude of ambitious, unprecedented laws, including the Clean Air Act (1970), the Toxic Substances Control Act (1976), the National Environmental Policy Act (1970), and the Surface Mining Control and Reclamation Act (1977), whose collective purpose was to compel through public policy a reversal of two centuries' environmental negligence and to force a new public responsibility for future environmental protection. Its inheritance is also an arduous, often frustrating, and extraordinarily difficult task of translating these statutes, among the most legally and technically complex laws ever enacted in the United States, into effective public policy.

Implementing environmental laws has been far more difficult, protracted, and costly than proponents of environmental reform had ever anticipated. "Neither easy nor cheap," the words of the president's commission, should be the first admonition in any catechism for environmental preservation. The tortured progress of EPA's sanctions against the states typifies the practical complications to which the commission refers. These are more than unanticipated problems, inevitable in any new program. Proponents of environmental reform often chose deliberately to ignore or to minimize the intimidating problems they fully recognized would arise. Determined to force solutions to problems through legislative formulas and persistence in enforcement, they refused to compromise ambitious regulatory goals through what they regarded as excessive caution for practical difficulties in implementation. Many difficulties common to environmental policy today testify that such a strategy was only partially successful.

The Limits to 'Pressing Technology'

During floor debate prior to the Senate's passage of the Clean Air Act, critics warned that the legislation would be unenforceable because it established air quality standards and compliance deadlines for pollution control then beyond the technical capacity of polluters to achieve. Edmund Muskie, D-Maine, the act's most prominent senatorial sponsor, responded with an argument that inspired a multitude of later congressional laws on environmental protection. "Predictions of technological impossibility or infeasibility are not sufficient as reasons to avoid tough standards and deadlines, and thus to compromise the public health. . . . Only clear and tough public policy can generate the needed effort." [14]

This determination to "press technology" rested upon a faith that regulated interests could be driven to obtain the required technical controls by statutory deadlines. It was a measure of congressional impatience with past strategies that had awaited the development of the necessary technologies before imposing stringent emission controls. Regulated interests often deliberately delayed development of the technologies as long as possible and thus avoided tougher standards. Now the approach was reversed. "Rather than regulate from the standpoint of what was technically feasible, it started from the point of determining what air

7

standards were necessary to protect public health and it required technology to meet these standards." [15] It was also shrewd politics. Congress, like the White House, was aware of the environmental movement's growing political strength in the early 1970s. Pressing technology powerfully appealed to the movement and afforded legislators a chance to wrap themselves in the mantle of environmentalism.

Soon pressing technology was almost axiomatic in writing federal environmental programs. The nation's major water pollution control law, the Federal Water Pollution Control Act, made no concessions to the limits of existing water pollution control technologies; it insisted that all the nation's major waterways should be made "fishable and swimmable" by 1983 and that "all discharges" of pollutants should be eliminated from navigable waterways by 1985. The Toxic Substances Control Act (1976) required, among other things, that the EPA create an inventory of all major chemical substances used in U.S. industry—a potential list exceeding 55,000 different substances—and demanded detailed information about the chemical, biological, and environmental characteristics of each chemical despite the absence of such data on a vast number of substances. In 1977 Congress amended the Federal Water Pollution Control Act by requiring industry-by-industry standards for the pretreatment of 65 toxics associated with 22 industries. At the time the technology essential for achieving such standards often did not exist or remained unreliable. [16] And so, in these and many other instances, Congress resolutely pressed technology on the presumption that the requisite technologies could be summoned if only enough regulatory pressure were applied.

Sometimes the approach worked. For instance, the technology to control auto hydrocarbon emissions had existed since the 1930s. But only after the federal government began enforcing stringent national emission standards for hydrocarbons through the Clean Air Act did the American automobile industry develop the positive crankcase ventilation technology and apply it to production models in time to satisfy emission deadlines mandated by the act. [17] The fuel-economy standards required by the Energy Policy and Conservation Act (1975) hastened the appearance of more fuel-efficient U.S. auto engines to the extent that General Motors and the Chrysler Corporation both are expected to exceed the required 1985 standards of 27.5 miles per gallon by several additional miles.

But the law often failed to press into existence the required technologies, operating at anticipated efficiency, within the allotted time.

Compliance deadlines for pollution emissions frequently passed unmet. Air and water quality standards, dependent upon undeveloped control technologies, were unattained. One reason why the United States did not attain "fishable and swimmable" waters by 1983 as required by the Federal Water Pollution Control Act was that a technology still does not exist to control nonpoint pollution sources, such as farmlands, forests, or construction sites, which pour as much as 79 percent of all nitrates and 92 percent of all suspended solids into U.S. surface waters.[18] The strategy of pressing technology has failed at some crucial phase in almost all major U.S. programs affecting air and water quality, hazardous substances, and nuclear energy regulation.

Despite its failures, however, pressing technology does often serve a useful purpose. It can put a regulated interest's "feet to the fire," forcing a faster pace of pollution management and greater innovation in emission control technologies than might occur without such persistent pressure. But there are costs to be paid for such pressure: (1) confusion and delay in implementing regulations; (2) expensive and time-consuming litigation over the appropriateness or feasibility of regulations; (3) frequent resort to technical "quick fixes" to meet statutory standards when more efficient and economical technologies might be available with more time; and (4) continual setbacks in compliance deadlines that diminish the credibility of programs and leave regulated interests uncertain about future policy.

Politics and Partisanship

EPA Administrator Burford's abrasive confrontations with congressional Democrats over the Clean Air Act's sanctions are a reminder that environmental policy making is, and always has been, a political affair. While the Reagan administration's determination to impose "regulatory relief" upon environmental programs provoked the bitterest partisan battles over environmental policy in a half century, every administration has its share of political conflicts and partisan squabbles over environmental management. Under Burford, the EPA leadership commonly assumed a viewpoint sympathetic to business and other regulated interests, whereas Congress often took an environmentalist position. But the political polarities between Congress and EPA can change. Under the Carter administration, for instance, the EPA was pressing for more stringent auto emission controls, and Congress was urging a relaxation of existing emission control deadlines.

Where the institutions stand on issues depends, in good part, on who sits in the White House. Although President Richard Nixon took considerable credit for initiating the Environmental Era, he also impounded more than $5 billion in congressional grants authorized by the Federal Water Pollution Control Act for water quality management when the expenditures violated his 1975 budget guidelines. President Gerald R. Ford aroused the ire of environmentalists and congressional liberals in both parties by twice vetoing legislation creating a national surface mining regulatory program. And President Jimmy Carter, the most environmentally sensitive of all recent presidents, nonetheless provoked controversy by bringing pressure on the EPA to relax auto emission standards for several pollutants in an effort to reduce regulatory costs to the U.S. auto industry.

Efforts have been made to design public laws and institutions that will free environmental policies, particularly at the implementation and enforcement stages, from politics. Persuasive arguments have been made for insulating environmental management whenever possible from the mischief of faction or political manipulation. Nevertheless, in any domain where public institutions assume authority, one can never wholly quarantine government from politics. There are many reasons why this is so. The major parties disagree about the priority of environmental issues among other national concerns, about the effectiveness of various regulatory strategies, about the relative burden the public and private sectors should bear for environmental restoration. As the estimated expenditures for environmental protection mount—total public and private spending is estimated to reach $518 billion between 1979 and 1988—party officials feel a strong responsibility to exert their influence throughout the governmental process to affect such massive allocations.[19] Presidents, particularly, occupy a strategic position for influencing environmental policy through executive powers such as budgeting, appointing executive branch officials, preparing legislative programs, and managing the executive branch.

The bureaucracy, where environmental programs are implemented, offers many opportunities for presidents, members of Congress, organized interests, and others with a stake in environmental policy to shape decisions to their advantage. Administrators invite such partisan pressure primarily because bureaucrats exercise "administrative discretion"—the authority to determine when, where, and how to interpret the law. Thus the administrative process is permeated by the play of political influence and conflict. Moreover, environmental programs are often bundles of distributive benefits—grants for waste treatment plants, new flood control projects, major scientific research facilities, and so forth—which members of Congress covet for constituencies. The aroma of political pork emanating from many environmental programs is sufficient to invite intense congressional bargaining and conflict over program design and implementation.

These competing forces impose costs on environmental management. Perhaps the most severe costs arise when the major parties strongly disagree over goals and procedures for environmental management. Such deep cleavages—when one party displaces another in the White House or congressional party alignments shift substantially—can lead to sharp discontinuities of policy, abrupt changes in program funding or management, and costly delay in program implementation. Leaders of both parties attempted in the early 1970s to create a tradition of bipartisan support reaching from Congress to the White House for environmental policy. Bipartisanship endured throughout the 1970s but largely evaporated with the advent of the Reagan presidency and the appearance of the first Republican majority in the Senate since 1955. The president's promised regulatory reforms were seen by critics as a sharp reversal of almost all major federal environmental programs enacted since 1970. Congressional debate over the proposals was strident and partisan; congressional Democrats, considering themselves guardians of the imperiled programs, regarded the president's regulatory agenda as an assault upon their legislative record. Environmentalists saw "regulatory relief" as the cutting edge of a massive administrative assault on the legislative foundations of the Environmental Era. They almost unanimously considered the Reagan administration as the most environmentally hostile presidency in a half century and rallied behind his Democratic critics.

In this polarizing milieu, debate over Reagan's environmental program was laced with the acid-dripped invective that became the usual style of address between the administration and its critics:

> I don't think they'll be happy until the White House looks like a bird's nest. (President Reagan about environmental critics).[20]

> We have witnessed across the board a pattern of lawlessness and heedlessness with regard to the nation's natural resources unequaled since the days of the robber barons a century ago. (An evaluation by the Sierra Club, Natural Resources Defense Council, Wilderness Society, and Solar Lobby).[21]

Efforts by Reagan administration officials to change policy and personnel in environmentally sensitive agencies such as the EPA and Department of the Interior produced the conflict, confusion, and congressional controversy illustrated by the sanctions conflict. Indeed, no agency suffered more severely or publicly from such disruptions than the EPA.

In a broader perspective, it is almost inevitable that politics will affect environmental policy in some manner no matter what party controls the White House or Congress, particularly when the EPA remains an executive agency whose leadership is appointed by the president. Executive managers appointed by the president to environmental agencies customarily come to their jobs with a zeal to carry out the president's environmental commitments; otherwise they would not have been cleared for their position by the usual White House review for such appointments. Moreover, such executives usually regard themselves as bearers of a public mandate, given at the presidential election, to make policy changes. And, as we shall often observe, there is ample opportunity in all environmental programs for such partisan influence to shape policies. This partisan bias to policy making, however, can create dangerous and irresponsible decisions when policy makers are willing to ignore or manipulate scientific information, expose the public to serious health risks, or disregard their mandated legal responsibilities to gain some partisan end.

Even without partisan conflict, implementing environmental policy would be complicated by the continual need to reconcile different interests and to build a broad consensus on policy among those with a stake in implementation. In fact environmental administration is, in large part, the business of reconciling conflicts and building supportive coalitions. All this is often tedious and time consuming; it often fails, and political conflict erupts. In short managing and reconciling political interests have become a continuing task in environmental regulation and an essential one for effective environmental programs.

The Cost of Progress

Total national spending for environmental quality, rising in absolute terms steadily through the last decade, will continue growing through the 1980s. The Council on Environmental Quality (CEQ) estimates that the nation spent approximately $271.7 billion on pollution abatement between 1972 and 1979. Between 1979 and 1988 the CEQ anticipates the nation will spend an additional $518.5 billion for the same purpose.[22] Table 1-1 indicates how this future spending will be allocated between

Table 1-1 Estimated Incremental Pollution Abatement Expenditures: 1979-1988[*] (billions of 1979 dollars)

Program	1979			1988			Cumulative (1979-1988)		
	Operation and maintenance	Annual capital costs[a]	Total annual costs	Operation and maintenance	Annual capital costs[a]	Total annual costs	Operation and maintenance	Capital costs[a]	Total costs
Air pollution									
Public	1.2	.3	1.5	2.0	.5	2.5	15.8	3.7	19.5
Private									
Mobile	3.2	4.9	8.1	3.7	11.0	14.7	32.1	83.7	115.8
Industrial	2.0	2.3	4.3	3.0	4.1	7.1	25.8	33.0	58.8
Electric utilities	5.5	2.9	8.4	7.6	5.7	13.3	62.3	42.7	105.0
Subtotal	11.9	10.4	22.3	16.3	21.3	37.6	136.0	163.1	299.1
Water pollution									
Public	1.7	4.3	6.0	3.3	10.0	13.3	25.1	59.2	84.3
Private									
Industrial	3.4	2.6	6.0	5.4	4.5	9.9	42.0	34.0	76.0
Electric utilities	.3	.4	.7	.3	.9	1.2	2.9	6.5	9.4
Subtotal	5.4	7.3	12.7	9.0	15.4	24.4	70.0	99.7	169.7
Solid waste									
Public	<.05	<.05	<.05	.4	.3	.7	2.6	2.0	4.6
Private	<.05	<.05	<.05	.9	.7	1.6	6.4	4.4	10.8
Subtotal	<.05	<.05	<.05	1.3	1.0	2.3	9.0	6.4	15.4
Toxic substances	.1	.2	.3	.5	.6	1.1	3.6	4.6	8.2
Drinking water	<.05	<.05	<.05	.1	.3	.4	1.3	1.4	2.7
Noise	<.05	.1	.1	.6	1.0	1.6	2.6	4.3	6.9
Pesticides	.1	<.05	.1	.1	<.05	.1	1.2	<.05	1.2
Land reclamation	.3	1.1	1.4	.3	1.2	1.5	3.8	11.5	15.3
Total	17.8	19.1	36.9	28.2	40.8	69.0	227.5	291.0	518.5

[*] Incremental costs are those made in response to federal legislation beyond those that would have been made in the absence of that legislation.

[a] Interest and depreciation.

Source: Council on Environmental Quality, *Environmental Quality 1980* (Washington, D.C.: Government Printing Office, 1981), 394.

the public and private sectors and among major pollution programs.

Although the CEQ estimates that pollution abatement costs in the early 1980s constituted only 1.5 percent of the Gross National Product (GNP), these costs will be growing at a real rate exceeding 7 percent annually through the 1980s. Continuing cost escalations have been a major concern of the private sector, which is expected to assume about 93 percent of the incremental costs for air pollution control and about 50 percent of similar costs for water quality controls between 1979 and 1988.[23] Equally important, experience over the last decade suggests that the projected costs of existing pollution programs are nearly always underestimated, while unanticipated new programs add unexpected billions to future spending.

Pollution costs exceed projections partially because the pervasiveness of environmental damage and the difficulty of removing pollutants from complex ecological systems are usually underestimated. This is perhaps inevitable when the nation lacks experience with pollution abatement. But proponents of pollution control often accept conservative estimates of program costs that prove, deliberately or not, deceptively low. It is also the habit of Congress continually to amend pollution abatement programs with expensive new provisions. Thus, unanticipated costs are almost predestined in any abatement program:

> The Federal Water Pollution Control Act (1972) authorized $18 billion in federal grants to the states to construct sewage treatment plants; with matching state grants, the program was estimated to cost approximately $24 billion. But by 1976 the National Commission on Water Quality, appointed by the president to evaluate the program, reported it would cost at least $39.2 billion more to achieve the program's minimal objectives. All the treatment goals would add another $309 billion. By the mid-1980s, Congress had committed about $36 billion to the program.[24]

Further inflating costs is the continuing discovery of new environmental degradation requiring quick remedial action. The Love Canal tragedy of 1977, followed rapidly by other revelations of recklessly abandoned toxic wastes menacing public health, compelled the federal government to enact the Comprehensive Environmental Response, Compensation and Liability Act (1980). Known as "Superfund," the bill authorized initial expenditures of $1.6 billion to clean up the nation's worst abandoned hazardous waste sites. As the magnitude of abandoned waste sites becomes more apparent, Congress confronts the possibility of having to assist in cleaning up more than 40,000 lethal chemical dumps

whose detoxification is likely to cost many times the Superfund investment.

Other contributors to cost inflation are the congressional mandates in
several major environmental programs that require administrators to
ignore costs in promulgating control standards for harmful substances or
to balance other considerations against costs. Statutory language in such
instances customarily requires, or strongly favors, giving primary or
exclusive consideration to public health in standard setting. One controversial example of a cost-oblivious approach is found in section 109(b) of
the Clean Air Act, which instructs the EPA administrator to set "primary
standards" for major air pollutants at a level that in his judgment is
"requisite to protect public health" and that incudes "an adequate
margin of safety." No cost considerations are explicitly mandated in the
act. "The purpose of this mandate," writes one of its principal authors, "is
to require the Administrator to resolve any doubts created by conflicting
or ambiguous evidence on the side of protection of health." [25]

Critics charge that criteria that ignore, or minimize, the importance
of cost considerations in setting environmental standards encourage
administrators to set standards so stringently in the interest of public
health that compliance costs are excessive when compared with public
benefits. Regardless of the merit in this argument, it is apparent that
congressional mandates ignoring cost-benefit balancing in setting pollution standards have contributed substantially to the rising costs of
pollution management.

Administration and Litigation

The legislative foundation for current public policy toward the
environment was laid in a great outpouring of environmental laws in the
1970s. With the exception of the Superfund bill, no major new environmental programs have emerged from Congress and relatively few are
likely in this decade. During the 1980s the administrative and judicial
branches of the federal government will be the primary governmental
arenas for environmental policy as it increasingly progresses from the
stages where Congress dominates—the business of agenda setting and
policy formulation—to policy implementation and appraisal, which
concern especially the bureaucracy and the courts. Congress continues to
exert considerable influence on environmental policy through the budget,
administrative oversight, investigations, and legislation; amendments to
existing environmental programs and perhaps a few new enactments are

15

still likely. Still, since the mid-1970s, the bureaucracy and courts have assumed an increasingly broad and visible role in making environmental policy.

It is not surprising, in this perspective, that the EPA should have been the focus of controversy swirling about enforcement of the Clean Air Act's sanctions. And it is predictable that the controversy will eventually end in the federal courts. The complex task of translating broad legislative mandates into operational environmental programs and clarifying the language or intent of the law is the business of administrator and judge. This normal development of policy making in the U.S. political system invests the bureaucracy and courts with considerable power to make public policy in the act of implementing or interpreting legislative language. Indeed, environmental policy is essentially a set of paper promises sanctified by legislative majorities until it is implemented and interpreted.

The evolution of the environmental impact statement requirement in the National Environmental Policy Act of 1969 (NEPA) illustrates the importance of administrator and judge in policy development. The purpose of this requirement was to encourage federal agencies to consider more carefully the environmental consequences of their programs and to adopt more ecologically sensitive programs whenever possible. But the language of the law was broad and vague. NEPA's section 102 required all federal agencies to prepare impact statements for "all Federal actions significantly affecting the quality of the human environment" and specified the general content. But it was left to the CEQ, an executive agency, to create the guidelines for this complex and unprecedented procedure in collaboration with the administrative agencies that would implement it. In this manner, administrative agencies assumed a major responsibility for defining the law's scope and impact by making crucial decisions relating to the nature of specific agency programs to which impact statements would apply, the detailed content of the statements, and the appropriate review procedure within each agency.

By 1980 more than 45 federal agencies ranging from the Agriculture Department to the Veteran's Administration filed 966 draft and final impact statements with the CEQ.[26] These statements covered an enormous diversity of federal projects including highway and road construction, subsidized housing, location of historic sites, energy projects, and toxic substances. The agencies were largely responsible for the identification of their own programs subject to impact review and for the writing, circulating, and publishing of the statements. In this manner, the bureaucracy translated an abstract legislative mandate into operational programs.

The federal courts assumed an equally important role in the impact statement process. Federal judges very early insisted on careful and complete agency compliance with the law when some bureaucracies balked and stalled. Judges interpreted the law and its various administrative guidelines in a manner that ensured agencies would take their responsibilities seriously. "When enforcement from the Executive Office lagged," writes Fred Anderson of NEPA's first years, "the courts moved to fill the vacuum and began to review issues such as whether an impact statement had to be prepared or whether it was adequate." [27] Within a few years, he continues, "the courts had established a commanding presence as interpreter of the magnitude of 'procedural' questions of law presented by the legislation." By the end of that decade, notes another scholar, the courts had become "a highly visible influence on agency behavior" through interpretations of NEPA.[28]

Despite the importance of these and other events of the 1970s, the environmental policies of the 1980s will still be more than a newer edition of last decade's politics. Growing competition for capital between environmental regulation and other economic activity in both public and private sectors has provoked a new debate over the strategies and goals acceptable for environmental management. Concurrently, newly discovered sources of environmental deterioration, some highly toxic and eminently threatening, are fresh reminders that environmental restoration is still an urgent and complex task. Our growing technical capacity to identify, measure, and assess the risks to man and environment from low-level exposure to a multitude of widely dispersed hazardous substances has awakened growing concern about the adequacy of existing controls for such substances.

Emerging Issues of the 1980s

Environmental laws of the 1970s attacked the most visible and seemingly acute forms of environmental degradation: air contaminants such as sulfur oxides and photochemical smog, water pollutants such as dissolved organic chemicals producing lake eutrophication or the ubiquitous pesticide residue killing gamefish, shellfish, and their predators. In the process of acquiring the scientific data essential to establish environmental standards for such obvious pollutants, it has become apparent that other equally severe forms of environmental degradation have been caused, or intensified, by the dissemination of these early-recognized pollutants. Indeed, the agenda of new environmental problems in the 1980s is a confirmation of ecologist Barry Commoner's First Law of Ecology: "Everything Is Connected to Everything Else." [29] In tracing the intricate relationship between pollution and environmental quality, we have also come to appreciate Commoner's linking of obvious pollution processes with a more subtle, longer-lived but equally dangerous cycle of ecological deterioration with which we must reckon in this decade.

The nation's massive economic investment in environmental regulation and its broad legislative commitment to environmental restoration have produced significant achievements. Yet the nation's environment is still seriously polluted, its regulatory restraints on environmental degradation still somewhat brittle and incompletely tested, its appreciation of the full implications to continuing environmental pollution still comparatively primitive. A continuing public commitment to vigorous environmental regulation is needed in the 1980s.

By several conventional measures, the nation's air and waters have indeed improved. The total volume of regulated air pollutants such as suspended particulates, carbon monoxide, and sulfur oxides has diminished significantly since 1974. Progress has been particularly marked in urban areas where, for instance, the number of days measured as "unhealthful," "very unhealthful," or "hazardous" in the nation's 40 major metropolitan areas decreased from an average of 87 in 1974 to fewer than than 60 in 1980.[30] Data from the most comprehensive national monitoring of surface water quality, the National Stream Quality Accounting Network (NASQAN), show little deterioration in the last few years despite increasing population growth, greater production of water pollutants, and more competition for water use among industry, communities, and agriculture.[31] Such data suggest that the Clean Air Act, the Federal Water Pollution Control Act, and other regulatory programs of the 1970s are beginning to have an impact upon environmental quality.

It is becoming evident, however, that many regulated pollutants are not yet properly controlled and more importantly that new pollutants or newly discovered adverse impacts of known pollutants will probably require further controls. Growing awareness of new pollution problems is largely the result of research initiated to gather information for the first time on the human and environmental effects of pollutants scarcely studied until a decade ago.

Consider, for instance, suspended particulates, the microscopic particles of solid or liquid substances released into the air from fuel combustion, industrial processes, agricultural activity, and road transportation. Current air quality standards for particulates set a decade ago are based on total mass or weight in a cubic meter of air regardless of particle size. Recent research reveals that it is the smallest particles, three microns or less, that pass readily into the lungs with the most damaging effect.[32] Existing control technologies are largely ineffective in reducing the smallest particulates, and consequently the total mass of particulates can be reduced in ambient air without limiting the most dangerous types. Existing air quality standards, moreover, do not take into account the synergistic effect between two pollutants—that is, their impact in combination. A moderate amount of sulfur dioxide greatly enhances the damage done by suspended particulates; ozone and sulfur oxide also have adverse synergistic impacts. In this manner research forces a continuing reappraisal of existing air quality standards and pressure for more stringent control of known pollutants.

New Air Pollution Issues

Three major air pollution problems have come to full visibility only in this decade. If these problems are to be attacked, each will require major modification of existing regulatory programs, as later chapters will indicate.

1. *Hazardous Air Pollutants:* Although the Clean Air Act requires the EPA to establish national emission standards for air pollutants posing a particularly acute hazard to public health, only four of the suspected pollutants are currently regulated (beryllium, mercury, asbestos, and vinyl chloride). A great many other substances, including arsenic, benzene, radionuclides, and formaldehyde are currently under investigation; many will prove sufficiently dangerous to require new regulation.

2. *The Greenhouse Effect:* In 1982 the National Academy of Sciences warned that the "continued rise in atmospheric CO_2 (carbon dioxide) concentrations poses potentially severe long-term risks to the global climate and to the biological systems that depend upon it."[33] A decade ago, the so-called Greenhouse Effect was largely scientific speculation appearing to many responsible critics closer to science fiction than to science. The growing scientific evidence that continued carbon dioxide emissions worldwide from fossil fuel combustion may create a dangerous, and possibly cataclysmic, warming of the earth's atmosphere is now causing great concern that it may be necessary within a few decades to abate

much of the nation's currently unregulated carbon dioxide emissions.

3. *Acid Rain:* About 30 million tons of sulfur dioxide and 20 million tons of nitrogen oxide yearly rise into the atmosphere from the nation's industries, public utilities, and motor vehicles. High-level winds often transport these gases hundreds of miles from their origin; forming sulfate and nitrate aerosols, they combine with water vapor into precipitation returning to the earth as acid rain or snow.[34] Acid precipitation, now found throughout the United States, has become common in the northeastern United States and eastern Canada. A federal interagency task force reported in 1981 that the average northeastern rainfall had increased 10 times above normal acidity—in some areas, a thousandfold.[35] This continuing acid precipitation is suspected of rendering hundreds of mountain lakes in the United States and Canada ecologically sterile and disrupting the related forest ecosystems. Acid precipitation appears to be growing in severity and dispersion. Current U.S. air emission standards are apparently inadequate to control the precursors of acid precipitation, and measures may be necessary in this decade to prevent the continuing loss of productive land and water to acid from the sky.

Continuing Water Quality Problems

Protecting the nation's water quality often presents a more formidable problem than regulating air pollution because the nation's surface and underground waters can assimilate literally thousands of potential pollutants: organic and inorganic chemicals, suspended solids, metabolic waste and other biological contaminants, heavy metals, agricultural and urban runoff, and more. Both surface and underground water, moreover, must be monitored. The continual proliferation of new chemicals in the United States and elsewhere means that protecting the nation's water is a continual race against technological innovation to achieve water quality standards before new hazardous substances become widely distributed. It is hardly surprising, then, that the nation faces in the 1980s water quality problems yet to be satisfactorily resolved:

1. *Nonpoint Pollution:* The Federal Water Pollution Control Act authorized the EPA to regulate nonpoint sources of water pollution; but the agency, faced with the enormous difficulty, largely ignored the job in order to attack more immediately threatening and manageable pollution problems. Last decade's unfinished business must be confronted in the 1980s. "For the nation to have clean waters," declared the CEQ in 1981, "it must become a high national priority to ensure that nonpoint controls are properly installed, maintained and operated." [36] More than half the pollutants entering the nation's waters originate in nonpoint sources such as agriculture, silviculture, urban runoff, and septic tank systems. Nearly every U.S. water basin is affected.

2. *Toxic and Hazardous Substances:* In recent years, growing awareness of many

hazardous or toxic substances in ground water has led to greater emphasis upon their regulation. Among the toxic substances that EPA has identified recently as priority pollutants (those posing potentially serious risks to human and aquatic life) are arsenic, cadmium, chromium, copper, cyanide, lead, silver, mercury, and the synthetic chemical groups—PCBs and phthalate esters.[37] Studies of water supplies in major U.S. urban areas also suggest the widespread presence of many synthetic organic compounds suspected of being hazardous to human and animal life. Data on the risk of exposure to these synthetic chemicals are often fragmentary and inconclusive, but the growing dispersion of these materials throughout the ecosystem adds urgency to the quest for understanding and control of those whose effects are proven dangerous.

Toxics: An Emerging Menace

Perhaps the most universally recognized environmental threat of the 1980s, however, invades every aspect of the ecosystem. Toxic substances—more precisely, hazardous and toxic substances—have become the most widely publicized environmental issue of the 1980s as a result of nationwide revelations of abandoned hazardous waste sites, recklessly dumped toxic chemicals, and proven or suspected deaths and severe injuries attributable to exposure to hazardous substances in home or workplace. Each year about 90 percent of the 77 billion pounds of additional hazardous waste generated in the United States is unsafely disposed. More than 43,000 chemicals used in U.S. commerce are now subject to safety review by the federal government.

Although the federal government obtained in the 1970s authority to regulate the manufacture, sale, distribution, and eventual disposal of hazardous chemicals through legislation such as the Toxic Substances Control Act and the Resource Conservation and Recovery Act, public and governmental concern about hazardous substances lagged until the 1980s. Moreover, the nation has yet to identify and use a safe permanent repository for more than 85,000 tons of high-level radioactive waste accumulating since World War II in temporary, often poorly managed, sites from military research and weapons development, nuclear power plants, and civilian research. One statistic emerging from a fog of uncertainty about hazardous waste suggests the magnitude of the problem facing the United States: the EPA estimates, with considerable conservatism, that at least 1,200 to 2,000 known waste sites across the country may pose significant risks to human health and the environment. Lethal landfills, however, may vastly exceed this number when those presently forgotten, abandoned, or buried are finally revealed.

The Cost-Benefit Controversy

In the 1980s a major concern reaching across all branches and levels of government has arisen over the acceptability of costs associated with environmental protection. The controversy concerns a set of related issues. First, can environmental regulations, or at least some specific programs, be economically justified? As the President's Commission for a National Agenda explains, the issue isn't simple:

> Some critics maintain that tighter pollution controls will cause higher unemployment and consumer prices and lead to unproductive use of capital. Others defend pollution control standards by claiming that they help create jobs, cause only a relatively minor, one-time increase in consumer prices, and offer the economy benefits such as lower future clean-up costs or the encouragement of innovation. Potential costs are likely to be exaggerated by those subject to the stricter standards, while advocates of the standards are inclined to minimize the economic burdens. The actual cost of complying with a pollution control standard is an elusive figure and usually in dispute.[38]

A related matter is whether current methods of controlling pollution, rather than the goals, are economically efficient. Opponents of current regulatory programs have been harshly critical of the "command-and-control" or "standards-and-enforcement" procedure through which the government traditionally has attempted to regulate environmental quality. This approach, requiring the government to set environmental standards, prescribe the necessary control technologies, monitor pollution emissions, and enforce penalties upon violators, has been criticized as economically wasteful and inefficient; a better procedure, assert many economists and other critics, would be to create economic incentives through arrangements—such as a pollution tax—that offer more economic rewards for pollution control.

Finally, proponents of regulatory reform usually maintain that federal and state regulatory agencies should be required routinely to evaluate proposed new regulations, or changes in existing ones, by a cost-benefit analysis—a practice, we have earlier observed, not widely sanctioned in existing federal law. The presumption animating this enthusiasm for cost-benefit analysis is that agencies would be more likely to select cost-effective, or benefit-maximizing regulations, measured in monetary terms, if disciplined by a cost-benefit consciousness.

The Carter administration attempted in its latter years to awaken some cost awareness among regulation writers through arrangements such as inspection of federal regulations by the White House's Regulatory Analysis Review Group, but the most outspoken and aggressive champion of cost-benefit thinking in federal regulation since the 1970s became the Reagan administration. Indeed, the administration's "regulatory relief" gospel was largely a shorthand for cost-benefit analysis practiced almost universally by federal regulation writers.

The Reagan administration had been in office little more than a month when the president issued Executive Order 12291, which was intended to ensure that cost-benefit thinking would forthwith inspire the bureaucracy. Among the principles mandated by the order was that, in writing new regulations, the federal regulatory agencies should ensure that "the potential benefits to society of implementing regulatory action must outweigh the potential costs. . . ." All agencies were expected to "adhere to these requirements to the extent permitted by law." The order, however, fell short of requiring a rigorous cost-benefit analysis in purely monetary terms; many agencies also escaped strict compliance through responsibility for regulatory programs that required other statutory standards. As the years progressed, the administration found it easier to extol than to practice the virtues of cost-benefit analysis. But its determination to force cost-benefit thinking upon regulatory agencies set the administration on a collision course with many legislators, particularly congressional Democrats, and the majority of environmental groups. Opponents regarded cost-benefit, like other Reagan programs aimed at reducing the costs of environmental regulation, as a covert effort to weaken environmental laws to the benefit of the business community, which the administration candidly recognized as one of its principal constituencies. So cost-benefit analysis and other programs for "regulatory relief" became chronic sources of bitter controversy between environmental groups and the Reagan administration.

The controversy has had other impacts. It has stimulated a critical reexamination of many economical yet equally effective ways of achieving environmental quality. It has also encouraged studies revealing more clearly the strength and direction of public support for environmental policies as well as public tolerances for the costs involved. Finally, the controversy has significantly shifted environmental policy within agencies such as the EPA and the Department of the Interior away from earlier practices and towards goals strongly favored by the Reagan administration. We shall examine these implications further in later chapters.

A Global Perspective

The world ecosystem compels the United States to share with the world's other nations a common environmental responsibility and ecological destiny. Most environmental problems currently confronting the United States are, in fact, global; almost all nations contribute to global degradation and will share the consequences in an ecosystem where national boundaries cannot insulate a people from ecological interdependence. It has become increasingly evident in the last decade that the United States cannot expect to remedy its own ecological ills unless it is prepared to collaborate internationally in research, control, and education on environmental problems. As the developing countries industrialize and acquire a growing diversity of new technologies, existing stresses upon the global ecosystem introduced by population pressures will be compounded. With growing sophistication in methods of forecasting world ecological trends, the need for immediate, worldwide collaboration in environmental protection appears more obvious. "If present trends continue," warned the CEQ in its *Global 2000 Report* of 1980, "the world of 2000 will be more crowded, more polluted, less stable ecologically, and more vulnerable to disruption than the world we live in now. Serious stresses involving population, resources, and the environment are clearly visible ahead." [39] This was no doomsday pronouncement, for the council foresaw methods that, initiated early enough, might reverse some of these trends through international cooperation. But time is fleeting.

The global scale of U.S. environmental problems can be illustrated by briefly examining the nation's air quality. The mounting concentration of carbon dioxide in ambient air across the United States is part of a global trend; concern for the Greenhouse Effect should be a world issue. Global energy production is expected to rise throughout the remainder of the century by 1.5 percent to 3 percent yearly; this newer energy will be generated largely by fossil fuels responsible for most of the increased carbon dioxide emissions expected globally. Thus, the United States cannot unilaterally expect to diminish significantly the accumulation of global carbon dioxide or to ensure its own climatological protection; other industrialized and developing countries must also abate their own carbon dioxide emissions. The need for international action prompted the United Nations General Assembly in 1981 to list the atmospheric carbon dioxide problem as high priority for its ecological agenda of the decade. Scientists have also been concerned for almost a decade with the possibly serious ozone depletion in ambient air worldwide as a result of increasing international use of chlorofluorocarbons (CFCs) in aerosol containers, air conditioning equipment, and industrial processes. Atmospheric ozone is believed essential to protect humans from dangerous exposure to ultraviolet light currently screened by upper atmosphere ozone. CFCs are suspected of depleting this free atmospheric ozone by chemical alteration. While evidence of this depletion remains inconclusive, a number of nations, including Canada, Norway, Sweden, Japan, Australia, and the United States have agreed to limit continued CFC production. Any long-term management of CFCs, however, requires a far more comprehensive and difficult global collaboration among more nations.

Finally, acid precipitation is a worldwide issue. Research suggests that more than half the volume of acid gases that become the precursors of acid precipitation in Canada may originate in the United States and perhaps a third of the volume affecting the United States may, in turn, originate in Canada. The nations of western and northern Europe currently afflicted by acid precipitation, particularly the Scandanavian countries, seem to have inherited truly multinational degradation because complex, high-level wind streams often mix the gaseous emissions of many European nations before depositing a portion on each.

Many other environmental ills have global impacts, including the disappearance of ecological diversity, the progressive deforestation of mountains and rainforests, and the dissemination of persistent hazardous substances. Even among the world's environmentally progressive institutions, priorities for international cooperation remain underdeveloped in comparison with structures for purely national pollution abatement. The development of a global perspective on environmental management remains both a challenge and an essential step in the 1980s for the truly effective conservation of each nation's environmental heritage.

The Continuing Primacy of Politics

No domain of public authority in the United States has expanded more rapidly, nor has any embraced more ambitious goals, than has environmental regulation in the last decade. Environmental management, already a major governmental responsibility, will command a progressively larger future share of public resources measured in tax dollars, public employees, and governmental activity. This expansion of governmental stewardship for environmental quality, while most visible at the federal level, has progressively permeated lower levels of government until ecological issues are routine agenda items for governments ranging the whole federal spectrum from Washington to local communities. As the magnitude of ecological ills increases and our understanding of their complexity advances, we are depending primarily upon the nation's governments, and the political structures in which they are embedded, to assume leadership in environmental management and responsibility for future environmental planning.

The implications of this progressive politicizing of environmental quality are profoundly important. We have come to depend upon public institutions largely to define from the welter of important environmental tasks which ones will assume public priority. "Pollution is what government says it is." [40] Thus the environmental agenda for the nation is governmentally defined.

Moreover the manner in which the agenda is translated into public policies—the quality of that intricate interplay of political implementation, enforcement, and revision—will be determined by public institutions and the constellation of political forces that shape this institutional behavior. Finally, the capacity of public institutions, officials, and laws to deal with environmental management will determine in large measure whether environmental quality can be restored and protected and the nation's magnificent ecological inheritance remain for another generation. Thus environmental protection involves a testing of the resiliency in the nation's governments when faced with problems whose successful resolution requires continual innovation in a constitutional order more than two centuries old.

In short environmental protection is so inexorably bonded to the political process that it is impossible to understand, or affect, environmental quality in the United States without reference to the political structures that define environmental management today.

Notes

1. Anne McGill Gorsuch, single at the time she became EPA administrator in 1981, married Robert Burford, then head of Interior's Bureau of Land Management, on February 23, 1983, shortly before her resignation in October 1983.
2. *U.S. Statistical Abstract,* 1982.
3. See section 110(a) (2) (I) of the Clean Air Act for ban on "new sources" and sections 176 and 316 for other sanctions.

4. The 31 states receiving nonattainment warnings actually had until 1987 to adopt the needed control measures under the 1977 amendments. The 1982 deadline referred only to SIPs demonstrating that the states had taken measures necessary to meet the 1987 deadline.

5. *Congressional Quarterly*, December 4, 1982, 2970.

6. Congressional Research Service reportedly informed Congress also that EPA was making several questionable interpretations of the act. See the *New York Times*, July 9, 1982.

7. See, for instance, comments in the *National Journal*, November 13, 1982.

8. *Environmental Reporter*, July 23, 1982, 395-396.

9. Ibid.

10. *Environmental Reporter*, July 9, 1982.

11. *Environmental Reporter*, December 17, 1982.

12. One factor attenuating the process would have been the many months required by law for giving states proper notice and opportunity to respond to official sanction notification.

13. President's Commission for a National Agenda for the Eighties, *The American Economy, Energy and Environment in the Eighties* (Englewood Cliffs, N.J.: Prentice-Hall, 1981), 89.

14. John E. Bonina, "The Evolution of 'Technology Forcing' in the Clean Air Act," *Environmental Reporter*, monograph no. 21, July 25, 1975.

15. Ibid.

16. Lawrence Mosher, "Environmentalists, Industry Left Cold by EPA Bid for New Pretreatment Rules," *National Journal*, June 12, 1982.

17. Eugene P. Seskin, "Automobile Air Pollution Policy," in *Current Issues in U.S. Environmental Policy*, ed. Paul R. Portnoy (Baltimore: Johns Hopkins University Press, 1978), 84.

18. A. Myrick Freeman III, "Air and Water Pollution Policy," in *Current Issues in U.S. Environmental Policy*, 51.

19. Council on Environmental Quality (CEQ), *Environmental Quality 1980* (Washington, D.C.: Government Printing Office, 1981), 397.

20. *New York Times*, March 12, 1983.

21. *New York Times*, April 1, 1982.

22. CEQ, *Environmental Quality 1980*, 397.

23. Ibid.

24. Freeman, "Air and Water Pollution Policy," 60-61.

25. Bonina, "The Evolution of 'Technology Forcing' in the Clean Air Act."

26. CEQ, *Environmental Quality 1981*, 178.

27. Frederik R. Anderson, *NEPA in the Courts* (Baltimore: Johns Hopkins University Press, 1973), 276.

28. Richard A. Liroff, "NEPA: Where Have We Been and Where Are We Going?" *APA Journal* (April 1980): 156.

29. Barry Commoner, *The Closing Circle* (New York: Alfred A. Knopf, 1971), chapter 1.

30. CEQ, *Environmental Quality 1981*, 23.

31. Ibid., 52-56.

32. Freeman, "Air and Water Pollution Policy," 34.

33. *New York Times*, July 21, 1982.
34. General Accounting Office, "The Debate Over Acid Precipitation: Opposing Views, Status of Research," report no. EMD-81-131, September 11, 1981.
35. *New York Times*, January 25, 1981.
36. CEQ, *Environmental Quality 1981*, 133.
37. CEQ, *Environmental Quality 1980*, chapter 5.
38. A National Agenda for the Eighties, *The American Economy, Energy and Environment*, 126.
39. CEQ, *Global 2000 Report to the President, Executive Summary*, vol. 1 (Washington, D.C.: Government Printing Office, 1980).
40. Barbara S. Davies and J. Clarence Davies, *Politics of Pollution*, 2d ed. (Indianapolis: Bobbs-Merrill, 1975).

Under ... Anne McGill Burford, the Environmental Protection Agency division that oversees the Toxic Substances Control Act (TSCA) maintained an Industry Assistance Office. Under new broom William D. Ruckelshaus, the name has been changed to TSCA Assistance Office.... The office now furnishes environmental groups with advance notices of submissions to the Federal Register, *a service long provided industry groups.*

—News Item

The Politics of Environmental Policy

The Reagan administration had been in office but six months when it blundered into a series of incidents that embarrassed the White House and sent its widely advertised new public lands policy into instant disarray. The debacle illustrates some enduring characteristics of environmental policy making in the United States and offers useful insights about the institutions shaping such policy.

The issue was energy exploration on the public lands. A repeated theme in candidate Ronald Reagan's campaign had been the need to open more federal land to energy development. "This nation has been portrayed too long a time to the people as being energy poor when it is energy rich," he complained during a nationally televised debate with President Jimmy Carter.[1] The problem, he asserted, was the excessive energy resources "locked up" in public lands. After the election President Reagan looked to his newly appointed secretary of the interior, James Watt, to open major portions of the National Wilderness System, more than 15.3 million acres of wholly undeveloped and largely protected territory, to oil, gas, coal, and uranium exploration. Watt, whose department's jurisdiction embraced these wild and open places, felt a special mission. "I will," he promised, "seek to remove the government impediments and let the marketplace bring on development.... There is no greater wisdom than the marketplace." [2]

In July 1981 Watt announced that he would encourage more energy exploration in the National Wilderness System under the control of Interior's Bureau of Land Management (BLM) by giving BLM district offices greater authority to issue exploration leases. On September 1 the Albuquerque, New Mexico, district office issued what was probably the first oil and gas development lease in a designated federal wilderness and, in November, two more leases, all extending into 34,000 acres of New Mexico's Capitan Mountain Wilderness Area.

The Higher Wisdom of the Marketplace, however, had failed to enlighten New Mexico's representative Manuel Lujan, Jr. Lujan, the ranking Republican on the House Interior Affairs Committee whose jurisdiction included Interior, was irate upon discovering from the newspapers the existence of the leases. The Capitan Mountain Wilderness Area was in his district, and Lujan was an ardent conservationist. Charging that the secretary had failed to consult Congress as required by law before ordering the new BLM policy, Lujan threatened to use his committee's authority to withdraw all wilderness land from any future prospect of development leases through the BLM. Faced with nasty and unprofitable conflict over the respective constitutional powers of Congress and the executive branch, Watt rescinded his order, promised to consult Congress before permitting future exploration into wilderness regions, and assured Congress that full environmental impact assessments would accompany new leasing proposals.

By slowing the administration's early drive to open public domain to energy production, the confrontation had been a politically costly setback even though a later Supreme Court ruling, *Immigration and Naturalization Service v. Chadha* (1983), suggests that such a congressional "veto" might have been unconstitutional.[3] At the time, however, Watt could ill afford the time consuming and politically acrimonious conflict he would have invited by defending his order. Moreover, a coalition of environmental groups, alerted by the New Mexico incident, was preparing to bring the federal courts into the fray by initiating suits against Watt—a sure sign that the issue could become enormously complicated.

Environmental policies usually develop less tempestuously than this, but some characteristics common to most environmental policy can be observed. First, policy making is a process involving a number of related decisions originating from different institutions and actors ranging across the whole domain of the federal government and private institutions. As Hugh Heclo observes, policy is "a course of action or inaction rather than a specific decision or action. . . ."[4] Moreover, policy making is continuous; once made, decisions are rarely immutable. Consequently, environmental policy is always in some respects fluid and impermanent, always in metamorphosis. Finally, the restraints on Secretary Watt's freedom of action emphasize that the policy maker's discretion is bounded and shaped by a combination of restraints: constitutional prescriptions, institutional rules and biases, statutory laws, shared understandings about "the rules of the game" for conflict resolution, inherited culture, and more. Collectively, these restraints are givens in the policy setting that mean government never resolves issues in wholly new ways.

One useful way to understand public policy, and environmental policy specifically, is to view the process as a cycle of interrelated phases through which policy ordinarily evolves. Each phase involves a different mix of actors, institutions, and constraints. While somewhat simplified, this approach does illuminate particularly well the interrelated flow of decisions and the continual process of creation and modification that characterize governmental policy development.

The Policy Setting: Cycles and Constraints

Public policies usually develop with reasonable order and predictability. Governmental response to public issues—the business of converting an issue into a policy—customarily begins when an issue can be placed upon the governmental agenda. Successful promotion of issues to the agenda does not ensure that public policies will result, but this step initiates the policy cycle.

The Cycle of Policy Development

An environmental issue becomes an environmental policy as it passes through the following policy phases.

1. *Agenda Setting:* Charles O. Jones aptly called this "the politics of getting problems to government."[5] It is, more particularly, the politics of imparting sufficient importance and urgency to an issue that government will feel compelled to place the matter on the "official agenda" of government, the "set of items explicitly up for the serious and active consideration of authoritative decision-makers."[6] This means getting environmental issues on legislative calendars, before legislative committees, on a priority list for bill introduction by senator or representative, on the schedule of a regulatory agency or among the president's legislative proposals. In brief, getting on the agenda means placing an issue where institutions and individuals with public authority can make a response and feel the need to do so.

2. *Formulation and Legitimation:* Governmental agendas can easily become a graveyard for public problems. Only a small portion of issues reaching the

governmental agenda, environmental or otherwise, reach the stage of policy formulation or legitimation. Policy formulation involves setting goals for policy, creating specific plans and proposals for these goals, and selecting the means to implement such plans. Policy formulation in the federal government is particularly associated with the presidency and Congress; the State of the Union message and the avalanche of bills annually introduced in Congress represent the most obvious examples of formulated policies. Policies, once created, also must be legitimated—invested with the authority to evoke public acceptance. Customarily, this is done through constitutional, statutory, or administrative procedures such as voting, public hearings, presidential orders, or judicial decisions upholding the constitutionality of laws—all rituals whose purpose is to signify that policies have now acquired the weight of public authority.

3. *Implementation:* Public policies remain largely statements of intention until they are translated into operational programs. Indeed, the impact of policies largely depends upon how they are implemented. Thus, what government is "doing" about environmental problems relates in large part to how the programs have been implemented. Eugene Bardach has compared implementation with "an assembly process." It is, he writes, "as if the original mandate . . . that set the policy or program in motion were a blueprint for a large machine that has to turn out rehabilitated psychotics or healthier old people or better educated children. . . . Putting the machine together and making it run is, at one level, what we mean by the 'implementation' process." [7] Policy implementation involves especially the bureaucracy, whose presence and style shape the impact of all public policies.

4. *Assessment/Reformulation:* All the procedures involved in evaluating the social impact of government policies, in judging the desirability of these impacts, and in communicating these judgments to government and the public can be called "policy assessment." Often the federal courts assume an active role in this process, as do the mass media. The White House, Congress, and the bureaucracy continually monitor and assess the impacts of public policy also. Consequently once a policy has been formulated, it may pass through many phases of "reformulation." All major institutions of government may play a major role in this process of reformulation.

5. *Policy Termination:* The "deliberate conclusion or succession of specific governmental functions, programs, policies or organizations," suggests Peter deLeon, amounts to policy termination. [8] Terminating policies, environmental or otherwise, is such a formidable process that most public programs, in spite of intentions to the contrary, assume virtual immortality. More characteristically, policies change through repeated reformulation and reassessment.

Because policy formulation is a process, the various phases almost always will affect each other, an important reason why understanding a policy often requires a consideration of the whole development pattern. For instance, many problems encountered by the Environmental Protection Agency (EPA) when enforcing the Federal Water Pollution Control Act arose from congressional failure to define clearly in the law what was meant by a "navigable" waterway to which the legislation applied. The oversight was deliberate, intended to facilitate congressional passage of the extraordinarily complicated legislation. In turn the EPA sought early opportunities to bring the issue before the federal courts—to force judicial assessment of the law's intent—so that the agency might have reliable guidance for its own implementation of this provision. Additionally, it often happens that aspects of environmental policies, like most other complex federal laws, may appear simultaneously at different phases in the policy cycle. While the EPA was struggling to implement portions of the "Superfund" legislation allocating grants to the states for cleaning up abandoned toxic waste sites, Congress was considering a reformulation of the law to increase funding authorization for more state grants.

There are, however, common constraints shaping governmental response to environmental issues throughout the policy cycle. Permeating the governmental style of policy making, they are among the most powerful and persistent influences on environmental policy.

Constitutional Constraints

The design of governmental power intended two centuries ago for a nation of farmers still rests heavily upon the flow of policy making in a technological age. Like other public policies, environmental programs have been shaped, and complicated, by this enduring constitutional formula.

Checks and Balances. The Madisonian notion of setting "ambition against ambition," which inspired the constitutional structure, creates a government of countervailing and competitive institutions. The system of checks and balances disperses power and authority within the federal government among legislative, executive, and judicial institutions and thereby sows tenacious institutional rivalries. Yet, as Richard E. Neustadt observes, these are separated institutions sharing power; effective public policy requires that public officials collaborate by discovering strategies to transcend these institutional conflicts.[9]

Federalism disperses governmental power by fragmenting authority between national and state governments. Despite the growth of vast federal powers, federalism remains a sturdy constitutional buttress supporting an edifice of authority—shared, independent, and counter-vailing—erected from the states within the federal system. "It is difficult," writes one observer, "to find any governmental activity which does not involve all three of the so-called 'levels' of the federal system." [10] And no government monopolizes power. "There has never been a time when it was possible to put neat labels on discrete 'federal,' 'state' and 'local' functions." [11]

Federalism also introduces complexity, jurisdictional rivalries, confusion, and delay into the management of environmental problems. These are partially the result of authority over environmental issues being fragmented among a multitude of different governmental entities and partially the product of Washington's attempts to administer federal environmental regulations through state and local governments. Management of water quality in the Colorado River basin, for instance, is enormously complicated because seven different states have conflicting claims upon the quantity and quality of Colorado River water to which they are entitled. No overall plan exists for the comprehensive management and protection of the river, and none can exist in this structure of divided and competitive jurisdictions. The federal government often attempts to reduce administrative complications in programs administered through the states by the use of common regulations, guidelines, and other devices to impose consistency in implementation. However, the practical problems of reconciling so many geographic interests within the arena of a single regulatory program often trigger major problems in program implementation.

Organized Interests. The Constitution also encourages a robust pluralism of organized interests. Constitutional guarantees for freedom of petition, expression, and assembly promote constant organization and political activism at all governmental levels among thousands of economic, occupational, ethnic, ideological, and geographic interests. To make public policy in the United States requires public officials and institutions to reconcile the conflicting interests of organized groups whose claims not only to influence but to authority in making public policy have resulted in an unwritten constitutional principle. The constitutional architecture of the U.S. government also provides numerous points of access to public power for such groups operating in a fragmented governmental milieu. The political influence broadly distributed across this vast constellation of organized private groups clouds the formal distinction between public and private power.[12] Instead, the course of policy making moves routinely and easily between public institutions and private organizations mobilized for political action.

These constitutional constraints have important implications for environmental policy. Generally, it is easier to defeat legislation and other governmental policies than to enact them, to frustrate incisive governmental action on issues than to create it. Further, most policy decisions result from bargaining and compromise among institutions and actors all sharing some portion of diffused power. Policy formulation usually means coalition building in an effort to engineer consensus by reconciling diverse interests and aggregating sufficient strength among different interests to support effective policies. For instance, administrative agencies have a "thirst for consensus," as James DeLong observes:

> Agencies like to achieve consensus on issues and policies. If they cannot bring everyone into the tent, they will try to get enough disparate groups together so as to make the remainder appear unreasonable. If the interested parties are too far apart for even partial consensus, then the agency will try to give everybody something. . . .[13]

Bargaining and compromise often purchase consensus at the cost of disarray and contradiction in the resulting policies. "What happens," remarks Graham Allison, "is not chosen as a solution to a problem but rather results from compromise, conflict and confusion among officials with diverse interests and unequal influence." [14]

Incrementalism

Public officials strongly favor making and changing policy incrementally. "Policy making typically is part of a political process in which the only feasible political change is that which changes social states by relatively small steps," writes Charles A. Lindblom. "Hence, decisionmakers typically consider, among all the alternative policies that might be imagined to consider, only those relatively few alternatives that represent small or incremental changes from existing policies." [15] Generally, incrementalism favors reliance on past experience as a guide for new policies, careful deliberation before policy changes, and a rejection of rapid or comprehensive policy innovation.

Incrementalism is politically seductive. It permits policy makers to draw upon their own experience in the face of unfamiliar problems and encourages the making of small policy adjustments "at the margins" to reduce anticipated, perhaps irreversible, and politically risky consequences. But incrementalism can also become a prison to the imagination by inhibiting policy innovation and stifling new solutions to issues. Especially when officials treat new policy issues as if they were familiar ones and deal with them in the accustomed ways, a futile and possibly dangerous repetition of the past in the face of issues requiring a fresh approach can result.

The Clean Air Act (1970), the National Environmental Policy Act (1970), and the other innovative legislation of the early 1970s came only after Congress repeatedly failed in dealing with environmental issues incrementally.[16] Beginning with the Water Pollution Control Act of 1956, the first significant federal effort to define a role for Washington in pollution abatement, Congress and the White House continued into the late 1960s to write legislation that treated pollution management as a "uniquely local problem" in which a "partnership" between federal and state governments was considered the appropriate model. This deference to the states was a prescription for inaction; few states voluntarily wrote or enforced effective pollution controls. In the Water Quality Act (1965) and the Air Quality Act (1967) Congress prodded the states a bit more vigorously by setting compliance deadlines for state pollution control plans, yet the legislation was so burdened with ambiguities and constraints on federal action that the legislation was ineffective.

By the early 1970s Congress felt compelled to break with this incrementalism. The environmental movement had grown rapidly in political strength. Although to many observers environmentalism appeared to have been swept to political prominence in a few months, its rise on the national policy agenda had been prompted by years of increasingly skilled, patient, and persistent promotion by a multitude of groups. The Clean Air Act, for instance, had been supported for almost five years by a national environmental alliance, the Clean Air Coalition, before it achieved national attention. Also, the growing severity of environmental degradation was creating a climate of opinion congenial to aggressive, new approaches to pollution abatement. Environmentalists were aided powerfully in their quest for new federal approaches to pollution abatement by the presence of veteran conservationists who assumed crucial congressional positions during this period: Sen. Edmund S. Muskie, D-Maine, Sen. Henry M. Jackson, D-Wash., Sen. Philip A. Hart, D-Mich., Rep. Morris Udall, D-Ariz., Rep. Paul McCloskey, R-

Rep. Paul Rogers, D-Fla., and many others. Equally important, environmentalism had become a major media preoccupation.

The time consumed in attempts to attack problems incrementally, the degree of environmental damage necessary to convince Congress that new approaches were needed, and the effort invested by the environmental movement in political action all testify to the tenacity of incrementalism in the policy process. Indeed, one risk in the new environmental programs of the 1970s is that with time they also may settle into an incremental mold resisting necessary changes.

Interest Group Liberalism

It is an implicit principle in American politics, assumed by most public officials as well as those groups seeking access to them, that organized interests affected by public policy should have an important role in shaping those policies. Few interests enjoy such a pervasive and unchallenged access to government as business, for reasons soon to be elaborated, but almost all major organized groups enjoy some measure of influence in public institutions. Many officials, in Theodore Lowi's terms, conduct their offices "as if it were supposed to be the practice of dealing only with organized claims in formulating policy, and of dealing exclusively through organized claims in implementing programs." [17]

Structuring Groups into Government. Arrangements exist throughout governmental structures for giving groups access to strategic policy arenas. Lobbying is accepted as a normal, if not essential, arrangement for ensuring organized interests a major role in lawmaking. More than 1,000 advisory committees exist within the federal bureaucracy to give interests affected by policies some access and voice in agency deliberations. Hundreds of large, quasi-public associations bring together legislators, administrators, White House staff, and private group representatives to share policy concerns, thereby blurring the distinction between public and private interests. The National Rivers and Harbors Congress, for example, looks after water resource projects, the Highway Users Federation for Safety and Mobility diligently promotes the Interstate Highway System, and the Atomic Industrial Forum pursues the interests of commercial nuclear power corporations. Successful, organized groups so effectively control the exercise of governmental power that, in Grant McConnell's words, significant portions of American government have witnessed "the conquest of segments of formal state power by private groups and associations." [18] In effect, group activity at all governmental levels has been practiced so widely that it has become part of the constitutional order.

An Unusual Kind and Degree of Control. No interest has exploited this right to take part in the governmental process more pervasively or successfully than has business. In environmental affairs, the sure access of business to government assumes enormous importance, for business is a major regulated interest whose ability to represent itself and secure careful hearing before public agencies and officials often delays or complicates such regulation. But historically and institutionally the influence of business upon government has transcended the agencies and officials concerned with environmental affairs. Business has traditionally enjoyed what Lindblom has called a "special relationship" with government.

Business weighs especially heavy in the deliberations of public officials because its leaders collectively manage much of the economy and perform such essential economic functions that their failure would produce severe economic disorder and widespread suffering. "Government officials know this," observes Lindblom. "They also know that widespread failure of business . . . will bring down the government. A democratically elected government cannot expect to survive in the face of widespread or prolonged distress. . . . Consequently, government policy makers show constant concern about business performance." So great is this concern that public officials usually give business not all it desires but enough to ensure its profitability. Out of this grows the "privileged position" of business in government, its widely accepted right to require that government officials often "give business needs precedence over demands from citizens through electoral, party, and interest-group channels." [19]

Business also enjoys more practical political advantages in competition with other interests for access and influence within government: far greater financial resources, greater ease in raising money for political purposes, and an already-existing organization available for use in political action. These advantages in strategic resources and salience to public officials do not ensure business uncompromised acceptance of its demands upon government nor do they spare it from defeat or frustration by opponents. But business often, if not usually, is able to exploit its privileged status in American politics to ensure that its views are represented early and forcefully in any policy conflicts, its interests are pursued and protected carefully at all policy stages, and its forces are mobilized effectively for long periods of time. These are formidable advantages, often enough to give a decisive edge in competitive struggles with environmental or other interests that have not the political endurance, skill, or resources to be as resolute in bringing pressure on government when it counts.

Environmental Groups and Governmental Access. Environmental groups have been no less diligent than others in organizing. Prior to the 1970s environmentalists were at a considerable disadvantage in achieving effective access to government when compared with environmentally regulated interests, particularly business. However, environmental groups—along with public interest groups, consumer organizations, and others advocating broad public programs—were quick to promote a number of new structural and legal arrangements, often created deliberately for their advantage by Congress and administrative agencies. Of these, three were particularly important: (1) liberal provisions for public participation in the implementation and enforcement of environmental regulatory programs as required by statute or administrative regulation; (2) expanded "standing to sue" public agencies, often created within the legislation authorizing environmental programs such as the Clean Air Act, which gave environmental groups far greater access to the courts than in prior years; and (3) the provision by several regulatory agencies for "intervenor funding" to pay the often-substantial fees for lawyers and expert witnesses to represent environmental interests in agency proceedings where such groups provided an important, and otherwise unrepresented, interest. Environmental groups continue to defend these arrangements against the Reagan administration's effort to limit their scope.

Political Feasibility

"What considerations enter into the selection of priorities and the specific program designed to meet them?" mused veteran Washington observer Ralph Huitt. The answer was political feasibility. That means, notes Huitt, "Will it 'go' on the Hill? Will the public buy it? Does it have political 'sex appeal?' " [20] Policy deliberations involve more than calculations of political feasibility, but there is often a large component in them. Political feasibility involves an intuitive and often highly subjective judgment by public officials concerning what policies and programs can be enacted and implemented in some reasonably effective way, given the political realities as they are understood. It is often a judgment quite different from determinations of rationality, economy, or fairness to a policy. The irrationality, vagueness, and apparently sloppy draftsmanship in legislation, environmental or otherwise, are often explicable as an effort to make the law feasible. Calculations of political feasibility affect presidents, judges, and administrators as well as legislators in policy making. In short political feasibility is another test, and another constraint, on policy.

Examples abound in environmental policy. Political feasibility convinced Congress, when it enacted the original $18 billion federal sewage treatment grant program in 1972, that it must also provide a statutory allocation formula ensuring every state, regardless of size or need, a guaranteed and substantial minimum authorization. Political feasibility, in the guise of congressional opinion, dissuaded the Reagan administration from attempting to abolish the $20 billion synthetic fuels program authorized under President Carter. Uncounted thousands of executive orders, presidential addresses, congressional bills, and agency regulations have perished unissued because they bore the stigma of political infeasibility.

Policy makers are influenced not only by these general constraints but also by the characteristics of the various governmental institutions that make policy. Each institution has its own characteristic constraints on policy. This is particularly important in understanding environmental policy making in Congress, the bureaucracy, and the courts where different institutional constraints—what we shall call policy "styles"—prevail.

The Institutional Setting

In the United States the tasks of policy formulation, implementation, and assessment are invested largely in the White House, Congress, bureaucracy, and courts. Because the latter three institutions play such a prominent role in environmental policy making, the institutional bias characteristic to each assumes a crucial role in explaining Washington's response to environmental issues.

Congress: Policy Formulation by Fragmentation

The Constitution invests Congress with the principal legislative powers in the federal government. While twentieth century realities compel the president, bureaucracy, and courts to share these powers, Congress remains preeminent in policy formulation and legitimation. Despite the panoply of party organizations, legislative leaders, and coordinating committees, Congress remains largely an institution of fragmented internal powers and divided geographic loyalties. Legislative power is dispersed in both chambers among a multitude of committees and subcommittees; local or regional concerns often tenaciously claim legislative loyalties. The electoral cycle intrudes imperiously upon policy deliberations. The public interest and legislative objectivity compete with equally insistent legislative concerns to deliver something, if possible, from Washington to the "folks back home." In environmental affairs Congress is an assembly of scientific amateurs enacting programs of great technical complexity to ameliorate scientifically complicated environmental ills most legislators but dimly understand.

Committee Decentralization. Congress has been aptly described as a "kind of confederation of little legislatures." [21] In both chambers the committees and subcommittees—those little legislatures wielding the most consistently effective power in the legislative system—are dispersed and competitive in environmental matters. In the House, 38 committees and subcommittees claim some authority over environmentally sensitive energy issues; 10 committees and several dozen subcommittees share such jurisdiction in the Senate. Water policy is even further decentralized with 70 congressional committees and subcommittees sharing some jurisdiction.

Competition among committees, within and between chambers, commonly occurs in formulating environmental programs. The result is protected bargaining and compromise. With authority over environmental policy fragmented among a multitude of committees in each chamber, competition and jurisdictional rivalry commonly occur as each committee attempts to assert some influence over environmental programs. The result is that environmental legislation evolves only, as a rule, through protracted bargaining and compromising among the many committees. This time-consuming process often results in legislation that is vague or inconsistent. Divided jurisdictions, however, provide different interest groups with some point of committee access during environmental policy formulation, and consequently these groups resist efforts to reduce the number of committees with overlapping jurisdictions and otherwise to concentrate authority in a few major committees.

Groups hostile to the Clinch River Breeder Reactor, for instance, were aided greatly in their battle to terminate the project by House reforms in 1976 removing jurisdiction over the project from the exclusive control of the Joint Committee on Atomic Energy, the breeder's premier legislative champion, and vesting it in several other less supportive committees. Subsequently, these groups fiercely resisted efforts to reorganize the House committee structure lest they lose their access in the process.

Localism. During a crucial Senate vote on funding the highly controversial, multimillion-dollar Tennessee-Tombigbee Waterway, a reporter was impressed by what he called "the unabashed display of horse trading among Senators not wanting to endanger their own project." The funding finally passed because many senators of both parties had bartered their support for the project in return for assurances that the project proponents would return the favor when other projects were considered. "But that's nothing new," replied Sen. Howell Heflin, D-Ala., to a critic. "It's happened in the United States Senate since the beginning." [22]

The Senate's unapologetic loyalty to reciprocity in voting for local public works projects, known as political pork, is driven by a powerful tradition of localism in congressional voting. In American political culture, legislators are treated by constituents and regard themselves as ambassadors to Washington from their own geographic areas. They are expected to acquire skills in the practice of pork-barrel politics, capturing federal goods and services for the constituency. They are also expected to be vigilant in promoting and protecting local interests in the national policy arena. Congressional tenure is more likely to depend upon a legislator's ability to serve these local interests than upon other legislative achievements. While not the only influence upon congressional voting, it is deeply rooted and probably the single most compelling force in shaping voting decisions.

This localism affects environmental policy in different ways. By encouraging legislators to view environmental proposals first through the lens of local interests, it often weakens a sensitivity to national needs and interests. At worst it drives legislators to judge the merits of environmental policies almost solely by their impact upon frequently small and atypical constituencies. The Reagan administration learned about the costs of failing to recognize legislators' instinctive localism when, through the Interior Department, it acted to propose in late 1981 the approval of two lease applications for oil exploration in the Los Padres National Forest near Big Sur, one of California's most spectacular coastal vistas. The White House found itself confronting united opposition—regardless of party affiliation—from the entire 22-member California House delegation. Thus did geographic loyalty, awakened by fear of environmental devastation to Big Sur, unite California Republicans against their own party leader and with the opposition Democrats.

Localism also whets the congressional appetite for federal distributive programs freighted with local benefits. Not surprisingly, federal grants to build pollution control facilities, such as sewage treatment plants, have instant legislative appeal. Even the comparatively tiny federal program for such grants to the states in the mid-1960s appealed. "The program was immensely popular.... Congressmen enjoyed the publicity and credit they received every time they announced another grant for another community in their district." [23] The huge $18-billion waste treatment facilities program authorized in 1972, the second largest public works program in U.S. history, was even more popular. By 1982 the $10.5 billion obligated under the program had generated 4.5 million worker-years of employment supporting about 7.3 million Americans. The EPA estimated that for every $1 billion spent, about 50,900 worker-years of employment would be generated in plant and sewer construction. [24]

Elections. The electoral cycle also dominates the legislative mind. The constitutionally mandated electoral cycles of the federal government—two years, four years, six years—partition the time available for legislative deliberation into periods bound by different elections. Within these time frames, policy decisions are continually analyzed for their electoral implications and often valued largely for electoral impacts. This affects congressional policy styles in several ways. First, the short term becomes more important than the long term when evaluating programs; legislators often attribute more importance to a program's impact on the next election than to its longer-term effects upon unborn generations. Second, policies are tested continually against public opinion. While a weak or badly divided public opinion often can be ignored, a coherent majority opinion related to an environmental issue usually wields significant influence on congressional voting, especially when legislators can associate the opinion with their own constituencies.

Bureaucracy: Power Through Implementation

Federal agencies concerned with environmental affairs and closely related matters such as energy, consumer protection, and worker health have grown explosively in the last two decades. More than 130 major new federal laws, most concerned with broad regulation of business and the economy in the interest of public health and safety, have been enacted since 1970. More than 20 new regulatory agencies have been created to implement these programs, including the EPA, Occupational Safety and Health Administration (OSHA), and the Interior Department's Office of Surface Mining Reclamation and Enforcement.

The Power of Discretion. The significance of these agencies rests less upon their size and budget than upon the political realities obscured by a constitutional illusion. The Constitution appears to vest the power to formulate policy primarily in Congress while leaving to the president and the executive branch the task of seeing that the laws be "faithfully executed." Although implemented and enforced principally in the bureaucracy, public policy develops in both branches of the government.

Delegated authority and administrative discretion provide the well-springs of the bureaucracy's power. Congress routinely invests administrators with responsibility for making a multitude of decisions it can not or will not make itself about the implementation of policy; often this becomes legislative power delegated to the executive branch. Even when delegation is not clearly intended, administrators assume the power to make public policy when they choose how to implement policies permitting different options; hence the existence of administrative discretion. Consider, for instance, how delegated authority and administrative discretion coalesce as the Forest Service deals with routine responsibilities:

> In recommending approval of leases for mining exploration in Los Padres National Forest, the U.S. Forest Service must decide if drilling roads are "potentially erodable," and whether each project lies in "unstable bedrock." The Forest Service landscape architects and area supervisors must also approve the location of drilling and other exploration equipment, the routes of all drilling roads and the types of vehicle used.[25]

Congress and the president, using a variety of constitutional and statutory powers, attempt to discipline the exercise of administrative discretion. Congress usually includes with grants of delegated authority statutory guidelines intended to give administrators various criteria for the exercise of authority. Congress may assert its inherent powers of legislative oversight, budget review and authorization, legislative investigation as well as others to ensure administrative responsibility in program implementation. The White House, drawing upon the president's powers as chief executive and many congressionally delegated powers, can influence administrative discretion. Still this oversight holds no certain rein on administrative discretion, particularly in light of the vast number and complexity of environmental programs, the elephantine size of the bureaucracy, and competing demands upon presidential and congressional time. The federal bureaucracy, assured of generous discretionary authority well into the future, will continue to be an independent and largely self-regulated influence in environmental policy.

Bureaucratic Competitiveness. The bureaucracy is no monolith. Its powers in environmental affairs, although collectively vast, also are dispersed and competitive. One source of this fragmentation is the federalizing of environmental administration. Many major environmental laws enacted in Washington are administered partially or wholly through state governments; others give states an option to participate. Under the Federal Water Pollution Control Act, for instance, 27 states currently administer their own water pollution permit systems; all but 6 states and the District of Columbia administer the Safe Drinking Water Act. The Clean Air Act permits the states to participate in several major aspects of the program including the control of pollutants and the establishment of emission standards for stationary sources.

Another cause of fragmented administrative authority is the chronic division and overlapping of responsibility for environmental programs among federal agencies. Twenty-seven separate federal agencies, for example, share major regulatory responsibility in environmental and occupational health. Regulating even a single pollutant often necessitates a bureaucratic convention. Toxic substances are currently regulated under 20 different federal statutes involving five agencies. To address all the problems in human exposure to vinyl chloride, notes David Doniger, would require the collaboration of all five agencies working with 15 different laws.[26]

Dispersed authority breeds conflict and competition among agencies

45

and their political allies over program implementation, authority, and resources—the "turf fighting" familiar to students of bureaucracy. While collaboration is common, it is never dependable. State environmental agencies, for instance, often disagree with Washington and among themselves over the proper implementation of the same program. Such a disagreement led to a 1982 suit filed against the EPA by the attorney general of New York charging that the agency was responsible for increasing acid rain in the Northeast by failing to enforce air pollution limits on West Virginia, Michigan, Tennessee, Illinois, Indiana, and Missouri.

Federal agencies are notoriously fitful collaborators in environmental affairs. When the Energy Department, the EPA, and the Nuclear Regulatory Commission (NRC), all sharing responsibility for the regulation of nuclear power plants, attempted to fashion a procedure for safely closing the plants, the prospect of the NRC becoming the lead agency provoked resistance from the others. "The underlying reason for their disagreement," explained the U.S. Comptroller General's Office, "was that such an action would give NRC additional regulatory authority over their programs." [27]

In this milieu of dispersed and competitive agency authority, policy implementation often resolves into a continual process of collaboration and conflict between coalitions of agencies and their allies shaping and reshaping policy as the relative strengths of the conflicting alignments change. Moreover, administrative conflict crosses the institutional divisions of the federal government, spreads downward through the federal system to state and local governments and outward from government to organized private groups. Indeed, agencies failing to enlist diverse and active allies in their policy struggles may frustrate their own mission and leave their future hostage to more politically skilled opponents.

The Courts: The Role of Appraisal

Judges actively participate in the environmental policy process in several ways. They continually interpret environmental law, an inevitable task in light of the ambiguities and silences common to environmental legislation. This statutory interpretation often amounts to policy making by the judicial branch. Judges also attempt to ensure that agencies discharge their mandated responsibilities under environmental legislation and otherwise comply with administrative obligations. Additionally, the federal courts enforce the Administrative Procedures Act, the code of administrative procedure applicable to all federal agencies. Finally, the courts ensure that environmental laws and their administrative implementation comply with constitutional standards.

The Courts and Environmental Policy. The federal courts, particularly the Supreme Court, have made several significant contributions to environmental policy. During the 1970s the courts greatly expanded opportunities for environmental groups to bring issues before the bench by a broadened definition of standing to sue. Prior to the 1970s environmental interests were greatly inhibited in using the courts by the traditional requirement that "standing" —the right to have one's suit heard by the court—could be obtained in environmental issues only when states were a party or when the private party initiating the action had suffered a clear injury or property loss. This precluded judicial consideration in cases where plaintiffs charged another party with environmental harm (this was not a personal injury) or attempted to sue governmental agencies for failure to discharge environmental responsibilities (personal injury or loss was difficult to document). Beginning with the Scenic Hudson case (1971) the Supreme Court gradually expanded standing over the next few years until a generous variety of individuals and environmental groups were able to initiate litigation to protect various public interests.[28] In more recent years the courts have not always been consistent or generous in their definition of standing. Nonetheless, the earlier decisions enabled environmental interests to use litigation effectively to bring pressure on Congress, administrative agencies, and regulated interests for more effective environmental policies during a crucial decade when major environmental laws were being written.

The federal courts' substantive interpretations of environmental laws during the 1970s also had a major impact in strengthening the scope and impact of many programs. The federal district court's 1972 *Sierra Club v. Ruckelshaus* decision, for instance, interpreted the goals of the Clean Air Act to require that all states prevent the degradation of any airsheds with ambient air quality higher than national standards. This decision in effect forced EPA and Congress to create the Prevention of Significant Deterioration (PSD) policy to protect all high-quality airsheds throughout the United States. According to R. Shep Melnick, "PSD was born in the courtroom and has resided there almost constantly for the past decade." [29] Indeed, as his meticulous study of the federal courts and the Clean Air Act indicates, the courts have been a major factor in the evolution of extremely stringent air pollution control standards by Congress and the EPA.[30]

Environmentalists, impatient at the faltering pace of the EPA's development of a priority list of hazardous pollutants for examination as required under the Toxic Substances Control Act, used the federal courts—particularly the District Court for the District of Columbia, an especially sympathetic forum for environmentalists—to force the EPA to greater speed in its priority setting. While environmentalists also suffered defeats in federal litigation during the 1970s, generally it was a period when judicial interpretation of environmental law worked to the environmentalists' advantage.

The federal courts also have been extremely instrumental in enforcing strict procedural compliance and reasonable adherence to the intent of the law in enforcing the requirement of the National Environmental Policy Act (NEPA) for "environmental impact statements" (EISs) in the federal bureaucracy. Perhaps in no other area of environmental law have the federal courts been more consistent. "Judicial enforcement of NEPA has resulted in increased administrative disclosures by federal agencies, more detailed analysis of environmental considerations by these agencies, and more thoughtful future planning in this area on their part."[31] The EIS process has been particularly useful to environmentalists by disclosing the implications of administrative issues that otherwise might not have been apparent, by serving as an early warning system to alert environmental groups to impending new issues, and by compelling federal agencies to give environmentalists an opportunity to influence decisions with environmental consequences.

The Growth of Business Litigation. In the latter 1970s business and other regulated interests began to use the federal courts to their advantage far more adeptly than they had earlier. During the 1970s environmentalists had been the primary beneficiaries of federal litigation; in the 1980s this advantage seems to have been substantially diminished.

One major reason for the increased effectiveness of business interests in federal litigation was the great growth in number and activity of specialized not-for-profit legal foundations representing regulated industries in environmental litigation. Reasoning that the devil should not have all the good tunes, business patterned these associations after the public interest legal foundations created in the 1970s to represent environmental interests. The most effective of these regionally organized business foundations have been the Pacific States Legal Foundation and the Mountain States Legal Foundation. The Midwest Legal Foundation and the Northeast Legal Foundation are two others. Like environmental public interest groups, these business associations maintain they are suing the government in the public interest and enjoy tax-exempt status. However, business public interest groups are financed principally by organizations, such as the Adolph Coors Company and the Scaife Foundation, who have fought vigorously against most of the major environmental regulatory programs that have been passed during the last two decades.

While business legal foundations have been highly aggressive in initiating cases against federal and state environmental regulations, the growing strength of business in environmental litigation also has been the result of greater skill and more attention by individual corporations and trade associations. Initially many corporations had little experience with environmental litigation, but they learned quickly.

"Starting in 1970," observes Lettie Wenner, "environmentalists were the most active groups at both the trial and appellate levels [of the federal courts]. . . . However, as the decade progressed and business corporations and trade associations added attorneys conversant with environmental law to their staffs, the numbers of economic interest groups' demands on the courts increased dramatically." [32] Suits initiated by business organizations were most often directed against emission standards established by EPA under air and water pollution control legislation. In the early 1980s both the number and success of these business challenges to EPA emission standards appeared to be increasing.

The benefit to business interests from this growing strength in environmental litigation does not solely rest upon an ability to win cases. Exhaustive and relentless challenges to federal regulation can delay enforcement of environmental laws for many years and throw environmental groups on the defensive, compelling them to invest scarce resources in protracted legal battles. Often the battles are won ultimately not by the side with the best case but by the side with the best endurance. With its much greater legal and financial resources and capacity to sustain litigation, business has gradually eliminated many of the organizational and legal advantages once enjoyed by environmental interests in the federal courts.

Litigation as a Political Tactic. The impact of the courts upon policy, as the previous discussion suggests, arises not only from the

49

substance of court rulings but also from the use of litigation as a tactical weapon in policy conflict. The courts become another political arena where losers in prior policy battles fought in Congress, the bureaucracy, or the White House seek yet another opportunity to prevail. For instance, when the major U.S. automakers failed to persuade the EPA to delay for a year the enforcement of the 1975 auto emission standards required by the Clean Air Act, they appealed successfully to the federal courts for a judicially imposed delay. The federal court asked the EPA to conduct further hearings and to assemble more evidence justifying its decision. Faced with this prospect and the likelihood of further litigation, the agency granted a delay in the compliance deadline rather than invest further resources in a struggle of very uncertain outcome. Not surprisingly, environmental groups specializing in litigation, such as the Environmental Defense Fund, have increased their activity during the Reagan administration in an effort to counteract through the courts what they allege to be massive regulatory resistance to their interests within the Reagan administration.

Litigation is also a stall in the policy process, a frustration to the opposition. Litigation creates a bargaining chip to be bartered for concessions from the opposition. Both environmentalists and their opposition have used the obstructive capacities of litigation to good advantage. When the Interior Department attempted in late 1981 to sell for energy exploration 111 tracts of offshore land in California's coastal zone, the state of California and numerous environmental groups joined in litigation blocking the sale of 32 tracts, among the most desirable, thereby freezing sale of the others also. This persuaded the department to reconsider the leases rather than risk a prolonged freeze on the sale of all the valuable tracts. Litigation initiated in the mid-1970s by environmental opponents of the Seabrook, New Hampshire, nuclear power plant cost the facility owners almost $15 million monthly in delay and almost succeeded in shutting the facility permanently.

Many critics have pegged NEPA's requirement for EISs as an especially productive source of lawsuits working to the advantage of environmentalists, but the data suggest otherwise. The number of lawsuits challenging federal agency actions under NEPA has been decreasing generally since 1970 and remains relatively low. Between 1970 and 1980 more than 10,000 impact statements were filed by federal agencies, yet only 1,911 lawsuits challenging the adequacy of the statements were initiated—many by business, state and local governmental entities, and other nonenvironmental organizations. This litigation seems particularly modest in light of the large number of impact statements actually written in the past decade and the much greater number of agency decisions that might have been challenged on grounds that EISs should have been written for them. In 1975 alone, federal agencies assessed more than 30,000 decisions to which NEPA might apply. In short, environmentalists did not appear to have gained an especially strategic legal advantage from NEPA.[33]

Though the institutional styles of Congress, the bureaucracy, and the courts all contribute to shaping environmental policy, the Reagan administration's especially crucial role in policy implementation during the 1980s imparts a special importance to the agencies most active in this implementation. These agencies have become perhaps the decade's most visible institutions in environmental policy making. Their attributes, consequently, deserve more detailed consideration.

The Administrative Setting

The bureaucratic complexity in managing environmental policy is suggested in Table 2-1, which identifies the major agencies involved and their statutory responsibilities. Both the Interior and Agriculture departments have wide-ranging authorities, but of them all the EPA is the most important and usually the most controversial.

The EPA

Created by an executive order of President Richard Nixon in 1970, the EPA is Washington's largest regulatory agency in budget and personnel. Its responsibilities embrace extraordinarily complicated and technical programs ranging across the whole domain of environmental management. The size of EPA's regulatory burden is suggested by a few of the major programs for which the agency is responsible: the Clean Air Act; the Clean Water Act; the Noise Control Act; the Safe Drinking Water Act; the Resource Conservation and Recovery Act; the Toxic Substances Control Act; the Marine Protection, Research and Sanctuaries Act; and the Federal Insecticide, Fungicide and Rodenticide Act. Beginning with a staff of approximately 8,000 and budget of $455 million in 1972, the EPA steadily grew to almost 13,000 employees and a budget of $1.35 billion until 1981 when the Reagan administration severely reduced its budget and personnel, as shown in Table 2-2. The agency,

Table 2-1 Federal Agencies With Environmental Regulatory Responsibility

Agricultural Stabilization and Conservation Service (ASCS). Administers various voluntary land-use programs to protect, expand and conserve farmlands, wetlands and forests. *(Agriculture Department)*

Army Corps of Engineers. Regulates all construction projects in the navigable waterways of the United States; promulgates regulations governing the transportation and dumping of dredged materials in navigable waters; develops, plans and builds various structures — dams, reservoirs, levees, harbors, waterways and locks — to protect areas from floods, supply water for municipal and industrial use, create recreational areas, improve water and wildlife quality, and protect the shorelines of oceans and lakes. *(Defense Department)*

Bureau of Land Management (BLM). Administers public lands located mainly in the western United States and Alaska. Resources managed include timber, minerals, oil and gas, geothermal energy, wildlife habitats, endangered plant and animal species, rangeland vegetation, recreation areas, wild and scenic rivers, wild horses and burros, designated conservation and wilderness areas and open space lands. *(Interior Department)*

Consumer Product Safety Commission (CPSC). Establishes mandatory safety standards governing the design, construction, contents, performance, and labeling of consumer products; develops rules and regulations to enforce standards. Hazard-related programs include acute chemical and environmental hazards.

Federal Aviation Administration (FAA). Established and enforces rules and regulations for safety standards covering all aspects of civil aviation, including noise and exhaust emissions from aircraft (in cooperation with the EPA). *(Transportation Department)*

Federal Energy Regulatory Commission (FERC). Issues licenses for hydroelectric power and wildlife and water quality and provides for recreational opportunities, flood control, and the efficient and safe operation of project dams. *(Energy Department)*

Federal Highway Administration (FHWA). Sets functional safety standards for the design, construction and maintenance of the nation's highways and establishes safety standards for commercial motor carriers in interstate or foreign commerce; regulates the movement of dangerous cargoes on highways and administers programs to reduce motor carrier noise. *(Transportation Department)*

Federal Maritime Commission (FMC). Certifies the financial responsibility of vessels that carry oil or other hazardous material to cover costs of cleaning up spills in navigable waters of the United States and adjoining shorelines.

Federal Trade Commission (FTC). Protects the public from false and deceptive advertising, particularly that involving food, drugs, cosmetics and therapeutic devices. Issues report on "tar" and nicotine contents of cigarettes.

Food and Drug Administration (FDA). Administers laws to ensure the purity and safety of foods, drugs, and cosmetics. Develops programs to reduce human exposure to radiation; conducts research on the effects of radiation exposure. Conducts research on the biological effects of potentially toxic chemical substances found in the environment. *(Health and Human Services Department)*

Materials Transportation Bureau. Develops and enforces equipment and operating safety regulations for the transportation of all materials by pipeline; carries out inspection, compliance, and enforcement actions for transport of all hazardous materials (including radioactive materials) by air, water, highway, and rail. *(Transportation Department)*

Mine Safety and Health Administration (MSHA). Develops and promulgates

Table 2-1 (Continued)

mandatory mine safety and health standards and ensures compliance with such standards. Aims to prevent and reduce mine accidents and occupational diseases. *(Labor Department)*

National Bureau of Standards (NBS). Conducts research and provides technical information on the protection of public health and safety, environmental quality, the improvement of industrial productivity and the promotion of better materials use. *(Commerce Department)*

National Institute for Occupational Safety and Health (NIOSH). Researches and develops occupational safety and health standards. *(Department of Health and Human Services)*

National Oceanic and Atmospheric Administration (NOAA). Describes, monitors, and predicts conditions in the atmosphere, ocean, sun, and space environment; disseminates environmental data through a system of meteorological, oceanographic, geophysical, and solar-terrestrial data centers; manages and conserves living marine resources and their habitats, including certain endangered species and marine mammals. *(Commerce Department)*

National Park Service. Administers programs to conserve the scenery, natural and historic objects, and wildlife in the nation's parks. *(Interior Department)*

National Transportation Safety Board (NTSB). Investigates and reports on the transportation of hazardous materials. *(Transportation Department)*

Nuclear Regulatory Commission (NRC). Licenses the construction and operation of nuclear reactors and other facilities; licenses the possession, use, transportation, handling, and disposal of nuclear materials.

Office of Conservation and Renewable Energy. Directs energy conservation programs; expands use of biomass, alcohol fuels, and urban waste; studies the problems involved in acid rain and carbon dioxide associated with coal burning. *(Energy Department)*

Office of Surface Mining Reclamation and Enforcement. Protects society and the environment from the adverse effects of coal mining operations; establishes minimum national standards for regulating surface effects of coal mining; promotes reclamation of previously mined lands. *(Interior Department)*

Office of Water Research and Technology. Supervises the nation's water quality and quantity; research support includes controlling the quality and quantity of ground water and surface water; conservation techniques and technologies; protection of fragile water ecosystems and other natural resources; and water management planning. *(Interior Department)*

Soil Conservation Service (SCS). Administers national program to develop and conserve soil and water resources; offers technical assistance on agricultural pollution control and environmental improvement projects. *(Agriculture Department)*

U.S. Coast Guard. In the area of water pollution, works with Materials Transportation Bureau to ensure that shipowners clean up oil or hazardous materials discharged into navigable waters. *(Transportation Department)*

U.S. Fish and Wildlife Service. Regulates the development, protection, rearing, and stocking of wildlife resources and their habitats; protects migratory and game birds, fish and wildlife, endangered and threatened species; enforces regulations for hunters of migratory waterfowl; preserves wetlands as natural habitats. *(Interior Department)*

U.S. Forest Service. Manages the national forests and grasslands and regulates the use of forest resources; regulates activities of commercial foresters working in national forests to ensure that the methods employed do not substantially damage the environment. *(Interior Department)*

Table 2-1 (Continued)

U.S. Geological Survey (USGS). Classifies and manages mineral and water resources on federal lands, including the Outer Continental Shelf. Maintains the Earth Resources Observation System (EROS) Data Center that conducts and sponsors research to apply data findings in areas including mapping, geography, mineral and land resources, water resources, rangeland, wildlife and environmental monitoring. *(Interior Department)*

Water and Power Resources Service. Develops and manages water and power resources in the western states. Projects include flood control, river regulation, outdoor recreation opportunities, fish and wildlife enhancement, and water quality improvement. *(Interior Department)*

Source: *Environment and Health* (Washington, D.C.: Congressional Quarterly, 1981), 130-131.

---

whose administrator is appointed by the president, consists of a Washington headquarters and 10 regional offices, each headed by a regional administrator. Unlike most regulatory agencies the EPA administers both regulatory and distributive programs such as the huge federal waste treatment grants, the Superfund program, and varied research activities.

As the nation's principal environmental regulator, the EPA always has been controversial. During the early Reagan administration, however, bitter controversies catapulted the agency into the national limelight.

The president had violated a tacit bipartisan understanding among his predecessors that the EPA should be headed by an individual acceptable to environmentalists and generally sympathetic to the agency's mission. The president's first administrator, Anne Burford, was a former Colorado legislator and corporate attorney whose clients included many industries hostile to federal environmental regulations. Environmentalists interpreted her appointment as a deliberate signal that the White House intended to move the agency's sympathies toward business and other regulated interests and away from the environmental groups that considered themselves the agency's natural constituency. Early on Burford appointed to the agency's upper management individuals exclusively associated with past opponents of EPA programs: 11 of the 15 subordinates named by Burford had been lawyers, lobbyists, or consultants for industries regulated by EPA.

Between 1981 and 1983 the administration sharply reduced EPA's budget and personnel across nearly all programs. Critics charged that the changes had reduced the agency's budget by 30 percent and its employees by 23 percent between 1980 and 1983.[34] Environmental groups and their congressional allies, now a strong and durable coalition, were particularly unsettled by the severe reductions in the agency's resources for the crucial task of program enforcement. By mid-1983 the enforcement budget apparently had been reduced by 45 percent; in the first nine months of 1981 the number of cases sent by EPA to the Justice Department for prosecution had declined to 50 compared with 230 cases the previous year.[35] Defenders of these cutbacks asserted that the EPA could get its regulatory job done better without the "confrontational mode" used in litigation; moreover, they argued, greater efficiency would more than compensate for reductions in budget and manpower.

Further controversy was stirred by allegations that the administration's appointees were actively intervening in programs to relieve from regulation interests sympathetic to the president or to help them receive preferential treatment. Evidence began to accumulate suggesting widespread political chicanery: Superfund grants intended to assist states in cleaning up abandoned toxic waste dumps had been manipulated to help Republican candidates for election; a "hit list" appeared, allegedly intended to purge EPA advisory committees of scientists unfriendly to the administration; the administrator conducted private conferences with industries regulated by the Toxic Substances Control Act to assure them of friendly consideration; and so forth.

Table 2-2 Environmental Protection Agency: Personnel and Budget, Fiscal 1980 to Fiscal 1984 (millions of dollars)

Expenditures[a]	*Fiscal 1980*	*Fiscal 1981*	*Fiscal 1982*	*Fiscal 1983*	*Fiscal 1984 (proposed)*
Abatement, control and compliance	506.4	534.8	373.0	369.1	293.9
Salaries, expenses	524.8	561.7	555.1	548.6	540.4
Research, development	233.5	250.5	154.3	119.0	111.7
Buildings, facilities	2.2	4.1	3.6	3.0	2.6
TOTAL	1,266.9	1,351.1	1,086.0	1,029.7	948.2
Personnel	10,700	12,700	11,450	10,900	10,400

[a] Budget authority.

Source: Executive Office of the President, Office of Management and Budget, *The Budget of the United States Government* (Washington, D.C.: Government Printing Office), fiscal years 1980, 1981, 1982, 1983, and 1984.

By 1983 EPA's internal changes had badly disrupted its programs and demoralized its personnel. The agency's credibility appeared to be damaged and its leadership increasingly preoccupied with congressional investigations or running battles with environmental groups. The situation, already a White House embarrassment, threatened to be a liability during the upcoming presidential election. Finally, with White House prompting, Burford resigned, and soon thereafter most of the other early Reagan appointees within the agency followed. On the day she departed, Harry's Liquor Store in the mall adjacent to EPA headquarters filled an order from the EPA General Counsel's office for eight cases of champagne.

In a more enlightened effort to manage the agency, the president next appointed William D. Ruckelshaus as its administrator. Ruckelshaus, the agency's first administrator, was widely regarded among environmentalists and others as an able and concerned environmental administrator; his considerable support among both congressional parties and within the EPA itself seemed to promise a period of greater stability, less partisan bickering, and possibly more White House support for the agency's programs. Yet Ruckelshaus also had strong personal and professional ties with business and other interests regulated by his department; he had left an executive position with the Weyerhaeuser Company, a timber industry giant, to take the administrator's job. Many environmentalists doubted that he would be able, even if willing, to push environmental programs aggressively in an administration so unsympathetic to most environmentalist values. Ruckelshaus's unsuccessful efforts to persuade the president to support immediate new controls on fossil fuel emissions associated with acid rain, one of the administrator's first policy initiatives, seemed to confirm these suspicions. To many environmentalists Ruckelshaus seemed destined to become a frustrated and futile figure in a political environment so inhospitable to his agency.

In its first term the administration successfully bled many EPA programs of the personnel and resources essential for their effective operation through administrative and budgetary strategies. The administration's early attack on the agency and its environmental defenders had so deeply embittered the relationship between the White House and the environmental movement that the conflict, already the most severe in a half century, would continue so long as Reagan remained president. While his administration had not achieved many of the legislative victories over EPA's programs it had sought, such as major revision of the

Clean Air Act, it had forced some measure of "regulatory relief" on the agency by other means; in this respect, it had achieved at least a portion of its environmental objectives.

While failing to achieve most of its major legislative objectives in environmental policy, the administration had managed to fashion firmly for itself an antienvironmental image. The administration's environmental frustrations stemmed from its failure to appreciate some fundamental political realities. The White House and its initial EPA managers had badly underestimated the environmental movement's political strength, the durability of its bipartisan congressional support, and the symbolic importance attached to environmental programs by the public. Perhaps beguiled by their own rhetoric, Republican managers within the agency waited vainly for an outpouring of public and congressional support for their vigorous attack upon existing environmental legislation.

Moreover, making substantial program changes administratively, while simultaneously attacking career personnel, practically ensured the agency's vigorous resistance. Like other large federal bureaucracies, the EPA could fight back against White House opponents by mobilizing its congressional and interest group allies.

Finally, the initial Reagan management team in EPA attempted to turn too many sensitive technical determinations to partisan advantage by insisting upon political criteria for decisions—as, for example, when deciding which states were most endangered by abandoned hazardous waste sites.

Although the proper boundaries are often difficult to define, most interests concerned with environmental policy share the belief that scientific and political considerations should be kept apart in the making of technical determinations.

Council on Environmental Quality

The National Environmental Policy Act included a provision for the establishment of a commission to advise the president on environmental matters. To be headed by three members appointed by the president, the Council on Environmental Quality (CEQ) was to be part of the president's staff. Among the major responsibilities prescribed for the council in section 203 of NEPA were (1) to gather for the president's consideration "timely and authoritative information concerning the conditions and trends in the quality of the environment both current and prospective"; (2) "to develop and recommend to the President national policies to foster and promote the improvement of environmental quality"; and (3) "to review and appraise the various programs and activities of the Federal Government" to determine the extent to which they comply, among other things, with the requirement for writing EISs. Thus the CEQ was created, like other major presidential advisory commissions, to provide policy advice and evaluation from within the White House directly to the president.

Ever since its first year of operation in 1971, the CEQ has published a widely distributed and densely documented annual report, a periodic appraisal of major environmental trends, issues, and new developments. The council also administers the process for writing and reviewing EISs within the federal government. Although the CEQ is a small agency with no regulatory responsibilities or major environmental programs beyond modest research activities, it assumes enormous symbolic importance and political value to environmental interests. Its presence within the White House implies a high national priority to environmental programs, and the council's opportunities to influence the president directly mean that it can act, in the words of environmental leader Russell Peterson, as "the environmental conscience of the executive branch." Nonetheless, like all other presidential advisory bodies, it can exercise no more influence in White House decisions than the president cares to give it; it may carry on its NEPA-mandated activities, but the president is free to ignore any of its recommendations or other initiatives.

The CEQ's rapid decline in status between the Carter and Reagan administrations illustrates how much its effectiveness depends upon presidential favor. While the council enjoyed considerable influence under President Carter, a strong environmentalist himself, its influence plummeted rapidly with the Reagan administration. One of Reagan's earliest acts after his inauguration was to reduce the council's staff to 15 from 49 and its budget by 50 percent: the symbolism was obvious to environmentalists.[36] The severe reductions in the council's resources caused an immediate decline in the CEQ's publications and other research activities. Moreover, two and a half years after he entered the White House, the president still had not appointed the third member of the council. The new chairman asserted that the council, despite its emasculated condition, still could do its job. He maintained that the CEQ would function in a "neutral corner" in the formation of environmental policy with "no axe to grind." [37] Environmentalists regarded such rhetoric as evidence that under the Reagan administration the council would become little more than White House decoration, tolerated only because it could not be abolished.

Despite its banishment to the nether regions of the Reagan White House, the CEQ is likely to assume again an important role within an administration more sympathetic to ecological issues. Its continuing statutory placement within the White House and its important responsibilities ensure that the CEQ's members and staff over time will be strategically placed to influence environmental decisions at the highest levels within the executive branch.

The Interior Department

Established as a cabinet-level department in 1845, the Interior Department has acquired responsibilities for more than a century that leave few national environmental issues untouched. The department's important environmental responsibilities include (1) protection and management of more than 549 million acres of public land—roughly 28 percent of the total U.S. land area—set aside by Congress for national parks, wilderness areas, forests, and other restricted use; (2) administration of Indian lands and federal Indian programs, including authority over western tribal lands containing a very large proportion of the coal, petroleum, uranium, and other largely unexploited energy resources in the western United States; (3) enforcement of federal surface mining regulations through its Office of Surface Mining; (4) conservation and management of wetlands and estuarine areas; and (5) protection and preservation of wildlife, including endangered species. Headed by a cabinet secretary appointed by the president, the department's programs historically have been a primary concern to environmentalists; the interior secretary, although not always identified with the environmental or conservationist movements, in recent decades has been compatible with their interests.

At the beginning of the Reagan administration, the Interior Department—and particularly Reagan's first choice as the department's secretary, Watt—became the source of continual controversy as a result of its efforts to make sweeping changes in personnel and programs. Critics charged that the department's programs to protect the environment had been placed on the agenda for an administration "hit list" applied by Secretary Watt. The secretary, more than any other official, epitomized to environmentalists all that seemed wrong with the Reagan administration's environmental record; he became the movement's archvillain. Watt, who seemed to relish bare-knuckle political brawls, insisted he had a public mandate to accomplish long-overdue reforms thwarted—until the Reagan administration—by a small clique of selfish and narrow-minded environmental interests. With his environmental opposition he expressed little patience:

> The environmentalists who were so vocal and shrill in opposition to me have lost much of their credibility with Congress. Seldom are these shrill groups for any person. They're against people.... These groups are not a positive force in the political scene....[38]

The controversies were rooted in strong convictions held by environmental groups about the nature of the department and its mission. Environmentalists maintain that Interior's leadership—like EPA's—should be acceptable to the environmental movement and reasonably supportive of the department's programs. Although the secretary was known as an able administrator who had extensive experience with Interior and the Federal Power Commission, prior to his appointment he had served as the head of the Mountain States Legal Foundation, a conservative public interest group representing a number of corporate and state governmental interests opposing federal environmental regulations. Further, he regarded himself as a westerner come to Washington to restore more control of federal lands to state governments and private interests anxious to use the vast resources on the public domain.

Environmentalists were disturbed as well by the appointment of numerous individuals who had been critical of programs to guard resources to administer those very programs. Environmentalists particularly criticized administrative changes that appeared to emasculate environmental programs through starvation: rather than overtly oppose these programs, opponents within Interior were gutting them by denying them money and manpower. Within the first six months of the Reagan administration, for example, personnel in Interior's Office of Surface Mining had been reduced to 628 from 1000, and 28 lawyers had been fired from the department's Solicitor's Office.[39] To most environmentalists the secretary's departmental agenda seemed the opposite of their own conservation goals: he intended to accelerate oil and gas exploration on the outer continental shelf, open more federal lands to fossil fuel development, give concessionaires in the national parks wider influence in making park policies, and give the states greater control over federal lands within their boundaries.

The department, as we shall observe frequently in later chapters, has always been caught between interests seeking to conserve the resources in the public domain and those seeking at least limited access to them. The department's responsibilities customarily include an obligation to ensure "balanced use" of resources between conservation and development—a mandate that continually places the department and its secretary in the middle of controversies concerning what use shall dominate in issues such as grazing, exploring for minerals, or timbering on federal lands. Moreover, the department's programs serve a clientele that includes not only environmentalists but also the timber and cattle industries, mining companies, sportsmen, a multitude of private corporations, and many other interests who expect the department to be equally solicitous of their viewpoints. Finally, the western states historically have maintained that they have been given insufficient influence in the administration of the federal lands that often constitute the vast majority of land within their boundaries. The desire of these states to assume greater control over the public domain within their jurisdictions and the resulting tensions with Washington will outlive any administration.

In October 1983 James Watt resigned from his position, the victim of his own ideological and rhetorical intemperance; he had finally accumulated too many enemies to be an administration asset. His replacement, William P. Clark, proved far less controversial in his public behavior but no less committed to the Reagan administration's environmental program than his predecessor. Few significant policy changes were expected in the department's management.

The Nuclear Regulatory Commission

The NRC was created by Congress in 1976 to assume the regulatory responsibilities originally vested in the Atomic Energy Commission. An independent agency with five commissioners appointed by the president, the NRC regulates most nonmilitary uses of nuclear facilities and materials. The commission's major activities related to the environment include the (1) regulation of the site choice, construction, operation, and security of all civilian nuclear reactors; (2) designation and supervision of all nuclear waste repositories; (3) regulation of uranium mining and milling facilities; and (4) closing of civilian nuclear facilities after their use (called decommissioning). In 1984 the NRC employed about 4,000 individuals with a budget of approximately $500 million.

Environmental groups have been most concerned with the NRC's supervision of nuclear power plants and repositories for radioactive wastes. Although more than 80 nuclear plants were approved for construction in the early 1980s, the majority of those under construction in 1984 have been criticized by environmental groups for alleged deficiencies in structural safety, control of radioactive emissions, and waste storage.[40] Additionally, environmental groups often have been very aggressive in seeking NRC safety reviews of operating plants and personnel training. The federal government has not yet designated a permanent repository for the nation's steadily mounting nuclear wastes, and until 1982 it lacked a clear process for designating such a site. With the passage of the Nuclear Waste Act (1982) the federal government in collaboration with the states will be planning for the designation and construction of the nation's first permanent nuclear waste sites before 1990. The NRC will assume a major responsibility for the review of the site selection and the supervision of the waste disposal on the sites; environmental groups regard the process for the site selection and disposal of these nuclear wastes as a major issue of the decade.[41]

The NRC and environmental groups have been adversaries and allies. The environmental movement generally has supported the NRC's stricter enforcement and review of regulations for operating nuclear facilities and its increasingly rigorous standards for new facility licensing. Yet environmentalists also have criticized the NRC for allegedly siding too often with the nuclear power industry against its critics, for bureaucratic inertia and conservatism, and for ignoring technical criticism and data from sources not associated with the nuclear power industry or the commission. Like other regulatory agencies, the NRC is bound to its own clientele—the nuclear power industry—by professional associations, common technical and economic concerns, and historic sympathies; it is also committed to regulating the industry in the public interest while maintaining sufficient objectivity and disengagement from the nuclear power movement to do that job. These often conflicting responsibilities lead the NRC into controversies with environmental interests. Nonetheless, the NRC and its mission remain among the most environmentally significant elements in the executive branch.

The Energy Department

Despite its size and importance the Energy Department has been the stepchild of the executive branch. Widely criticized, burdened with difficult and often unpopular programs, the department continues to exist largely because Congress cannot agree upon how to replace it. The department was created in 1976 when Congress combined a number of independent agencies with programs already operating in other departments in order to bring the federal government's sprawling energy activities within a single bureaucratic structure. Under the Energy Department's jurisdiction are a number of regulatory activities and energy programs affecting the environment. Among these, the more important include the (1) promotion of civilian nuclear power activities; (2) regulation of military nuclear facilities and radioactive wastes; (3) administration of the federal government's research and development programs in energy production and conservation; (4) regulation of price controls for domestic petroleum and natural gas; and (5) administration of federal research and development grants for commercial synthetic fuels production in the United States. With approximately 18,000 employees and a budget of $6.5 billion in 1984, the Energy Department is the principal executive agency involved in the regulation and production of many different energy technologies with significant environmental impacts.

From its inception the department has lacked strong leadership and internal stability.[42] Its important research and development programs often have been plagued by delays, maladroit administration, and controversies. Constant internal reorganizations have left the agency's staff demoralized and confused about its mission and viability. Nonetheless, the agency's authority embraces a multitude of programs with potentially significant impacts for the 1980s, especially the synthetic fuels program, the research and development activities associated with energy conservation, and the job of siting nuclear waste facilities.

In addition to these agencies many other executive branch bureaucracies have some significant regulatory responsibilities or programs affecting the environment. Included in this group are the Commerce Department's National Oceanic and Atmospheric Administration (NOAA), intended to promote environmentally sensitive land-use planning in the coastal areas of the United States; the Defense Department's U.S. Army Corps of Engineers, the nation's primary builder of civilian water resource projects; and the Agriculture Department's U.S. Forest Service, whose jurisdiction includes most of the national forests. Indeed, it is a rare federal department or independent agency whose responsibilities do not in some manner affect the environment. This multitude of bureaucratic entities daily involved in environmental administration leads, as we shall see, to many of the difficulties in interpreting and enforcing environmental programs throughout the federal government.

The Public Setting

Public officials and agencies are highly sensitive to organized interests and public attitudes related to environmental affairs. The priorities assigned to environmental issues and the substance of environmental policy depend substantially upon the character of these political pressures generated from the public sector. Public opinion often provides a cue to legislators concerning which environmental issues possess the public salience and intensity to require attention on the legislative agenda. Public attitudes also may determine limits to alternatives explored through the policy process or strongly move policy in specific directions. Organized interests are particularly important in environmental affairs because they constitute the continually active, informed, and vigilant "public" clearly involved with governmental policy making— organized interests are the constituency to which public policy makers usually respond in the course of daily decision making. Moreover, interest groups form a political communications network through which policy issues are translated into terms relevant to concerned citizens and by which individuals can be mobilized for political action in environmental issues. In short the public sector must be considered an essential element in the environmental policy process.

Public Opinion and the Environment

During a 1981 congressional committee hearing on proposed amendments to the Clean Air Act, a committee member asked pollster Louis Harris what he had discovered about public opinion on the issue. Any member of Congress who voted to weaken the act, replied the pollster, did so "at the risk of losing his seat." Shortly thereafter President Reagan's own pollster, Richard Wirthlin, reminded the Republican Senate staff that his own polls supported such a conclusion "emphatically." Largely because of this public mood Congress ended its 97th session without amending the act, despite Republican pledges to do so.[43]

A decade earlier few observers, including most environmentalists, would have predicted the public would remain highly supportive of environmental values for more than a few years; environmentalism, however fashionable, in the end would be perishable.[44] Perhaps the most significant aspect of public opinion concerning the environment is that environmental protection has become a "consensual value" in the years since 1970: a broadly and strongly held public belief that indicates environmental protection has become part of the nation's dominant policy priorities.

A *New York Times*/CBS poll in late 1981 suggests the strength of this concern. According to this poll, 67 percent of the public expressed a willingness to maintain current environmental laws "even at the cost of some economic growth."[45] The general high regard for environmental groups also provides evidence of support for their values. One major poll, for instance, suggested in 1982 that the public had greater confidence in environmental groups (74 percent) than in university professors (72 percent), their state governments (70 percent), the president (59 percent), or the news media (47 percent).[46] Table 2-3, which traces expressions of public interest in numerous issues between 1972 and 1980, suggests the enduring concern for environmental issues.

In light of this environmental consciousness it is hardly surprising that members of Congress should consider amending the Clean Air Act— widely regarded as the legislative symbol of the Environmental Era—so warily.

The broad social base of support for the environmental movement is equally significant. Environmentalists have been sensitive to accusations that ecology is the respectable packaging used by the privileged middle class to legitimate to the underprivileged, who will be the economic victims of environmentalism, the largely self-serving goals of the movement. Social writer William Tucker, voicing a common indictment among critics of the environmental movement, asserts that environmentalism is little more than camouflaged elitism: "Environmentalism, because it is oriented toward the status quo, had an inevitable appeal to people toward the top of the social ladder, and a negative appeal to those nearer the bottom. . . . At heart, environmentalism favors the affluent over the poor, the haves over the have nots." [47] However, while evidence suggests that the less advantaged are likely to care more about other issues, environmentalism nonetheless evokes considerable approval among virtually all socioeconomic groups. A 1980 poll sponsored jointly by the CEQ and EPA suggests, as do many other public surveys, this breadth of support.

Table 2-3 Public Concern with Environmental and Other Domestic Issues, 1972-1980[a]

Question: How worried are you about the:	1972 June	1974 April	1976 May	1980 Jan.-Feb.	1980 Mar.
a. Rise in prices and the cost of living?					
A great deal	—	83%	75%	81%	86%
Not much, not at all	—	4	4	3	3
b. Shortages of oil, gasoline, coal, natural gas, electricity, or other fuels?					
A great deal	—	57	—	73	—
Not much, not at all		17		7	
c. Disposal of industrial chemical wastes that are hazardous?					
A great deal	—	—	—	—	64
Not much, not at all					9
d. Cleaning up of our waterways and reducing water pollution?					
A great deal	61	51	57	39	54
Not much, not at all	8	12	9	16	12
e. Presence of toxic chemicals such as pesticides or PCBs in the environment?					
A great deal	—	—	—	—	46
Not much, not at all					20

		1,802	1,865	1,071	1,576	2,003
f. Problems of the poor?	A great deal	—	—	—	—	44
	Not much, not at all	—	—	—	—	13
g. Purity of the drinking water in your community?	A great deal	—	—	—	—	42
	Not much, not at all	—	—	—	—	29
h. Reduction of air pollution?	A great deal	60	46	55	36	—
	Not much, not at all	10	15	11	23	—
i. Reduction of the amount of unnecessary noise in this community?	A great deal	—	—	—	—	11
	Not much, not at all	—	—	—	—	68
N=		1,802	1,865	1,071	1,576	2,003

[a] Data for 1972-1976 are from the "State of the Nation" studies done by Potomac Associates. A dash indicates that the item was not included in a survey. The data labeled January-February are from the Resources for the Future survey for the Council on Environmental Quality and include 287 additional interviews in late March. The data labeled March 1980 are from a regular Roper survey. The four items asked in March were included in March because two of them had been inadvertently omitted in the January-February survey. The other two, on inflation and water pollution, were included in the January-February survey for comparative purposes.

Source: Council on Environmental Quality, *Public Opinion on Environmental Issues* (Washington, D.C.: Government Printing Office, 1980), 26-27.

Public support for environmentalism also is evident in the substantial portion of the population that appears willing to make significant sacrifices, or to accept rather costly trade-offs, for environmental protection. Thus a 1982 Roper poll found that almost 46 percent of the public was "on the side of protecting the environment" if the United States were forced to choose between environmental protection and adequate energy supplies.[48] Generally public opinion polls indicate surprisingly strong public support of environmental protection even when it involves major social costs, such as reduced economic growth, smaller energy supplies, or factory closings. These sentiments do not guarantee, however, that the public correctly understands and accepts the real implications of these trade-offs. Still, the polls impress many public officials as a demonstration of ecology's political strength.

Moreover, the environment may be an enduring public concern, but it is not necessarily an all-consuming one. The salience of environmental matters varies. A national poll between 1965 and 1980, which asked individuals to identify the three national issues to which they thought government should give the most attention, reflects the volatility of public preoccupation with environmental issues. Among the 10 issues mentioned by respondents, "reducing air and water pollution" was ranked ninth in 1965, second in 1970, and sixth in 1980. In another poll, public concern for pollution during this same period also widely varied; while 53 percent of the public thought pollution a major problem in 1970, by 1980 only 24 percent thought so.[49]

One might also wonder about the firmness of public tolerances for environmental protection when significant and visible costs are inflicted upon an individual or community. For instance, one poll asking the public "Would you favor or oppose keeping air pollution laws as tough as they are now, even if some factories might have to close?" found that 68 percent of the respondents would accept the factory closings.[50] But in another poll only a month later respondents were asked how they felt about "closing factories in a local area until they make the necessary changes to meet clean air standards even if it results in unemployment and hurts the economy of the area." Faced with the possible social costs of environmental protection to their own communities, 63 percent of the respondents opposed the factory closing.[51]

These variations in public opinion raise important issues for the environmental movement in the 1980s. Public support for environmental protection may be "soft" in the face of a severe crisis that appears to force

Figure 2-1 Public View of the Environmental Movement, 1980

Question: "In recent years, the environmental movement has been very active. Do you think of yourself as: an active participant in the environmental movement, sympathetic towards the movement but not active, neutral or unsympathetic towards the environmental movement?"

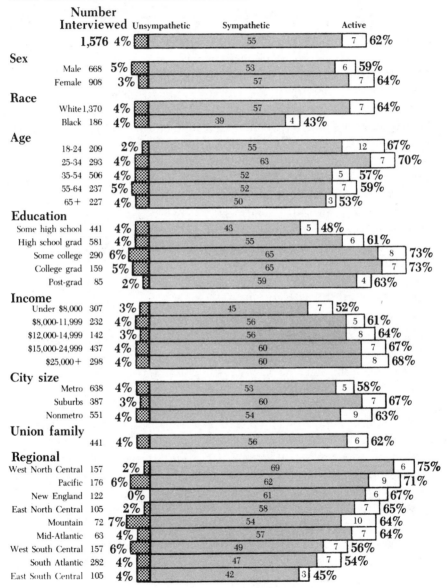

Note: Categories not shown in this figure and the national percentages are: Neutral (31%) and Unsure (3%).

Source: Council on Environmental Quality, *Public Opinion on Environmental Issues* (Washington, D.C.: Government Printing Office, 1980), 44-45.

a choice between environmental values and other national priorities, particularly energy supply and economic growth. Indeed, opinion polls strongly suggest that the public is most likely to waver in its support of environmental protection when it is forced to choose between environmental values and economic growth or energy supply. (Environmentalists insist, however, that the nation can reconcile these values without any significant sacrifice.) Without constant crises or other dramatic evidence of continuing environmental dangers, there remains the possibility of renewed public apathy as the environmental issue sinks further from public awareness and other preoccupations dominate the media and the public mind. Finally, environmental leaders are aware that the costs of environmental protection are high and will continue to rise as the full scope of environmental degradation is appreciated through new research into matters such as toxic wastes or acid rain. Public acceptance of the costs for responsible environmental management may become brittle when the cost is immediate and personal—when the factory to be closed is down the street or the electric bill must rise to pay for pollution control. Thus, environmentalism is a consensual value whose durability has yet to be fully tested.

The Environmental Movement

Viewed at close range the environmental movement shows a diversity of viewpoints, social support, and political strategies common to most large interests in U.S. society, such as business or agriculture; environmentalism encompasses a great pluralism of environmentalists.

The Organizational Base. The large national environmental organizations have approximately 5 million members and about 3,000 local organizations. A 1980 estimate suggests that as much as 7 percent of the U.S. population may be involved in some type of environmental organization.[52] If state and local environmental groups, as well as relatively short-lived ad hoc organizations, are added to the national totals, the number of active groups and individuals appears to be even larger and, as we shall see, growing.

Socially, the national environmental organizations attract primarily a white, well-educated, and relatively affluent membership. As sociologist Robert Mitchell has documented, the average member of a major national environmental group tends to be strongly liberal; in a 1980 survey of environmental group members, 80 percent of those surveyed supported civil rights activism, the antiwar movement, and the women's movement.[53]

Organizationally, the environmental movement can be divided into a core coalition, close allies, and fellow travelers. The core coalition consists of the national organizations, usually with state and local chapters, most consistently active and vocal in environmental matters. The core coalition, however, is no church singing one hymn. Within this coalition are a plurality of environmental viewpoints. One ideological grouping, represented by the Sierra Club and the Wilderness Society, promotes hard-line preservation. Preservationism, inspired by the great American naturalist John Muir, stresses the importance of protecting and preserving open space and natural resources against all forms of economic exploitation or other "development"; it is generally hostile to uncontrolled population growth and urban expansion and to any forms of technological or economic development that seem to threaten a major disruption in the existing ecological order. Preservationists have been the conservatives of the environmental movement, those least willing to make accommodations and compromises with continued conversion of open space and natural resources to economic development.

A second significant component of the core coalition is recreationists, such as the large, 1.5 million-member National Wildlife Federation or the Izaak Walton League, concerned principally for the preservation and development of resources for hunting, fishing, and other activities. Recreationists, unlike preservationists, often have been willing to tolerate economic development of natural resources and "multiple" use of public lands so long as game and recreational opportunities are not harmed.

Another important segment of the core coalition might be called protectionists, to emphasize their concern with the preservation of endangered species and wildlife habitat. This group includes the National Audubon Society—among the oldest, most active, and most well known of all organizations associated with environmental protection in the United States. Within this center coalition of the movement are organizations that attempt to conduct broad research, publication, and lobbying activities representing all the major concerns of the movement. The best known among this group is probably the Conservation Foundation, whose competence has led some environmental leaders to call it the "Vatican of the Environmental Movement."

Lastly, several national organizations specialize almost exclusively in initiating litigation or intervening in administrative procedures of federal and state governments for the purpose of establishing important legal precedents or creating significant legal issues. Two organizations, the Environmental Defense Fund and the Natural Resources Defense Council, have established preeminent reputations in this field.

Other interests, although not explicitly environmental, are strongly sympathetic to environmental causes. Liberal public interest groups such as the League of Women Voters, Common Cause, and Ralph Nader's Public Citizen are among these organizations. Also commonly associated with environmental causes are a variety of organizations, which can be called "forensic science groups," that speak professionally for scientists and other technicians concerned with public issues. The Boston-based Union of Concerned Scientists and Washington's Center for Science in the Public Interest frequently have been active collaborators with environmental organizations in urging stronger state and federal control of toxic materials, more regulation of workplace hazards, and other technical issues. State and local government agencies concerned with environmental affairs often work with environmental groups in areas of mutual concern, such as increased federal support for state and local pollution regulation.

Less closely associated with environmental causes, yet often strong allies, are several major fellow travelers in the political arena. When job security is not threatened, organized labor often vigorously supports environmental programs, particularly those concerned with air and water pollution control or the regulation of hazardous substances. Thus, while the AFL-CIO's national headquarters is a strong proponent of the Clean Air Act, the United Auto Workers union often has favored relaxation of deadlines for auto emission controls when strict enforcement appears to create economic difficulties for Detroit. Environmental organizations have made a particularly strong appeal to organized labor, blue-collar employees, and agricultural workers through campaigns for greater workplace safety and control of hazardous substances to which workers may be exposed. The campaign to regulate toxic substances has become an effective means of broadening the movement's social base and blunting accusations of "social elitism" directed at the movement. The antinuclear movement also has joined the environmental coalition when common cause could be made for nuclear regulation.

However, environmental groups have been adept at forming alliances with almost any interest whose collaboration might be a political advantage. In the environmental division of Politics Makes Strange

Bedfellows, for instance, one might ponder the coalition that opposed in 1981 renewed funding of the Clinch River Breeder Reactor project: major environmental organizations such as the Natural Resources Defense Council and the Friends of the Earth were joined by the International Association of Machinists and Aerospace Workers, the Methodist church's General Board of Church and Society, Rural America, the Union of Concerned Scientists, and conservative groups such as the Heritage Foundation and the National Taxpayers Union. (The latter two organizations, especially, have rarely been accused of vigorous environmental sympathies).

Growth and Change. Significant changes have occurred within the environmental movement in the 1980s. Most national environmental groups experienced a major growth surge in the 1980s, inspired by the movement's alarm at what it perceived to be the Reagan administration's aggressive antienvironmentalism. Extremely vigorous recruitment drives found a responsive audience. In 1981, for example, the Sierra Club grew at a rate unprecedented in its history; by the mid-1980s it said it had more than 250,000 members. Many other groups, especially state and local organizations, formed and expanded to deal with the regulation of hazardous substances—an issue creating intense public interest and apprehension.

Many environmental groups are becoming more politically active in elections, and this is a change with unknown ramifications. Several organizations, such as the Sierra Club and Friends of the Earth, have formed their own political action committees (PACs) through which money can be contributed directly to candidates. The League of Conservation Voters, an umbrella organization for many environmental groups, has become increasingly active in congressional and presidential elections; its list of congressional candidates targeted for defeat is a widely publicized focus of its activities. Although environmental groups risk a loss of income and internal dissatisfaction at "going partisan," most environmental leaders believe the strategy has been and will continue to be more successful than earlier political tactics that emphasized primarily legislative lobbying and public education. This electoral collaboration demonstrates a growing tendency toward the formation of common political strategies among the major environmental groups; in recent years groups also have worked together to initiate litigation and to campaign for various state referendums.

During the 1970s several national environmental organizations increased the size of their technical staffs to provide scientific research and expert testimony on environmental issues. This structural change was expected to contribute significantly to the groups' political impact. In 1984 almost half of the Environmental Defense Fund's staff and a substantial portion of the NRDC's had scientific or technical training. The Conservation Foundation has added an economics staff enabling it to provide in-house economic analyses of important issues. The growing technical capacity of environmental organizations relieves them from depending upon expert testimony or scientific studies provided solely by government agencies or regulated interests in policy making. Moreover, an in-house technical staff provides expert witnesses available to testify in court cases or administrative hearings, where the credibility of the organization's viewpoints may depend heavily upon the competence of its witnesses in highly technical disputes. In environmental policy, as the next chapter will emphasize, issues often turn upon technical disputes and conflicting expert testimony. The growing capacity of environmental groups to enter these controversies competently provides an additional source of influence and access to government for such groups.

The Political Environment of Environmentalism

In an important sense, environmental degradation is a twentieth century problem resolved according to eighteenth century rules: fundamental governmental arrangements such as institutional checks and balances, interest group liberalism, congressional localism, and much else reviewed in this chapter are explicitly created by the Constitution or implicit in its philosophy. In contrast bureaucracy has imparted to environmental policy making, as to other federal policies, a distinctly twentieth century character; administrative politics are now as fundamental in shaping environmental policy as any other, older element in the Constitution.

The explosive growth within the last few decades of federal environmental legislation, together with a specialized environmental bureaucracy, has added distinctly new elements to the federal policy cycle and indicates that environmental management has become a permanent new policy domain within federal and state governments with its own set of institutional and political biases. In short environmental policy making today occurs within a context of many political givens whose collective impact upon the substance of environmental policy has been the focus of this chapter.

Notes

1. *New York Times*, October 30, 1980.
2. Lawrence Mosher, "Reagan and the GOP Are Riding the Sagebrush Rebellion—But for How Long?" *National Journal*, March 21, 1981, 479.
3. The Supreme Court did not rule specifically on the constitutionality of the congressional veto as it applied to Secretary Watt.
4. Hugh Heclo, "Issue Networks and the Executive Establishment," in *The New American Political System*, ed. Anthony King (Washington, D.C.: American Enterprise Institute, 1979), 89.
5. Charles O. Jones, *An Introduction to the Study of Public Policy* (North Scituate, Mass.: Duxbury Press, 1978), chapter 2.
6. Roger W. Cobb and Charles D. Elder, *Participation in American Politics* (Baltimore: John Hopkins University Press, 1972), 86.
7. Eugene Bardach, *The Implementation Game* (Cambridge, Mass.: MIT Press, 1971), 36.
8. Peter deLeon, "A Theory of Termination in the Policy Process: Rules, Rhymes and Reasons" (Paper delivered at the annual meeting of the American Political Science Association, Washington, D.C., September 1-4, 1977), 2.
9. Richard E. Neustadt, *Presidential Power* (New York: John Wiley and Sons, 1960).
10. Morton Grodzins, "The Federal System," in *American Federalism in Perspective*, ed. Aaron Wildavsky (Boston: Little, Brown, 1967), 257.
11. Ibid., 260.
12. The mingling of public and private power is well explored in Grant McConnell, *Private Power and American Democracy* (New York: Vintage Books, 1967).
13. James V. DeLong, "How to Convince an Agency," *Regulation*, September/October, 1982, 31.
14. Graham Allison, *The Essence of Decision* (Boston: Little, Brown, 1971), 163.
15. Charles A. Lindblom, "The Science of 'Muddling Through,'" *Public Administration Review* (Spring 1959): 86.
16. The reasons for this departure are examined carefully in J. Clarence Davies III and Charles F. Lettow, "The Impact of Federal Institutional Arrangements," in *Federal Environmental Law*, ed. Erica L. Dolgin and Thomas G. P. Guilbert (St. Paul, Minn.: West Publishing, 1974), 26-191.
17. Theodore Lowi, "The Public Philosophy: Interest Group Liberalism," *American Political Science Review* (March 1967): 18.
18. McConnell, *Private Power*, 162.
19. Charles A. Lindblom, *The Policy Making Process*, 2d ed. (Englewood Cliffs, N.J.: Prentice-Hall, 1980), 73.
20. Ralph Huitt, "Political Feasibility," in *Policy Analysis in Political Science*, ed. Ira Sharkansky (Chicago: Markham Publishing, 1970), 410.

21. Ibid., 414.
22. *New York Times*, November 5, 1981.
23. R. Douglas Arnold, *Congress and the Bureaucracy* (New Haven: Yale University Press, 1979), 133.
24. Lawrence Mosher, "Clean Water Requirements Will Remain Even if the Federal Spigot Is Closed," *National Journal*, May 16, 1981, 874-878.
25. *National Journal*, November 21, 1981, 2078.
26. David D. Doniger, *The Law and Policy of Toxic Substances Control* (Baltimore: Johns Hopkins University Press, 1978), 3.
27. U.S. General Accounting Office, "Cleaning Up Nuclear Facilities—An Aggressive And Unified Federal Program Is Needed," Report No. GAO/EMD-82-40 (May 25, 1982), v.
28. Werner J. Grunbaum, *Judicial Policymaking: The Supreme Court and Environmental Quality* (Morristown, N.J.: General Learning Press, 1976), 31.
29. R. Shep Melnick, *Regulation and the Courts: The Case of the Clean Air Act* (Washington, D.C.: Brookings Institution, 1983), 73.
30. Ibid., especially chapter 4.
31. Grunbaum, *Judicial Policymaking*.
32. Lettie McSpadden Wenner, "Interest Group Litigation and Environmental Policy," *Policy Studies Journal* (June 1983): 674.
33. See summaries of NEPA litigation in the 1980 and 1981 Council on Environmental Quality annual reports; see also Richard A. Liroff, "NEPA Litigation in the 1970s: A Deluge or a Dribble?" *Natural Resources Journal* (April 1981): 315-330.
34. Details on the Reagan administration's early budgetary attack on environmental programs may be found in the Conservation Foundation, *State of the Environment 1982* (Washington, D.C.: Conservation Foundation, 1982), chapter 9.
35. *New York Times*, October 15, 1982.
36. Lawrence Mosher, "Environmental Quality Council Trims Its Sails in Stormy Budget Weather," *National Journal*, July 24, 1982, 1306-1307.
37. *New York Times*, May 23, 1982.
38. *Public Opinion*, February 3, 1981, 13.
39. Lawrence Mosher, "Regulatory Striptease—Watt Takes Aim at Surface Mining Regulations," *National Journal*, May 30, 1981, 971-973.
40. The environmentalist viewpoint may be found in Ralph Nader and John Abbotts, *The Menace of Atomic Energy* (New York: W. W. Norton, 1979); and Stephen Hilgartner, Richard C. Bell, and Rory O'Connor, *Nukespeak: The Selling of Nuclear Technology in America* (San Francisco: Sierra Club Books, 1982).
41. On the general problems of nuclear waste disposal, see the balanced discussion in the Ford Foundation, *Nuclear Power Issues and Choices* (Cambridge, Mass.: Ballinger Publishing, 1977), chapter 8.
42. Christopher Madison, "The Energy Department At Three—Still Trying to Establish Itself," *National Journal*, October 4, 1980.
43. *New York Times*, November 3, 1981.
44. See, for instance, Anthony Downs, "Up and Down of Ecology—the 'Issue-Attention' Cycle," *Public Interest* (Summer 1972): 38-50.
45. *New York Times*, October 4, 1981. See also William Schneider, "The Environment:

The Public Wants More Protection, Not Less," *National Journal*, March 26, 1983, 676.

46. *Public Opinion*, February/March 1982, 37.
47. William Tucker, "The Environmental Era," *Public Opinion*, February/March 1982, 44.
48. Schneider, "The Environment."
49. CEQ, *Public Opinion on Environmental Issues: Results of a National Public Opinion Survey* (Washington, D.C.: Government Printing Office, 1980), 7.
50. *Public Opinion*, February/March 1982, 35.
51. Ibid.
52. CEQ, *Public Opinion on Environmental Issues*, 44.
53. *National Journal*, December 13, 1980.

I just had an eight-hour briefing on fine particulate standards. These are the ones that get deep down into your lungs, rather than the bigger particulate standard we now have. Our scientists told me we could defend any standard between 150 and 250 parts per million. So pick a number.

—EPA Administrator William D. Ruckelshaus
on amending the Clean Air Act

'Pick a Number': Science, Politics, and Environment

In the fall of 1982 Environmental Protection Agency (EPA) technicians examining soil samples from roadways in the small suburban St. Louis community of Times Beach discovered extremely high levels of the chemical 2,3,7,8-tetrachlorodibenzo-p-dioxin, commonly known as dioxin. Times Beach evidently had been contaminated by one of the earth's most lethal poisons: this was national news. Less than two months later, while investigators were still estimating the extent of the contamination, the rain-gorged Merrimac River overflowed the community; fear of further contamination spread. More than 2,000 individuals apparently had become victims of another hazardous waste crisis, evoking memories of the Love Canal incidents in the late 1970s.

In March 1983 the EPA, under considerable pressure from Congress, allocated $33.6 million, to which the state of Missouri added $3.3 million, to purchase all the homes in Times Beach, confirming that dioxin was sufficiently dangerous to justify the permanent evacuation of the town's 700 families. Today Times Beach is virtually abandoned by its former residents and the media. But a disturbing and unresolved question remains: Has Times Beach become a multimillion-dollar memorial to a phantom crisis?

The Times Beach Controversy

Unquestionably there was dioxin in Times Beach. Sometime in 1972 waste oil laced with a large quantity of dioxin was sprayed, unknown to

79

the residents, on dirt roadways to control dust. Samples of affected soil taken more than 10 years later, shortly before the flood, showed concentrations of dioxin as high as 100 parts per billion, when the chemical was thought to be dangerous in concentrations exceeding 1 part per billion. But was it dangerous? From its initial discovery experts and public officials disagreed, and still disagree, about the gravity of dioxin's threat to community residents. Despite its reputation more is suspected of dioxin than has yet been proven.

Estimates of dioxin's virulence are based largely on animal studies. These, according to the Council on Environmental Quality (CEQ), rank dioxin as 100 times more deadly than strychnine. Like many other public agencies, the CEQ assumed that a substance believed to be so lethal ought to be considered a major environmental hazard:

> Research since 1970 has shown TCCD (dioxin) to be one of the most toxic substances ever studied. Fetotoxic effects have been seen in rats at levels of exposure at least as low as . . . 10 parts per trillion. . . . In monkeys, toxicity to the offspring of treated animals has been shown at doses as low as 2.5 parts per trillion. TCCD has also been shown to be carcinogenic to test animals at doses as low as 2.2 parts per billion.[1]

Largely on the basis of such animal studies, the EPA in early 1979 took the unprecedented action of issuing an emergency order temporarily banning most uses of two of the nation's most common herbicides containing dioxin until further tests of the products were made.

Yet in mid-1982, only weeks after dioxin had been discovered in Times Beach, the EPA was warning that dangers to the community may have been greatly exaggerated. An EPA official complained of "misleading and uninformed comment from outsiders," which confused and alarmed Times Beach residents. One of the "outsiders" was Dr. Barry Commoner, an internationally known biologist and environmentalist who had studied dioxin contamination in Missouri for decades. Commoner, warning that "strong actions" would be required if the initial test results proved accurate, had declared it "unconscionable" to expose residents to the dioxin for long periods.[2] In December the federal Centers for Disease Control issued a warning that the town should be completely evacuated on the basis of soil samples taken before the flood. Yet only a few weeks earlier, the director of the Missouri Department of Natural Resources complained that the biggest problem with the dioxin was that "we don't know how dangerous it really is." Community residents were confused and frustrated by such conflicting assessments. So were reporters, public officials, and others attempting to determine the magnitude of peril to Times Beach.[3]

Public officials responded finally to scientists and others advocating a conservative approach to the dioxin problem. In effect officials accepted the costs of evacuating the whole community, and later purchasing the homes, as preferable to the alternative of exposing residents to dioxin's unknown but possibly dangerous consequences. Yet the true extent of the community's risk remains uncertain and the wisdom of the solution arguable. Following the Times Beach affair the American Medical Association first condemned the news media for generating "unjustified public fright" and "hysteria" by conducting a "witch hunt" against dioxin. Yet the AMA later cited Times Beach and the controversy over the effects of the dioxin in the defoliant Agent Orange upon Vietnam veterans as reasons why public studies were needed to produce reliable evidence about the human risks of dioxin exposure. At almost the same time EPA's new administrator, William D. Ruckelshaus, was advocating the establishment of a national commission to find "some universal way" to measure the health risks from environmental hazards and to establish what the nation was willing to pay to reduce these risks. The controversy spawned at Times Beach is but a single episode in the continuing conflict over the proper means for measuring the risks and costs of exposure to a wide range of substances suspected to be environmentally hazardous.[4]

The Limits of Science in Environmental Policy

Environmental issues draw public officials and scientists into a treacherous zone between science and politics, where collaboration is essential and difficult. Public officials seek from scientists information accurate enough to indicate precisely where to establish environmental standards and credible enough to defend in the inevitable conflicts to follow. Scientists want government to act quickly and forcefully on ecological issues they believe to be critical. Yet science often cannot produce technical information in the form and within the time desired by public officials—indeed, it often cannot provide the information at all—leaving officials to make crucial decisions from fragmentary and disputable information. Scientists often discover that public officials and agencies are unwilling, or unable, to await the slow testing and validation of data before reaching decisions about scientific issues; data are needed now, or tomorrow. And policies often are made, and unmade, without resort to the scientific materials supposed to govern such decisions.

In short, environmental issues often raise difficult scientific and political questions. They compel public officials to make scientific judgments and scientists to resolve policy issues for which neither may be initially trained. The almost inevitable need to resolve scientific questions through the political process and the problems that arise in making scientific and political judgments compatible are two of the most troublesome characteristics of environmental politics.

Science Issues in Political Settings

The growth of environmental legislation in the last two decades is evidence of the federal government's increasing concern with science and technology since World War II.

Legislation concerning atomic power, air and water pollution, workplace and consumer safety, and hazardous wastes all have put before public officials and agencies the need to make determinations of public policy depending heavily upon scientific evidence and scientific judgments. Environmental issues, indeed, routinely require administrative agencies, Congress, judges, the White House staff, and even the president to make these determinations.

The range of scientific judgments required of administrative agencies in implementing environmental programs seems to embrace the whole domain of ecological research.

> The Coast Guard is authorized "in order to secure effective provisions . . . for protection of the marine environment . . . to establish regulations for ships with respect to the design and construction of such vessels . . . and with respect to equipment and appliances for . . . the prevention and mitigation of damage to the marine environment." *(Ports and Waterways Act of 1972)*

> The EPA is to set effluent standards for new sources of water pollution so that each standard reflects "the greatest degree of effluent reduction . . . achievable through application of the best available demonstrated control technology, process, operating methods, or other alternatives, including, where practicable, a standard permitting no discharge of pollutants." *(Federal Water Pollution Control Act of 1972)*

> The EPA is required to establish "standards of performance" for classes and categories of new air pollution sources "which contribute significantly to air pollution or contribute to endangerment of public health or welfare." *(Clean Water Act of 1970)* [5]

Congress, and particularly the congressional committees writing legislation, also may have to resolve a multitude of technical issues. When regulating hazardous substances, for instance, what is a reasonable period to specify for chemical manufacturers to produce reliable data on the human effects of potentially dangerous substances? Is it necessary to regulate air emissions from diesel trucks in order to reduce harmful air pollutants? Is it appropriate to include heavy metals in the list of water pollutants for which standards must be created by the EPA? Eventually judges will be compelled to weigh scientific evidence and render judgment upon environmental issues. Did the Interior Department have sufficient information to file a valid environmental impact assessment on a proposed coal mining lease on federal lands? Do federal standards for nuclear reactors adequately protect public safety as required by law? The fabric of environmental policy is so interwoven with scientific issues that it is impossible to exclude them at any stage of the policy process.

Policy Pressures and Scientific Method

Few public officials are scientists. Faced with the questions inherent in environmental policy, officials customarily turn to scientists and technicians for answers or for, at the least, a definition of alternative solutions that clarify choices. As a matter of practical politics, moreover, solving an issue by resort to credible scientific evidence can spare officials controversy and criticism they might otherwise endure—sometimes science alone legitimates policies. But the public official and the scientist frequently approach environmental issues with different perspectives growing from their differing professional values, responsibilities, and priorities. Often officials discover that science provides no sovereign or simple answers to troublesome issues because the logic of science does not readily fit the requirements of the policy process.[6]

There are, for instance, significant differences in the time frames for problem solving. Public officials often must act quickly; data are needed now, or very soon. The Clean Air Act of 1970 required the EPA administrator to set air standards for sulfur oxides and nitrogen oxide, for instance, within two years. When in 1980 an abandoned chemical waste site was discovered to be leaking many dangerous substances such as DDT and benzine into the ground water near St. Louis, Michigan, the community expected an immediate federal response. But reliable scientific data about environmental problems often appear only after decades of controlled experiment.

Further, the scientist tends to measure the correctness of a policy, when possible, by the standards of experimentation and empiricism. For example, the appropriate standard for an air pollutant would be determined by careful dose-response studies involving animals and perhaps human beings. The public official, in contrast, has to calculate a standard's correctness using several additional criteria: Will it satisfy enough public and private interests to be enforceable? Can it be enforced with existing governmental personnel and budget? Does the standard appear credible? (It must not be so controversial as to shake public confidence.) The public official may be content to set environmental standards within a range of acceptable figures, according to what best will balance political, economic, and administrative considerations. But the scientist may measure acceptability by the single standard of precision; accuracy, not acceptability, matters. Under these circumstances, it is understandable that policy makers and their scientific consultants often disagree about what data should be used, and in what manner, in policy decisions. Such situations are replete with opportunities for conflict over how accurately and appropriately information was used in arriving at policy prescriptions.[7]

Derelict Data and Embattled Expertise

Controversy among experts commonly arises in environmental policy making. Contending battalions of experts—all garlanded with degrees and publications, and primed to dispute one another's judgments—predictably appear at congressional and administrative hearings. Substantial expert consensus upon environmental issues is rare; policy makers more often are left to judge not only the wisdom of the policies but also the quality of the science supporting the policies.

Missing Data. Why is controversy so predictable? Frequently there is a void of useful data about the distribution and severity of environmental problems or possible pollutants. Many problems are so recent that public and private agencies have only begun to study them. Many pollutants—hazardous chemicals, for instance—have existed only a few decades; their ecological impacts cannot yet be reliably measured. Quite often the result is that nobody has basic information, the kind "somebody ought to have."

> There are no comprehensive national data on ground water contaminants, the number of exposed persons, or the health effects of exposure. Ground water

data obtained in the past by the states and the U.S. Geological Survey generally ignored the possible impact of hazardous waste disposal and synthetic organic compounds. Case study data from selected water basins examine only a few of several hundred possible compounds contaminating water, and then only when contamination is suspected.[8]

New York city officials really do not know the extent of carbon monoxide and ozone pollution in the city's air because of inadequate monitoring. Regional EPA officials admit that "there has not been really good carbon monoxide monitoring done in the city." In 1978 New York state assumed responsibility for monitoring; the six stations in the city created by the state are considered too few by almost all expert opinion.[9]

A recent federal government study of coal waste concluded: "Much of the information presented on coal wastes was speculative and not universally agreed upon.... Although coal has been around longer than nuclear [power], its environmental and health effects are not as fully understood. In fact, coal wastes were not even recognized as potentially hazardous until recent years."[10 ˙]

Lacking high-quality data, experts often extrapolate answers from fragmentary information; plausible disputes over the reliability of such procedures are inevitable. The scarcity of fundamental information on ecological trends and pollutant characteristics is a major reason why environmental monitoring is essential to prudent policies. However, monitoring is customarily underfunded and undervalued by government because it lacks the political "sex appeal" attracting public interest and official enthusiasm.

Late and Latent Effects. Disagreement over the severity of environmental problems also arises because the effects of many substances thought to be hazardous to humans or the environment may not become evident for decades or generations. The latency and diffusion of these impacts also may make it difficult to establish causality between the suspected substances, or events, and the consequences.

Asbestos, a hazardous chemical whose malignancy has been documented recently, illustrates these problems.[11] Since World War II approximately 8 million to 11 million U.S. workers have been exposed to asbestos, a mineral fiber with more than 2,000 uses; its heat resistance, electrical properties, immunity to chemical deterioration, and other characteristics made it appear ideal to a multitude of major industries. It has been used widely to manufacture break and clutch linings, plastics, plumbing, roofing tile, wall insulation, paint, paper, and much else. Asbestos is also highly carcinogenic. Among those highly exposed to asbestos, 20 percent to 25 percent died of lung cancer, 7 percent to 10 percent perished from mesothelioma (cancer of the chest lining or stomach), and another 8 percent to 9 percent died from gastrointestinal cancer.[12]

This toxicity has become apparent only recently because cancers associated with asbestos do not become clinically evident until 15 years to 40 years after exposure; illness may appear from 2 years to 50 years later. Added to the incalculable cost of human suffering is the immense economic impact of these delayed effects. By 1984 more than 12,500 liability suits had been filed by 35,000 plaintiffs against almost 300 companies involved in the past use or manufacture of asbestos. One major manufacturer, the Johns Manville Company, eventually may be involved in as many as 52,000 suits whose settlements might exceed $2 billion.

Many other substances used in American commerce, science, and domestic life are suspected of producing adverse impacts upon man or the environment.[13] These impacts may be diffuse and latent; conclusive evidence might appear in decades. Yet government must decide whether to regulate these substances now. In effect, experts are estimating the risks from continued use of a substance when the actual effects on man or the environment are largely unknown. Difficult as such calculations are, a failure to act, as in the case of asbestos, may eventually prove so costly in human suffering and economic loss that scientists may be reluctant to wait for conclusive data. Experts also must weigh in their risk calculus the possible irreversibility of anticipated future impacts. These complex and often tenuous determinations lead to honest disagreements over the validity of most risk assessments associated with hazardous substances.

The Risks in Risk Assessment. The current controversy within the scientific community over the "Greenhouse Effect" illustrates the difficulties inherent in determining the magnitude of risk from exposure to potentially hazardous substances. The Greenhouse Effect theory holds that an increase in the atmospheric content of carbon dioxide will result in heat becoming trapped in the earth's atmosphere, producing a dramatic warming of the earth. This theory has spawned predictions of polar ice caps melting, Miami Beach being awash in a foot of the Atlantic Ocean, and the gradual changing of the Midwest into a vast desert. Critics dismiss this scenario as wild speculation, yet responsible scientists can find reputable scientific studies suggesting such apocalyptic visions.

Disagreement arises over how latent and irreversible these effects of rising concentrations of carbon dioxide in the earth's atmosphere might be. The CEQ has estimated, for instance, that a doubling of the pre-industrial levels of carbon dioxide in the world's atmosphere would be a significant threshold at which major atmospheric changes are likely. But when will such a doubling occur? If global fossil fuel use were held at existing levels, it probably would not occur until the year 2175. But a rise of 2 percent annually in fossil fuel burning probably would advance the same doubling to the year 2050. And a 4 percent annual growth of world fossil fuel combustion, about the actual growth rate for the period 1940 to 1973, would produce the important threshold in the year 2025, within the lifetime of millions living today.[14]

Which figure is acceptable? The most conservative estimate leaves a considerable period for further study since the problem would not become critical for several generations. But if future world fossil fuel use holds to the pattern of the last quarter century, the problem may become acute within the lifetime of this generation and immediate abatement of world fossil fuel use may seem imperative. Should governments delay, in any case, taking action on the carbon dioxide issue in light of the disruptive and probably irreversible climatic changes to be expected whenever such a doubling happens? "When the 'signal' announcing the gradual global warming due to carbon dioxide has been clearly identified, the change will already be well established, if the climate models are correct," notes the CEQ.[15] By this time, governmental action would seem futile:

> It would then probably be too late to avoid continued climate change, should the countries of the world decide to do so. As a consequence of the ocean's extremely slow takeup of CO_2, it is estimated that centuries might then be required to restore present atmospheric temperatures, even if all CO_2 emissions were somehow to stop in the next century.[16]

Inevitably, differing estimates of the latency and diffuseness of the carbon dioxide problem, based on differing technical data, will yield conclusions so varied that one will often seem highly implausible compared with another. Perhaps most distressing to those seeking "objective" and "reliable" data, no such data may be available within decades of the time decisions about the Greenhouse Effect must be made.[17]

Animal and Epidemiological Experiments. Estimates of a substance's danger to human beings, particularly the cancer risks, based on animal or epidemiological studies are a rich source of controversy and confusion. Having rejected most controlled human studies as ethically repugnant, scientists are left with few alternatives in arriving at risk estimates. They may attempt to characterize a substance's danger based on existing knowledge of how chemical carcinogens affect human cells. Little knowledge exists about the precise way in which these chemicals alter the structure and chemistry of cells. One common alternative is controlled animal experiments in which test animals are exposed to substances, the effects monitored, and the risks to human beings extrapolated from the findings.

Animal studies are particularly controversial when estimating the human effects from low levels of chemical exposure—for instance, a dose of a few parts per million or billion of a pesticide or heavy metal in drinking water over 30 years. The human risks of cancer or other serious illnesses will be small, but how small? And how reliable is the estimate? Animal studies do not and can not use enough animals to eliminate possibilities of error in estimating the human effects of low-level exposure. To demonstrate conclusively with 95 percent confidence that a certain low-level dose of one substance causes less than one case of cancer per million subjects would require a "mega-mouse" experiment involving 6 million animals.[18] Instead researchers use high doses of a substance with relatively few animals and then extrapolate through statistical models the effect on humans from low-level exposure to the tested substance. But these models can differ by a factor as much as 100,000 in estimating the size of the dose that could produce one cancer per million subjects. A whole litany of other problems attend small animal studies. Failure to observe any response to a substance among a small group of animals does not imply a substance is safe. Animals, moreover, differ greatly in their sensitivity to substances; dioxin is 5,000 times more toxic to guinea pigs than to hamsters.[19] And so forth.

Epidemiological studies depend upon surveys recording the relationship between known human exposure to suspected hazardous substances and the known effects; the investigator does not deliberately expose humans to possibly dangerous substances but does attempt to capitalize upon exposure when it occurs. Such after-the-fact studies have been used to establish the cancer risks of exposure to cigarette smoke and asbestos, for example. Epidemiological studies can establish statistical relationships between exposure to suspected hazardous substances and adverse effects, but they cannot prove causality; consequently they are open to dispute.

Challenges often are raised because such studies can not be scientifically controlled to eliminate other possible factors affecting the results. Some connections between exposure to substances and effects often can be drawn for the general population, observes David Doniger, but "humans are exposed to too many different substances at unknown doses for unknown periods to permit statistically reliable conclusions to be drawn. Moreover, there are synergistic and antagonistic interactions between chemicals that drastically complicate drawing conclusions about the effects of each chemical." [20]

The Value of Science in Environmental Policy Making. Despite the scientific disputes attending environmental policy making, it remains important to recognize how often science provides useful and highly reliable guidance to policy makers. Often the scientific data relevant to an issue clearly point to the adverse impacts of substances and define the magnitude of their risk; this was certainly evident in the data leading to the federal government's decision to ban most domestic agriculture uses of the pesticides DDT, aldrin, and dieldrin, for instance. Furthermore, even when one set of data does not alone provide definitive evidence of human risks from exposure to chemicals, numerous studies pointing to the same conclusion together can provide almost irrefutable evidence; such was the case in the epidemiological evidence indicting asbestos as a human carcinogen. Often the reliability of data will be routinely challenged by those opposed to the regulation of some substance regardless of the ultimate merit to their case. Finally, public officials must make decisions on the basis of the best evidence available. For all their limitations, scientific data often enable officials to define more carefully and clearly the range of options, risks, and benefits involved in regulating a substance even when the data can not answer all risk questions conclusively.

Even if indisputable data were available on the risks of human exposure to all levels of a substance, controversy would continue over the acceptable level. It is asserted sometimes that science should be responsible for determining the magnitudes of risk from exposure to chemicals and that government should define the acceptability—that is, defining acceptable risk is largely a political matter. Such a division of labor is rarely possible. Scientists usually are drawn together with public officials into the nettlesome problem of determining what levels of exposure to substances ultimately will be acceptable.

What Risks Are Acceptable?

It is not surprising that William Ruckelshaus should begin his second season as EPA's administrator with a plea that Congress or some other authoritative institution establish guidelines for deciding what risks are acceptable in regulating hazardous substances. The EPA, like several other federal agencies, wrestles daily and inconclusively with the problem. Discretionary judgment also permeates the process of determining acceptable risks, which invites pressures and counterpressures for contending sides struggling to influence official decisions to their advantage. The language of the law may conceal it, but determining acceptable risk is ultimately an intensely political affair.

A Multitude of Risk Criteria

As Ruckelshaus implies, a multitude of different congressional standards guide regulatory agencies in making determinations of acceptable risk. Different substances are often regulated according to different standards. The same agency may have to use as many as six or seven standards depending upon which substances, or which laws, are involved. The same substance may be subject to one regulatory standard when dumped into a river and another when mixed into processed food. Statutory risk standards are commonly vague and sometimes confusing; congressional intent may be muddled, often deliberately. Agencies must, nonetheless, render from this confusion defensible judgments.

Generally, regulatory agencies encounter one or more of the statutory formulas listed below in determining the permissible exposure levels to various substances. The examples are drawn from existing legislation:

> 1. *No-Risk Criteria.* Regulatory agencies are to set standards ensuring no risks to human health from the use of a substance. These standards are also "cost oblivious" because they do not permit agencies to use the cost of regulation as a consideration in standard setting. "No additive shall be deemed to be safe if it is found to induce cancer when ingested in man or animal, or if it is found, after tests which are appropriate for the evaluation of the safety of food additives, to induce cancer in man or animal. . . ." [Food, Drug and Cosmetic Act (1938), 21 U.S.C.A. section 348 (3) (A)]

> 2. *Margin-of-Safety Criteria.* Congress orders regulatory agencies to set standards that protect human health with an additional margin for safety, which allows agencies to introduce an extra degree of control in case their original standards prove too lenient. "National primary ambient air quality standards

... shall be ... in the judgment of the [EPA] Administrator, based on [air quality] criteria and allowing an adequate margin of safety ... requisite to protect human health." [Clean Air Act (1970), U.S.C.A. section 7409 (b)(1)]

3. *Cost-Regarding Criteria.* Congress mandates that an agency consider, in varying extent, the costs of regulation alongside the benefits in setting a standard for human or environmental exposure; or Congress may permit cost considerations to be among other criteria an agency may consider. Statutes define how costs are to be weighed with other criteria differently:

A. *Cost-Sensitive Criteria:* Agencies are permitted but not necessarily required to balance the benefits for a given regulatory standard against the costs of its enforcement. Different formulas may be provided in assigning priorities to cost and benefit. "The Secretary [of Labor], in promulgating standards dealing with toxic materials or harmful physical agents under this subsection, shall set the standard which most adequately assures, to the extent feasible, on the basis of the best available evidence, that no employee will suffer material impairment of health or functional capacity ... other considerations shall be ... the feasibility of the standards, and experience gained under this and other health and safety laws." [Occupational Safety and Health Act (1970), 33 U.S.C.A. section 655(b)(5)]

B. *Cost-Benefit Criteria:* Agencies are ordered to balance the benefits against the economic costs in setting standards for exposure to a substance. "The Commission shall not promulgate a consumer product safety rule unless it finds ... that the benefits expected from the rule bear a reasonable relationship to its costs; and ... that the rule imposes the least burdensome requirement which prevents or adequately reduces the risk or injury for which the rule is being promulgated." [Consumer Product Safety Act (1972), 15 U.S.C.A. section (f)(3)(E)-(F)]

A close reading of these guidelines will reveal the enormous discretion customarily left to regulatory agencies in determining how to balance the various statutory criteria.[21] It is often difficult to separate scientific from nonscientific issues; scientists usually become activists in standard setting as well as in determining the magnitude of risks upon which the standards should be based. For instance, the Food and Drug Act's requirement that no food additive may be permitted in the United States if it is "found to induce cancer when ingested by man or animal" raises scientific issues even as it attempts to serve as a criterion for regulators in setting policy: Over what period of time must the risk of cancer exist? Must substances be banned even if they are used in quantities so small that only extremely small risks may exist to man? Are the cancers produced by a substance in animals the result of exposure to that substance alone? In the end, determining acceptable risks becomes both a political and a scientific question.[22]

Limited by its lack of scientific expertise yet reluctant to leave agencies with too much discretion in determining acceptable risk, Congress often packs regulatory laws with so many criteria for risk determination—lest any important consideration be ignored—that regulatory decisions become enormously cumbersome and technical. Consider, for instance, the criteria EPA is ordered to use in the Toxic Substances Control Act (1976) when deciding whether the risks from exposure to a substance are "unreasonable":

> The type of effect (chronic or acute, reversible or irreversible); degree of risk; characteristics and number of humans, plants and animals, or ecosystems, at risk; amount of knowledge about the effects; available or alternative substances and their expected effects; magnitude of the social and economic costs and benefits of possible control actions; and appropriateness and effectiveness of TSCA as the legal instrument for controlling the risk.[23]

Agencies often spend considerable time working out detailed internal regulations to translate these complexities into workable procedures. They may attempt to reach understandings concerning how criteria will be balanced with interest groups active in the regulatory process. But agencies often are faced with limited time for making regulatory decisions, with fragmentary information relevant to many criteria for standard setting, with disputes between interest groups concerning the validity of information and the priorities for criteria in policy making. In the first years of a new regulatory program, moreover, an agency can expect virtually all its major decisions to be challenged through litigation, usually by an interest alleging the agency has failed to interpret properly its statutory responsibilities. Agencies frequently encourage either openly or tacitly such litigation because it can work to their advantage. By interpreting the manner in which risk determinations should be made by agencies, judges often dissipate the fog of uncertainty about congressional intent and provide agencies with firm guidelines for future determinations.

Political Bias

Agency formulas for determining acceptable risks also have proven to be highly sensitive to political pressures and to ideological biases. Given the great discretion left with agencies in determining acceptable risks, it is possible for the process to be biased toward differing philosophies of regulation. During the Carter years the White House directed the

Occupational Safety and Health Administration (OSHA) to treat any suspected carcinogen as a proven hazard until tests proved otherwise—a stance well within OSHA's authority.[24] Moreover, a substance was deemed "suspect" if it induced either benign or malignant tumors in at least one laboratory study on animals. This approach, strongly biased toward regulation of workplace hazards, environmental protection, and strict control of suspected hazardous substances, fit comfortably into the activist regulatory bias of a liberal Democratic administration.

The Reagan administration, however, rapidly changed these guidelines. In the future much more convincing proof would be required before a substance was considered even "suspect." OSHA abolished its list of suspected workplace carcinogens regularly published during the Carter years. And the levels of acceptable risk from substances were raised by factors of 10 to 100 over the earlier Carter criteria. Not surprisingly, these new guidelines were far more compatible with the Reagan administration's determination to place fewer substances under regulatory control and to decrease the compliance costs for business and other regulated interests. These changes, too, generally could be reconciled with OSHA's discretionary authority in determining acceptable risks from workplace exposure to hazardous substances.

The Disappearing Threshold

One of the most politically controversial aspects of determining acceptable risk remains the *threshold problem,* a largely unanticipated result of three tendencies among Congress and agencies concerned with environmental regulation. First, in writing and enforcing most environmental legislation during the 1970s, officials remained *risk averse* in dealing with potential hazards; risk reduction was preferred to risk tolerance. Second, Congress generally assumed that with many, or most, regulated substances there would be some threshold of exposure below which the risks to humans or the ecosystem were negligible. Congress certainly did not anticipate removing *all* traces of human or ecological hazards. And third, legislators, who were largely indifferent to regulatory costs compared with health criteria in setting regulatory standards, discouraged agencies from using cost-benefit analyses when determining acceptable risks.

Economics and technology now present regulation writers with some very difficult decisions growing from these circumstances. Extremely sophisticated technologies enable scientists to detect hazardous substances in increasingly small concentrations, currently as small as parts per billion or trillion. It is usually impossible to assert scientifically that such low concentrations are wholly innocent of adverse risk, however slight, to humans or the environment. Further, the cost of controlling hazardous substances often rises steeply as progressively higher standards are enforced; after reducing, for instance, 85 percent of a substance in a waterway, it may cost half as much or more to remove an additional 5 percent to 10 percent. In effect, the risk threshold once presumed by policy makers vanished; all measurable concentrations of a substance apparently held some possible harm to humans or their environment. To eliminate conclusively *any* probable risks from such substances, regulators would have to require the total elimination of the substance—an extraordinarily expensive undertaking. The threshold problem thus was created: Should a trade-off be made between the costs and benefits of risk prevention, and, if so, what criteria should govern the choice?

Critics assert that regulators err in this trade-off by insisting upon extremely high standards for controlling risks out of all proportion to the benefits to man or the environment and without sensitivity to the economic burden imposed upon regulated interests.[25] This is, in critic Paul Johnson's terms, the "Custer Syndrome." Regulators "take action at any cost, do it as quickly as possible, and leave the thinking to afterwards." This leaves the public with "unrealistic expectations" about the benefits, which will in most cases be extremely small if not undiscoverable when regulators insist upon eliminating even minuscule risks from hazardous substances.[26] Advocates of strict risk management, however, usually will respond that the full extent of risk is unknown or may be greater than currently estimated; they may dispute the accuracy of opposing data. Often, they are especially indignant at the suggestion that human lives may be endangered if the cost of protection is deemed excessive—an assertion that, skillfully delivered, implies that officials are venal or inhumane for imperiling lives to save money for a regulated interest.

Elected officials are understandably wary in dealing with these publicly sensitive issues, especially when they may be cast as the villains by advocates of strict regulation. It is easy to make tolerance for even small risks appear to be a cruel gambling with the destinies of innocent people. When the Nuclear Regulatory Commission (NRC) proposed to set standards for reactor safety at a level that would make the risk of immediate death or lethal cancer from an accident 1,000 times smaller than the actual fatalities from all other causes, that may have seemed a negligible risk indeed. But when critics argued that this meant the NRC was tacitly accepting the possibility of 13,000 American deaths from reactor accidents in the next 30 years, the NRC found itself embroiled in a conflict.[27] In fact risk assessment deals in *probabilities*, not certainties, of accident, or death, or disease. Still, it is often politically difficult to defend some risk threshold, no matter what the economic advantages and despite the relatively few additional benefits that might occur from removing the threshold.

The threshold problem is likely to persist as one of the most frequent and difficult issues in all governmental assessments of acceptable risk. The ability to measure even finer concentrations of hazardous substances and to define more clearly the future risks of low-level exposure to such substances will increase throughout the decade, along with the costs of risk reduction.

The Politicizing of Science

Environmental issues place scientists in a highly charged political atmosphere where impartiality and objectivity, among the most highly esteemed scientific virtues, are severely tested and sometimes fail. Scientists are often consulted by public officials in good part because the scientists' presumed objectivity, as well as technical expertise, makes them trustworthy advisers. But impartiality may be an early casualty in the highly partisan and polarizing atmosphere of policy conflict. Even if a scientist can maintain impartiality, he can not prevent partisans of one or another policy from distorting technical information to their own advantage. Scientists often correctly suspect that their work will be misrepresented when used in political arguments and their credibility consequently diminished. In any case it is characteristic of environmental policy that scientific evidence and opinion are frequently divided for political reasons and that consequently expert disagreements tend to reinforce political conflicts; often these expert cleavages yield no conclusive answers to difficult issues.

Scientific disagreement in complex environmental issues is, in fact, almost predictable because so many opportunities exist for political issues to create, or exacerbate, technical disputes. One leading scientist has estimated that in routine risk assessment there are at least 50 areas left to the discretionary judgments of scientists and other experts.[28] Scientists, bringing to their work the full human measure of political bias and preconception, can not always purge scientific opinions of such influence. Especially when political conflict tends to polarize views and force division over issues, an expert can intentionally, or unwittingly, shade opinions to fit a favored position or manipulate materials until they fit a simplistic policy position. "Experts tend to behave like other people when they engage in a controversy," observes Allan Mazur, himself a sociologist and a physicist. "Coalitions solidify and disagreements become polarized as conflict becomes more acrimonious." [29]

Particularly when a technical issue involves ambiguous data or several plausible alternative explanations, experts often will select the viewpoint congenial to their political, social, or economic convictions. Mazur observes that experts favoring nuclear power tend to support the notion that there exists a threshold of radiation exposure below which human risks are negligible; opponents of nuclear power plants, in contrast, favor a linear conception of risk that permits no such threshold.[30] Apparently, there are Republican and Democratic theories of genetic chemistry. In the mid-1980s many Reagan administration officials and some experts sympathetic to the president's program to reduce environmental regulations were supporting the *epigenetic theory* of cell chemistry.[31] This theory asserts that many carcinogenic substances affect cell mechanisms other than the DNA strands with their genetically coded materials; such a theory could be interpreted to permit greater human exposure to known cancer-causing substances—and also less regulation of such substances—than previously had been federal policy. Under Administrator Anne Burford, the EPA did approve tolerance limits for several carcinogenic pesticides, including the potent pesticide permethrin, on the basis of this epigenetic theory. Under the Carter administration, however, the *genotoxic theory* had prevailed; it asserted that all carcinogens cause changes in genetic cell materials and hence must be considered dangerous. Although the genotoxic theory has been more generally accepted by experts, reputable scientists have supported the conflicting interpretation. One need not accuse either side of willful deceit in order to suggest that political and economic bias could, and probably does, play some part in convincing experts of the truth of a position.

Even when experts qualify their opinions appropriately, policy partisans often distort technical information for their own purposes. In policy conflict a piece of data becomes a weapon, science a bastion against one's critics. Policy advocates and public officials, constantly pressured to take positions and defend them convincingly, often attempt to force upon scientific data a clarity and a simplicity that do not exist. Indeed, torturing technical data to fit some partisan position can be considered an art form in policy debates.

Regulatory agencies, no less than individuals, are guilty of using scientific data selectively, sometimes with gross negligence. One of the worst examples became evident in the 1980s when it was revealed that the Atomic Energy Commission had suppressed deliberately and consistently for more than 20 years scientific evidence suggesting that radioactive fallout from nuclear weapons tests in Nevada may have endangered ranchers and others in its path during the 1950s. All agencies at some time practice a garden variety of data manipulation. One of the virtues in wide public exposure of regulatory proceedings is that opportunities will exist for experts to expose and challenge such manipulation.

The great potential in policy conflict for disrupting sound scientific inquiry and distorting data emphasizes the importance of permitting an open, prolonged, and comprehensive scientific review of major environmental policy decisions. Such a process does not ensure that any scientific consensus will emerge upon strategic issues. But it does permit the widest latitude for scientific debate—for the uncovering and publicizing of information as well as for challenging and refining interpretations of data. It encourages among policy makers greater clarity about the full range and limits of the technical information confronting them. It invites a public airing of issues that experts otherwise might keep to themselves or confine to a small cadre of governmental and scientific insiders who become by virtue of their privileged information a powerful technocratic elite. It helps to discriminate between plausible and unrealistic policy options. If the politicizing of science in environmental issues is inevitable, it should at least be exploited to advantage when possible.

Is the Evidence Itself a Risk?

One of the most disturbing developments in the 1980s stems from accusations that a potentially large volume of test data used by the EPA and other environmental agencies may have been falsified or otherwise corrupted. If these charges are true, the fundamental scientific documentation sustaining the government's decisions to permit public exposure to hundreds of substances under various controlled conditions would be suspect. Even though a small proportion of data might be tainted, the evidence could prejudice public and official opinion to the point where the reliability of almost all crucial scientific data in environmental disputes might become an issue. Such a situation would more than complicate the task of gathering reliable information for policy makers. It would vastly increase the time and complexity in making environmental decisions at a time when dispatch is essential.

The most frequent sources of allegedly unreliable test data have been the research institutions, public and private, hired by chemical manufacturers and other producers or users of hazardous substances to test product safety. These supposedly independent laboratories have been responsible for producing test data relevant to some of the most widely used and regulated substances in the United States. Thus, the following incidents were particularly unsettling.

> The Food and Drug Administration (FDA) charged in 1983 that Industrial Biotest Laboratory, one of the largest among 200 independent laboratories conducting safety tests on cosmetics, drugs, pesticides, and food additives, had falsified the results of numerous tests for corporate clients. At least four major studies were involved. The federal government announced it would prosecute the charges.[32]

> The EPA charged that two-thirds of the tests conducted by Bio-Test Labs on pesticides were scientifically invalid. Virtually all the 212 pesticides and herbicides cleared by the laboratory were allegedly subject to at least one invalid test.[33]

> The EPA asserted that newly proposed Clean Air Act standards for carbon monoxide were based on questionable, and perhaps falsified, research conducted by a doctor who was the director of cardiovascular research at a university medical center.[34]

These charges help to illuminate the dependence of federal regulatory agencies upon the producers of regulated substances for test information regarding a chemical's human and ecological impacts. Although the substance user or manufacturer is required to certify that all test data presented for regulatory consideration have been prepared by an independent source, agencies seldom have the time or ability to verify such assertions. While Congress and the White House both have acknowledged the problems this creates, relatively little money had been spent by the federal government until the late 1970s to provide agencies with the ability to conduct their own in-house testing of substances or to contract for such testing. An exception was the substantial funding for research activities provided to the EPA from the mid-1970s until the Reagan administration. This administration's efforts to reduce EPA's research budget by approximately 30 percent between 1981 and 1983 were criticized by environmental groups, consumer advocates, and others because they allegedly would burden the agency with a greater dependence upon the producers of regulated substances for scientific information at a time when this arrangement was increasingly suspect.[35]

The testing issue threatens to become a serious new problem for which the government is not prepared. Federal agencies are wholly unequipped to undertake, alone or collaboratively, the job of retesting the thousands of substances currently regulated on the basis of past independent laboratory data. Creating a federal capacity to perform such testing for all future regulated products would require massive funding and decades to accomplish. A more likely response would be a new program of governmental inspection and certification of independent testing laboratories, which itself would require many years to implement. One certainty, in any event, would be a massive mobilizing of environmental, consumer, and other public interest organizations to challenge existing federal regulatory standards established on the basis of suspect laboratory tests. The possibility exists that chemical manufacturers may be deluged with an avalanche of liability suits that would make the asbestos cases seem, by comparison, a modest affair. This, together with the other political and administrative complications sure to follow, undoubtedly would delay by years if not decades the process of environmental regulation already moving in many areas at a glacial pace. In short the emerging issue of test validity, however much it ultimately may advance the quality of environmental management, promises bleak prospects for advancing regulatory programs in the immediate future.

Gambling with the Future

The complex new problems of risk assessment in environmental regulation confirm that we live in a historically unique era of technocratic power. American science and industry, in common with that of other advanced industrial nations, now possess the capacity to alter in profound but often unpredictable ways the biochemical basis of future human life and thus to change future ecosystems radically. In its extreme form, represented by nuclear weapons, modern technology has the power to eradicate human society, if not humanity itself, as we know it. But modern technologies also can alter the future ecosphere in a multitude of less dramatic but significant ways: through the deliberate redesign of genetic materials in human reproduction, through the depletion of irreplaceable energy resources such as petroleum or natural gas, through the multiplication of long-lived hazardous substances whose biological impacts upon humans and the ecosystem may magnify through hundreds of years, and much more. We are practically the first generation in the world's history with the certain technical capacity to alter and even to destroy the fundamental biochemical and geophysical conditions for societies living centuries after ours. It is, as one social prophet noted, a power that men of the Middle Ages did not even credit to devils.

With this new technocratic power comes the ability to develop technologies, to manufacture new substances, and to deplete finite resources so that the benefits are largely distributed in the present and the risks for the most part displaced to the future. Future societies may inherit most of the burden to create the social, economic, and political institutions necessary for managing the risks inherent in this generational cost transfer. Such technical capacity can become an exercise of power undisciplined by responsibility for the consequences.

The status of nuclear wastes in many ways provides a paradigm for this problem. As of 1984 the United States consumed electric power from approximately 73 nuclear power plants whose average productive life was expected to be approximately 52 years. Because the wastes from these civilian nuclear reactors currently can not be recycled, as was assumed when the nuclear power industry began in the United States during the 1950s, the federal government now must find a safe and reliable way to dispose of the growing amount of nuclear wastes from these facilities.

Among the most dangerous of these substances are "high-level" wastes—those highly toxic to humans for long periods—found in the spent fuel rods from civilian reactors. Strontium 90 and cesium 137, for instance, must be isolated from human exposure for at least 600 years; other high-level wastes must be isolated for perhaps a thousand years. Equally dangerous and much more persistent are the "transuranic" wastes forming over long periods from the decay of the original materials in the spent fuel rods after they are removed from the reactors. Plutonium 239 remains dangerous to humans for at least 24,000 years, perhaps for as much as 500,000 years. This plutonium, notes one commentator generally sympathetic to the nuclear power industry, "will remain a source of radioactive emissions as far in the future as one can meaningfully contemplate." [36] Other transuranics include americum-241 (dangerous for about 433 years) and iodine-129 (dangerous for perhaps 210,000 years).

Practically speaking, such figures mean that hazardous wastes must be prevented from invading the ecosystem for periods ranging from centuries to hundreds of millennia. Not only must they be securely isolated physically, but human institutions also must survive with sufficient continuity to ensure their responsible administration throughout these eons. Many other chemicals created in the last few decades, including widely used pesticides such as DDT, 2-3-5-T, and dieldrin are not biodegradable and may persist throughout the world ecosystem indefinitely. Though less dangerous than nuclear wastes, these and other substances also represent a displacement of risks to human health and to the ecosystem well into the future.

This transfer of risk raises fundamental ethical and social questions for government. Should public institutions be compelled in some formal and explicit way to exercise regard—and how much?—for the future impacts of decisions concerning environmental management today? Should they be forced, if necessary, to consider not only the future ecological implications in developing dangerous technologies but also the ability of future societies to create institutions capable of controlling these technologies when deciding whether to develop them?

This issue, to be further discussed in the final chapter, is significant because governmental and economic institutions have a tendency to discount the future impacts of new technologies or newly developed chemicals when compared with the immediate impacts. In economic terms this is done in formal cost-benefit analysis by discounting future benefits and costs rather substantially. In political terms it amounts to adopting a strategy that favors taking environmental actions on the basis of short-term political advantage rather than long-term consequences. (Elected officials, especially, often treat as gospel the legendary advice of a former House Speaker to a new colleague: "Remember that when it comes time to vote, most folks want to know 'what have you done for me lately?' ") It is particularly difficult for public officials to develop a sensitive regard for the distant future when there are no apparent political rewards for doing so. At some time whispers the political cynic in practically all public officials: "What has posterity recently done for you?"

Science and Uncertainty in Environmental Policy

Scientific issues so permeate environmental problems that the scientist's substantial involvement in making environmental policy is essential. Science, however, has not proven to be an oracle in the environmental policy process. As we have seen, there are limits to the capacity of technical experts to resolve environmental problems and, sometimes, even to clarify them. These limitations arise from the frequent absence of essential technical data, or the ambiguity of available data, or disagreements among experts over the proper evaluation of scientific evidence relevant to environmental problems. Thus, expert opinions on environmental issues may run on a continuum from consensus to dissension; quite often differing opinions tend to leave public officials without any clear and immediate policy options to adopt. Further, many environmental issues involve policy choices that are, as one commentator has remarked, "transcientific." These are issues in which matters such as the acceptability of risks from alternative policies are involved—questions for which the scientist can claim no special competence or superior understanding.

It is also apparent that policy partisans, public agencies, and others attempting to advance one policy or another often will attempt to use scientific evidence, or the scientist's own opinions, to legitimate their policy bias. This tactic often can amount to willful, or unwitting, misrepresentation of technical materials; it is also an almost irresistible temptation to someone in the policy process. Thus major concerns in evaluating environmental policy should always be an alertness to the limits of scientific evidence in resolving policy issues and a sensitivity to the potential abuses of technical excerpts and evidence.

Often environmental policy must be formulated not only in the absence of definitive data concerning key issues but also with a likelihood that such data will not be available before a final decision must be made. In many cases, technical data that indisputably resolve scientific conflicts in environmental policy may never become available. Thus those who appeal for "more time to study the problem" or advise "waiting until more evidence is available" may only be attempting to prevent action as long as possible. It is among the most difficult, yet common, problems facing environmental policy makers that they must make prudent judgments concerning when "further study" will truly yield constructive new evidence and when it is only a pretext for prolonged inaction.

In the end science cannot relieve public officials and institutions from making many difficult and controversial environmental decisions. Nor are scientists and their work invulnerable to the pressures and prejudices of political life. Science can make essential and constructive contributions to environmental policy making by clarifying the impacts of policies, by identifying policy alternatives and suggesting their feasibility, and by suggesting new environmental issues for public consideration. There will always remain, however, a domain of choice for public officials that lies beyond the proper capacity of science to resolve, just as there are vast domains of scientific inquiry that ought to remain beyond the ability of politics to manipulate.

Notes

1. Council on Environmental Quality (CEQ), *Environmental Quality 1979* (Washington, D.C.: Government Printing Office, 1980), 210.
2. *New York Times*, November 19, 1982.
3. *New York Times*, November 20, 1982.
4. On the general problems of risk assessment, see CEQ, *Contamination of Ground Water by Toxic Organic Chemicals* (Washington, D.C.: Government Printing Office, 1981); and U.S. Congress, Senate Committee on Environment and Public Works, *Health Effects of Toxic Pollutants: A Report from the Surgeon General and a Brief Review of Selected Environmental Contamination Incidents with a Potential for Health Effects, August 1980*, 96th Congress, 2d session, 1980.
5. Cited in Erica L. Dolgin and Thomas G. P. Guilbert, eds., *Federal Environmental Law* (St. Paul, Minn.: West Publishing, 1974), 636, 709, 1071.
6. On the tensions between science and the policy process, see William W. Lowrence, *Of Acceptable Risk* (Los Altos, Calif.: William Kaufmann, 1976), especially chapter 4; Allan Mazur, *The Dynamics of Technical Controversy* (Washington, D.C.: Communications Press, 1981), chapters 4, 5, and 6.
7. See, for example, Thomas R. Dunlap, *DDT: Scientists, Citizens and Public Policy* (Princeton, N.J.: Princeton University Press, 1981), especially chapter 8.
8. CEQ, *Environmental Quality 1980* (Washington, D.C.: Government Printing Office, 1981), 92.
9. *New York Times*, May 26, 1981.
10. U.S. General Accounting Office, "Coal and Nuclear Wastes—Both Potential Contributors to Environmental and Health Problems," Publication No. EMD-81-132 (September 21, 1981), 2.
11. See CEQ, *Environmental Quality 1979* (Washington, D.C.: Government Printing Office, 1980), 194ff.
12. Ibid.

13. A useful compendium of such substances may be found in Samuel S. Epstein, Lester Brown, and Carl Pope, *Hazardous Waste in America* (San Francisco: Sierra Club Books, 1982), appendix I; and CEQ, *Environmental Quality 1979*, chapter 3.

14. CEQ, *Global Energy Futures and the Carbon Dioxide Problem* (Washington, D.C.: Government Printing Office, 1981), 5.

15. Ibid., 54.

16. Ibid.

17. A general review of the issues may be found in Sam H. Schurr et al., *Energy in America's Future* (Baltimore: Johns Hopkins University Press, 1979), chapter 14.

18. On the general problems of animal experiments, see David D. Doniger, *The Law and Policy of Toxic Substances Control* (Baltimore: Johns Hopkins University Press, 1978), part I.

19. Animal data are cited in the *New York Times*, June 25, 1983.

20. Doniger, *The Law and Policy of Toxic Substances Control*, 12.

21. I am indebted to my colleague Albert Matheny for these illustrations.

22. See Lowrence, *Of Acceptable Risks*.

23. CEQ, *Environmental Quality 1979*, 218.

24. *National Journal*, June 18, 1983.

25. A sampling of this literature may be found in the collection of articles by Peter Lewin, Gerald L. Sauer, Bernard L. Cohen, Richard N. Langlois, and Aaron Wildavsky in the *Cato Journal*, "Symposium on Pollution" (Spring 1982): 205ff.

26. Paul Johnson, "The Perils of Risk Avoidance," *Regulation*, May/June 1980, 17.

27. *New York Times*, February 12, 1982.

28. *National Journal*, June 18, 1983. Estimate by Lawrence E. McCray of the National Research Council, National Academy of Sciences.

29. Allan Mazur, *The Dynamics of Technical Controversy*, 29.

30. Ibid., 27.

31. *National Journal*, June 18, 1983.

32. *New York Times*, April 13, 1983.

33. *New York Times*, May 12, 1983.

34. *New York Times*, June 6, 1983.

35. See the Conservation Foundation, *State of the Environment 1982* (Washington, D.C.: Conservation Foundation, 1983), chapter 9.

36. On the problems of this risk transfer, see Walter A. Rosenbaum, "The Hidden Risks in Risk Assessment," in *Risk Assessment and Politics*, ed. Susan Hadden (Westport, Conn.: Greenwood Press, 1984).

The air accompanying this planet is not replaceable. . . . It may be cleaned in part if excessively spoiled. The passenger's lungs will help. . . . However, they will discover that anything they throw, spew, or dump into the air will return to them in due time. Since passengers will need to use the air, on the average, every five seconds, they should treat it accordingly.

Third Planet Operating Instructions
by David R. Brower

'Every Five Seconds': The Air We Breathe 4

"Clean air" is a powerful image to many Americans. Members of the environmental movement regard the Clean Air Act of 1970 as the foundation of the Environmental Era. Public opinion polls show that Americans universally recognize the nation's gravely degraded air quality as a major ecological problem. Clean air has become a symbol for environmental restoration that almost all Americans can approve. And so it is politically chic. Politicians so routinely assure constituents that they favor clean air—whatever that implies—that clean air has become a cliché long before it has become a reality.

It is not surprising, then, that the media have given considerable attention to the annual reports published by the Council on Environmental Quality (CEQ) suggesting there has been "a noticeable improvement in air quality." [1] Evidence suggests that in fact public concern has produced measurable improvements in the nation's ambient air. Nevertheless, the EPA was unprepared for the reaction when it decided that what Americans were pumping into their gas tanks had become as important to them as what they were inhaling into their lungs.

Early in 1982 the EPA announced its intention to use its authority under the Clean Air Act to relax a regulation limiting the amount of lead added to petroleum by large oil refiners to a half gram per gallon. [2] The regulation, created in 1980, was intended to reduce the amount of lead, a dangerous pollutant, from air and air residues in soil, vegetation, and water. The EPA asserted that the lead standard no longer was necessary because the use of unleaded gasoline, required as of 1975 for all new

105

automobiles using catalytic converters, would practically eliminate leaded fuel within a few years. Also, so argued the agency, enforcement of the lead standard was excessively costly to the government and the petroleum industry. Support for the new rule was expected to come not only from oil refiners, including smaller companies adding expensive lead substitutes to raise fuel-octane levels, but also from millions of U.S. motorists driving older cars for which lead additives would improve fuel economy.

The agency's timing could not have been worse. Less than a month after the EPA's announcement, the federal Centers for Disease Control reported that lead in blood samples of Americans showed almost a 37 percent decrease between 1976 and 1980, which they attributed in part to the reduced levels of leaded gasoline.[3] Faced with such widely publicized data and the resulting criticism of the intended change in regulations by environmental and scientific groups, the EPA decided in mid-1982 not to relax the lead standard for large refiners. But the agency persisted in retaining the existing regulations that exempted all small refiners and blenders from the lead limits. Exempting these groups was significant because the average amount of lead in all U.S. gasoline began rising in 1980, largely as a result of fuel produced by small refiners and blenders; many environmental and scientific spokespersons warned of dangers from increased lead ingestion, especially among children.

The agency's political timing remained miserable. Less than a month after EPA's decision concerning small refiners and blenders, the National Center for Health Statistics released a study indicating that 4 percent of all U.S. schoolchildren, including about 12 percent of all black preschoolers, had excessive lead levels in their blood. About 675,000 children were at risk to kidney or brain damage, anemia, retardation, and other ills associated with lead poisoning. The center's announcement noted that children, more vulnerable to lead ingestion than adults, probably acquired much of this lead by inhalation.[4] The announcement prompted the chairman of the House Government Operations Subcommittee on Environment, Energy, and Natural Resources to urge the EPA to consider immediately more stringent lead regulations for small refiners and blenders. The Environmental Defense Fund, the Natural Resources Defense Council, and several other environmental groups publicly chastised the agency and the lead industry for callousness about the lead problem. Recognizing belatedly that the issue was becoming an embarrassment, the EPA put the controversy momentarily to rest by proposing new regulations in late 1982 that would significantly reduce the amount of leaded gasoline produced by the small refiners.

The lead controversy illuminates the Clean Air Act's importance as the strategic policy structure within which the nation's governments are attempting to restore ambient air quality. It emphasizes the sensitivity of the air pollution issue in environmental affairs. And it demonstrates the continuing emergence of new air pollution issues making the task of restoring air quality a continuing effort. In this chapter we shall examine briefly the nature of air pollutants and their origins. We shall explore in greater depth the political structures, processes, and problems created by the "standards-and-enforcement" approach to regulation illustrated by the Clean Air Act. Finally, we shall examine the substance of the act itself and current controversies arising from its implementation.

Air Pollution: What Is It?

A multitude of substances, singly and combined, create air pollution. The Clean Air Act required the EPA to establish the maximum permissible concentrations for seven of the most common national air pollutants and for any additional air pollutants that "endanger public health." The first seven air pollutants for which the EPA established ambient air standards, the so-called criteria pollutants, generally are the most broadly distributed. These pollutants and their health risks are described in Table 4-1. In addition to these pollutants, section 112 of the act also requires the EPA administrator to identify "hazardous air pollutants" that "may cause, or contribute to, an increase in mortality or an increase in serious, irreversible, or incapacitating reversible illness" — pollutants likely to have a more immediate and grave effect on public health than the seven previously noted. For these hazardous pollutants the administrator is required to establish uniform national emission standards to protect public health "with an adequate margin for safety." As of 1984 the EPA had established national emission standards for four such hazardous substances: asbestos, beryllium, mercury, and vinyl chloride.[5]

An important political aspect of air pollution relates to where it originates, which determines what interests are affected by regulation. Table 4-2, which identifies the major sources of five important criteria pollutants, also shows that responsibility for air pollution and the consequent weight of regulation do not fall equally upon all sources. For example, almost all the sulfur oxide and almost half the nitrogen oxide air emissions originate with electric utilities. Carbon monoxide pollution is

Table 4-1 Major Air Pollutants and their Health Effects

Pollutant	Major Sources	Characteristics and Effects
Carbon monoxide (CO)	Vehicle exhausts	Colorless, odorless poisonous gas. Replaces oxygen in red blood cells, causing dizziness, unconsciousness, or death.
Hydrocarbons (HC)	Incomplete combustion of gasoline; evaporation of petroleum fuels, solvents, and paints	Although some are poisonous, most are not. Reacts with NO_2 to form ozone, or smog.
Lead (Pb)	Anti-knock agents in gasoline	Accumulates in the bone and soft tissues. Affects blood-forming organs, kidneys, and nervous system. Suspected of causing learning disabilities in young children.
Nitrogen dioxide (NO_2)	Industrial processes, vehicle exhausts	Causes structural and chemical changes in the lungs. Lowers resistance to respiratory infections. Reacts in sunlight with hydrocarbons to produce smog. Contributes to acid rain.
Ozone (O_3)	Formed when HC and NO_2 react	Principal constituent of smog. Irritates mucous membranes, causing coughing, choking, impaired lung function. Aggravates chronic asthma and bronchitis.
Total suspended particulates (TSP)	Industrial plants, heating boilers, auto engines, dust	Larger visible types (soot, smoke, or dust) can clog the lung sacs. Smaller invisible particles can pass into the bloodstream. Often carry carcinogens and toxic metals; impair visibility.
Sulfur dioxide (SO_2)	Burning coal and oil, industrial processes	Corrosive, poisonous gas. Associated with coughs, colds, asthma, and bronchitis. Contributes to acid rain.

Source: *Environment and Health* (Washington, D.C.: Congressional Quarterly, 1982), 21.

primarily associated with trucks and automobiles. Three sources appear to account for about three-fourths of the major air pollutants by weight: gasoline burning vehicles (transportation), electric power (stationary sources), and industry.[6]

As noted in chapter 1, the nation's air quality has improved since 1974. Between 1974 and 1980, for instance, the CEQ estimates that the emission of particulates declined by almost 50 percent; carbon monoxide, sulfur oxides, and hydrocarbon emissions appear to have declined slightly.

Table 4-2 National Air Pollutant Emissions: By Pollutant and Source, 1980 (million metric tons per year)

Source	Particulates	Sulfur oxides	Nitrogen oxides	Hydro-carbons	Carbon monoxide
Transportation	1.4	0.9	9.1	7.8	69.1
Highway vehicles	1.1	0.4	6.6	6.4	61.9
Aircraft	0.1	0.0	0.1	0.2	1.0
Railroads	0.1	0.1	0.7	0.2	0.3
Vessels	0.0	0.3	0.2	0.5	1.5
Other off-highway vehicles	0.1	0.1	1.5	0.5	4.4
Stationary source fuel combustion	1.4	19.0	10.6	0.2	2.1
Electric utilities	0.8	15.9	6.7	0.0	0.3
Industrial	0.3	2.3	3.3	0.1	0.6
Commercial-institutional	0.1	0.6	0.3	0.0	0.1
Residential	0.2	0.2	0.3	0.1	1.1
Industrial processes	3.7	3.8	0.7	10.8	5.8
Solid waste disposal	0.4	0.0	0.1	0.6	2.2
Incineration	0.2	0.0	0.0	0.3	1.2
Open burning	0.2	0.0	0.1	0.3	1.0
Miscellaneous	0.9	0.0	0.2	2.4	6.2
Forest fires	0.8	0.0	0.2	0.7	5.5
Other burning	0.1	0.0	0.0	0.1	0.7
Miscellaneous organic solvent	0.0	0.0	0.0	1.6	0.0
Total	7.8	23.7	20.7	21.8	85.4

Source: Environmental Protection Agency, *National Air Pollutant Emission Estimates, 1940-1980* (draft, November 1981), tables 2-6.

It is equally significant that emissions of major criteria pollutants apparently have not increased over this period despite expansion of these pollution sources. "Breaking even" during a growth decade suggests in itself a major achievement in controlling new air pollution sources. Data from 23 American cities measuring combined levels of pollution, the so-called pollutant standards index (PSI), show a generally decreasing incidence of days classified as "unhealthful," "very unhealthful," or "hazardous" by the PSI since 1974.[7]

Progress, however, has been uneven. Alongside encouraging evidence of the Clean Air Act's impact stands much to emphasize that serious air pollution is still pervasive. First, a great many of the nation's urban areas remain heavily and dangerously polluted after more than a decade of the Clean Air Act. Table 4-3 gives the rankings of 40 major U.S. urban areas using the PSI index to identify the severity of pollution from 1978 to 1980. According to this table, Los Angeles and its neighboring communities of San Bernardino, Riverside, and Ontario experienced air pollution classified as "unhealthful" or worse at least one day in every three during this period. Other major cities, including New York, Denver, Pittsburgh, and Houston, were only slightly better. Taken together, the data in Table 4-3 imply that a substantial majority of the U.S. population was exposed to moderately or severely polluted air for considerable periods during this time.

Second, many sources emitting large volumes of air pollution still remain in noncompliance with emission controls mandated by federal and state agencies. In 1981, for instance, 87 percent of integrated iron and steel facilities, 19 percent of other iron and steel factories, 21 percent of petroleum refineries, and 54 percent of primary smelters were failing to comply with emission limits.[8] The CEQ estimates that, in all, approximately 2,700 major pollution sources (those with a potential to emit more than 100 tons per year of pollutants) were not controlled adequately in 1981. Problems in enforcing emission controls have been particularly evident when existing stationary pollution sources, such as the iron and steel industry and power plants, had to be retrofitted with control technologies.

Finally, fewer than 30 states have completely approved plans, as required by the Clean Air Act, for achieving national air quality standards for all the major criteria pollutants. This means that many states have yet to achieve—or to demonstrate the will and capacity to achieve—the administrative and technical planning essential to translate

Table 4-3 Ranking of 40 Standard Metropolitan Statistical Areas Using the Pollutant Standards Index (PSI), 1978-1980

Severity Level (Days with PSI greater than 100)	Metropolitan Area	*Three-Year Average of Number of Days*	
		"Unhealthful," "Very Unhealthful," and "Hazardous" (PSI>100)	"Very Unhealthful," and "Hazardous" (PSI>200)
More than 150 days	Los Angeles	231	113
	San Bernardino, Riverside, and Ontario	174	89
100-150 days	New York	139	6
	Denver	130	36
	Pittsburgh	119	18
	Houston	104	23
50-99 days	Chicago	93	14
	St. Louis	89	19
	Philadelphia	74	6
	San Diego	72[b]	8[b]
	Louisville	70	4
	Phoenix	70[b]	6[b]
	Gary	68	33
	Portland	62	11
	Washington	62	3
	Jersey City	58[a]	0[a]
	Salt Lake City	58	18
	Seattle	52	3
	Birmingham	50[a]	8[a]
25-49 days	Cleveland	46	11
	Detroit	39	4
	Memphis	37[a]	3[a]
	Baltimore	36	2
	Indianapolis	34	2
	Cincinnati	28	1
	Milwaukee	28	2
	Kansas City	28[a]	1[a]
0-24 days	Sacramento	22	1
	Dallas	21	1
	Allentown	21	2
	Buffalo	20[b]	4[b]
	San Francisco	18	0
	Toledo	15	2
	Dayton	15	1
	Tampa	8	1
	Syracuse	7	1
	Norfolk	6[b]	0[b]
	Grand Rapids	6[a]	0[a]
	Rochester	5	0
	Akron	4	0

[a] Based on one year of data. [b] Based on two years of data.

Source: Council on Environmental Quality, *Environmental Quality 1981* (Washington, D.C.: Government Printing Office, 1982), 33.

the goals of the act into accomplishments. One of the most persistent problems in current air pollution policy concerns whether the states are able to create and implement the required State Implementation Plans (SIPs) within a reasonable period—an issue triggering the confrontation between EPA and the states that was used to introduce this book.

Beyond difficulties with implementing the Clean Air Act, there is growing evidence that several new forms of air pollution may require broad and rapid federal action for which the act may need revision. We have noted already the growing recognition that acid rain and the so-called Greenhouse Effect may require new regulations for carbon dioxide and further revision of existing regulations controlling nitrogen and sulfur oxides. New hazardous pollutants, including formaldehyde, arsenic, and several heavy metals, may be added to the regulatory agenda. The recognition of new air pollutants is likely to continue as research gradually uncovers the true extent and complexity of the nation's air quality problems.

Standards and Enforcement

Like all other regulatory programs affecting the U.S. environment, the Clean Air Act is based on the standards-and-enforcement approach to regulation, sometimes called "command and control." The structure and philosophy of this approach create many of the characteristic processes and problems associated with governmental management of the environment. In recent years this regulatory philosophy has been increasingly criticized as administratively and economically inefficient, excessively cumbersome, and counterproductive. Regulatory horror stories abound, many doubtless true, convincing believers that a better method lies in less direct governmental involvement and more economic incentives to encourage pollution abatement. The issues merit detailed attention in a later chapter, for virtues and liabilities exist in both approaches.

Understanding current issues in pollution regulation does require an appreciation in broad outline of the standards-and-enforcement method and some of its purposes. Essentially this method consists of five phases through which pollution policy evolves.

Goal Setting

In theory the first step in pollution abatement begins with a determination by Congress of the ultimate objectives to be accomplished through pollution regulation. In practice these goals are often broadly and vaguely worded. Sometimes, as when Congress decides to "press technology," goals deliberately are made extremely ambitious as an incentive to vigorous regulatory action. The principal goals of the Clean Air Act are, for example, to protect public health and safety. Vague goals are not as important in defining the operational character of a regulatory program as the more detailed specifications for the setting of pollution standards, emission controls, and enforcement—the real cutting edges of regulation. Statements of goals, however, may be very politically significant as signals to the interests involved in regulation concerning which pollutants and sources will be given priority and how vigorously Congress intends to implement programs. The Clean Air Act's goal of establishing national air quality standards for major pollutants, for instance, was an unmistakable signal that Congress would tolerate no longer the continual delays in controlling air pollution caused by past legislative willingness to let· the states create their own air quality standards. It was also evidence that regulated interests had lost their once-dominant position in the formation of air pollution policy.

Criteria

Criteria are the technical data, commonly provided by research scientists, indicating what pollutants are associated with environmental damage and how such pollutants, in varying combination, affect the environment. Criteria are essential to give public officials some idea of what pollutant levels they must achieve to ensure various standards of air or water quality. If regulators intend to protect public health from the effects of air pollution, for example, they must know what levels of pollution—sulfur oxides, for instance—create public health risks. In a similar vein, restoring game fish to a dying lake requires information about the levels of organic waste such fish can tolerate. Criteria must be established for each regulated pollutant, and sometimes for combinations of pollutants.

As we noted earlier, obtaining criteria frequently is difficult because data on the environmental effects of many pollutants still may be fragmentary or absent. Even when data are available, there is often as much art as science in specifying relationships between specific levels of a pollutant and its environmental effects because precise correlations may not be obtainable from the information. The reliability of criteria data also may vary depending upon whether they are obtained from animal studies, epidemiological statistics, or human studies. Criteria are often likely to be controversial, especially to those convinced that a set of data works to their disadvantage. Given the limitations in criteria data, regulatory agencies often have had to set pollution standards with information that was open to scientific criticism but still the best available.

Quality Standards

Goals and criteria are a prelude to the critical business of establishing air and water quality standards—the maximum levels of various pollutants to be permitted in air, soil, workplaces, or other locations. As a practical matter, defining standards amounts to declaring what the public, acting through governmental regulators, will consider to be "pollution." An adequate set of quality standards should specify what contaminants will be regulated and what variation in levels and combinations will be accepted in different pollutant categories.

Creating quality standards—in effect, another means of defining acceptable risk —is ultimately a political decision. Criteria documents rarely provide public officials with a single number that defines unambiguously what specific concentration of a pollutant produces precisely what effects. A rather broad range of possible figures associated more or less closely with predictable effects is available; which one is accepted may be the result of prolonged struggle and negotiation among interests involved in regulation. This battle over numbers is a matter of economics as much as science or philosophy. The difference between two possible pollution standards, only a few units apart, may seem trivial to a layman. But the higher standard may involve millions or billions of additional dollars in pollution control technologies for the regulated interests and possibly many additional years before standards are achieved. Sometimes Congress establishes a standard based on a number's political "sex appeal." The original requirements in the Clean Air Act that automobile emissions of hydrocarbons and carbon monoxide be reduced by 90 percent of the 1970 levels no later than 1975 was largely accepted because the 90 percent figure sounded strict and spurred the auto industry into action. In practical terms the figure might have been set at 88 percent or 85 percent, or some other number in this range, with about the same results. Air quality standards created by the EPA for the major criteria pollutants are identified, and their method of calculation explained, in Table 4-4.

Table 4-4 National Ambient Air Quality Standards

Pollutant	Averaging time	Primary standard levels	Secondary standard levels
Particulate matter	Annual (geometric mean)	75 μg/m^3	60 μg/m^3
	24 hrs [b]	260 μg/m^3	150 μg/m^3
Sulfur oxides	Annual (arithmetic mean)	80 μg/m^3 (0.03 ppm)	—
	24 hrs [b]	365 μg/m^3 (0.14 ppm)	—
	3 hrs [b]	—	1300 μg/m^3 (0.5 ppm)
Carbon monoxide	8 hrs [b]	10 μg/m^3 (9 ppm)	10 mg/m^3 (9 ppm)
	1 hr [b]	40 mg/m^3 [*] (35 ppm)	40 mg/m^3 [*] (35 ppm)
Nitrogen dioxide	Annual (arithmetic mean)	100 μg/m^3 (0.05 ppm)	100 μg/m^3 (0.05 ppm)
Ozone	1 hr [b]	240 μg/m^3 (0.12 ppm)	240 μg/m^3 (0.12 ppm)
Hydrocarbons (nonmethane) [a]	3 hrs (6 to 9 a.m.)	160 μg/m^3 (0.24 ppm)	160 μg/m^3 (0.24 ppm)
Lead	3 months	1.5 μg/m^3	1.5 μg/m^3

[*] EPA has proposed a reduction of the standard to 25 ppm (29 mg/m^3).
[a] A nonhealth-related standard used as a guide for ozone control.
[b] Not to be exceeded more than once a year.

Source: Council on Environmental Quality, *Environmental Quality 1980* (Washington, D.C.: Government Printing Office, 1981), 172.

Emission Standards

Standards for clean air or water are only aspirations unless emission standards exist to prescribe the acceptable pollutant discharges from important sources of air or water contamination. If emission standards are to be effective, they must clearly indicate the acceptable emission levels from all important pollution sources and should be related to the pollution control standards established by policy makers.

Congress has used two different methods of determining how emission standards should be set. In regulating existing air pollution sources under the Clean Air Act, Congress requires that emissions be

115

limited to the extent necessary to meet the relevant air quality standards; determining what emission controls are necessary depends upon where the quality standards are set. In controlling new air pollution sources, and most water polluters, the emission controls are based upon the available technologies. This "technology-based" approach sets the emission levels largely according to the performance of available technologies.[9]

There is a very direct and critical relationship between air quality standards and emission controls. For example, once EPA declares national ambient air quality standards, each state is required in its SIP to calculate the total emissions of that pollutant within an airshed and then to assign emission controls to each source of that pollutant sufficient to ensure that total emissions will meet air quality standards. In effect this calls for the states to decide how much of the total pollution "load" within an airshed is the responsibility of each polluter and how much emission control the polluter must achieve. This has become a bitterly controversial process. Experts often have difficulty in determining precisely how much of a pollution "load" within a given body of water or air can be attributed to a specific source; this compounds the problem of assigning responsibility for pollution abatement equitably among a large number of polluters.[10] Regulated interests, aware of the relationship between air quality standards and emission controls, will attack both in an effort to avoid or relax their assigned emission controls. Regulated industries also chronically complain that insufficient attention is given to the cost of emission controls when government regulators prescribe the acceptable technology. Polluters often balk at installing specific control technologies prescribed by governmental regulators. The scrubber wars between electric utilities and regulatory authorities, for instance, have been continuing for more than a decade. Alleging that the scrubbers prescribed by government to control their sulfur oxide emissions are inefficient and unreliable, coal-fired utilities have fiercely resisted installing the scrubbers until compelled to do so.

The full weight of the backlash against emission controls often falls upon state government officials who, under existing federal law, usually are responsible for setting specific emission levels, prescribing the proper technologies, and enforcing emission restraints upon specific sources. This is accomplished largely through the issuance of a permit to individual dischargers specifying the permissible emission levels and technological controls for their facility. Despite more than a decade's experience and substantial financial assistance from Washington, many state regulatory authorities still are understaffed and undertrained, chronically enmeshed in litigation over regulation, and otherwise inhibited from implementing emission controls with dispatch. Moreover, the political and economic influence of regulated interests often are far more formidable in state capitals than in Washington.

Enforcement

A great diversity of enforcement procedures might be used to ensure that pollution standards are achieved; adequate enforcement must carry enough force to command the respect of those subject to regulation. Satisfactory enforcement schemes have several characteristics: they enable public officials to act with reasonable speed—very rapidly in the case of emergencies—to curb pollution; they carry sufficient penalties to encourage compliance; and they do not enable officials to evade a responsibility to act against violations when action is essential. It is desirable that officials have a range of enforcement options that might extend from gentle prodding to secure compliance, at one end, all the way to litigation and criminal penalties for severe, chronic, or reckless violations. In reality, when it comes to enforcement, administrative authority is often the power to "make a deal." Armed with a flexible variety of enforcement options, administrators are in a position to bargain with polluters in noncompliance with the law, selecting those enforcement options they believe will best achieve their purposes. This bargaining, a common occurrence in environmental regulation, illustrates how political pressure and administrative discretion concurrently shape environmental policy; we shall shortly examine enforcement in greater detail.

In the end an effective pollution abatement program largely depends upon voluntary compliance by regulated interests. No regulatory agency has enough personnel, money, and time to engage in continual litigation or other actions to force compliance with pollution standards. Furthermore, litigation usually remains among the slowest, most inflexible, and inefficient means of achieving environmental protection. Administrative agencies prefer to negotiate and otherwise to maneuver to avoid litigation as the primary means of regulation whenever possible.

The Anatomy of Regulation

The standards-and-enforcement approach to regulation creates a number of characteristic political processes and issues regardless of which specific pollution program is involved. The technicality of pollution regulation frequently creates a language and style of action that conceals (sometimes deliberately) the extent to which political forces are operating behind the facade of regulatory procedures. Nonetheless regulation is fundamentally a political enterprise.

Opportunities for Political Influence. Political influence and conflict occur wherever administrative discretion exists in the regulatory process, just as they develop in any other aspect of bureaucracy. There are several characteristic points where such administrative discretion ordinarily is found in pollution regulation.

1. *When words, phrases, or policy objectives are unclear.* Congress may deliberately shift responsibility to administrators for settling disputes between interests in conflict over how a law should be phrased. Tossing this political "hot potato" to administrators ensures that partisans for all sides of an issue with something to gain or lose by the law's interpretation will scramble to influence whatever officials or bureaucracies resolve such obscurities. Sometimes this lack of legislative clarity results less from deliberation than from congressional confusion or ignorance. In any case, regulators usually find themselves caught between competing group pressures to interpret statutes or regulations in different ways. Such pressures, in fact, should be considered routine in the regulatory process.

2. *When technical standards must be created or revised.* Existing legislation regulating air pollution, water pollution, and hazardous substances ordinarily requires the EPA to define the standards and prescribe the appropriate control technologies necessary to meet mandated standards; often regulatory agencies also are required by such legislation to review periodically and, if appropriate, revise such standards or technology requirements. Legitimate disagreement often exists, as we noted in the previous chapter, over the technical and economic justification for most regulatory standards. In the presence of expert dissension about such issues, a large measure of discretion rests with regulatory agencies for resolving such disputes. This discretion, and the conflict it invites, will reappear when regulatory standards are reviewed. In fact virtually all major technical determinations by regulatory agencies are politicized by the activity of pressure groups, Congress, competing governmental agencies, and other interests seeking to shape discretionary decisions to their respective advantage.

3. *When compliance deadlines are flexible.* Pollution legislation may bristle with explicit compliance deadlines, but administrators almost always have authority to extend them. Legislation is particularly generous in granting the administrator authority to extend compliance deadlines when, in his opinion, economic hardship or other inequities may result from strict enforcement. Thus the Clean Air Act instructs the EPA to set emission standards for new air

pollution sources by considering, among other things, "the degree of emission limitation achievable through the application of the best system of emission reduction which (taking into account the cost of achieving such reduction) the administrator determines has been adequately demonstrated."[11] Such a fistful of discretionary authority in effect permits the EPA to extend compliance deadlines for specific air pollution sources by increasing the time allowed to search for pollution controls meeting these multiple criteria. In many cases a compliance deadline also may be relaxed if an agency determines that it is beyond the technical ability of a polluter to install the proper controls in the required time. Agencies sometimes can achieve "backdoor" extension of compliance deadlines by deliberately delaying the establishment of a standard long enough to permit the regulated interests to make adjustments to the anticipated standard. The EPA, for instance, waited until 1976—more than two and a half years after vinyl chloride was identified as a human carcinogen—before setting an exposure standard for that substance. The reason, the agency explained, was to avoid creating "unacceptably severe economic consequences" for the vinyl chloride manufacturers and users through an earlier standard establishing a more rapid deadline for controlling the chemical's emissions.[12]

4. *When enforcement is discretionary.* Few provisions in current pollution legislation compel federal officials to stop a polluting activity. Most often enforcement actions are discretionary, as in section 112 of the Clean Air Act, which instructs the EPA administrator to regulate any pollutant from a stationary source when "in his judgment" it "may cause or contribute to any increase in mortality or an increase in serious irreversible or incapacitating illness." Even when enforcement action is initiated, officials are usually given optional methods for securing compliance.

Federalism. That environmental programs almost always are federalized, and sometimes regionalized, in their implementation introduces another political dimension. Federal air and water pollution legislation is administered by the EPA's Washington headquarters, its 10 regional offices, and the majority of state governments, which assume the responsibility for issuing permits to pollution dischargers specifying the acceptable control technologies and emission levels. This two- and three-tiered design ensures that state and regional interests take part in the regulatory process and that, consequently, state and local governments, together with the various associated interests, actively pursue their individual and often competitive objectives during program implementation.

In practical terms this means that writing and enforcing regulations often involve bargaining between federal, regional, and state agencies. State governments, in particular, have a habit of using their own congressional representatives to influence federal environmental regulations to their own advantage. Conflict, delay, and confusion often arise in environmental regulation precisely because state governments have successfully persuaded their congressional delegations to intervene in the regulatory process on behalf of a state interest. All federal regulatory agencies are acutely aware that individual members of Congress are very likely to be sympathetic and articulate about their own state's viewpoint in administering regulatory programs.

Agency Conflicts. Regulatory politics involve not only frequent bargaining and conflict· between federal, regional, and state regulatory agencies but also quite often conflict and competition between differing federal regulatory agencies. Few environmental problems are within the jurisdiction of a single agency. More commonly several agencies—sometimes as many as nine or ten—will share responsibility for some aspect of environmental management. Organized interests with a stake in an environmental issue understandably will promote, if possible, a major role for whatever relevant agency is most sympathetic to their viewpoint. Conversely, various interests will fight grimly and persistently to keep sympathetic agencies from losing their regulatory influence on crucial issues. American farmers, for instance, fought long but largely in vain to prevent Congress from investing the newly created EPA with the Agriculture Department's traditional authority for pesticide regulation. The farmers correctly reasoned that Agriculture would be considerably more sympathetic to the viewpoint of pesticide users and hence less likely to restrict agricultural chemicals than would the EPA. Often regulating environmental pollutants becomes primarily a struggle between different federal bureaucracies—perhaps state agencies as well—each with a different viewpoint and constituency.

The following story illustrates this point. In mid-1981 farmers sprayed more than 200,000 acres of eastern Montana wheatlands with the acutely toxic pesticide endrin. High levels of endrin subsequently were found in a variety of migratory and native fowl. Sixteen states along the central and Pacific migratory flyways, including South Dakota, North Dakota, Idaho, Washington, Oregon, Kansas, and Nebraska, eventually might be affected by the contaminated birds; several Canadian provinces also were involved. The Montana Department of Agriculture asserted that local residents would be seriously endangered if they were exposed to contaminated soil or ate the tainted birds. The U.S. Fish and Wildlife Service in the Interior Department agreed. But the EPA found the pesticide levels in birds and soil well below the human danger level, with an adequate margin for safety. Other Interior officials decided that the affected states would have to decide for themselves whether to curtail hunting seasons because of the pesticide. The Canadian Wildlife Service, not waiting, immediately ordered hunters in Alberta and Saskatchewan province to eat no more ducks or geese. This multitude of squabbling bureaucracies is a testimony to the overlapping authority and competitive clientele that routinely politicize the administration of most environmental programs.

Beyond Public View. It is worth noting that the implementation of most environmental regulatory programs does not routinely involve the public, or public opinion, in the process. Unlike the White House and Congress, the federal bureaucracy is neither highly visible nor readily understood by the public; regulation operates, in the words of Francis Rourke, behind an "opaque exterior" that the public seldom cares to penetrate. A 1981 public opinion poll that indicated 31 percent of the public knew "nothing at all about the Clean Air Act" and another 39 percent "knew a little" at a time when the act was a topic of major congressional debate typifies public attention to most regulatory matters.[13] This dearth of dependable public interest means that the constellation of political forces and actors involved in regulatory politics ordinarily is confined to organized interests, governmental officials, scientists, technicians, and other "insiders." Given the complexity and technicality of environmental issues, this situation is not surprising. But it emphasizes the extent to which regulatory politics tend to involve a process highly specialized and commonly closed to public involvement.

Politics and Administration: The Enforcement Problem. The intermingling of administrative discretion and political pressure in regulatory policy making is evident in the enforcement of environmental law. Typically, air and water pollution laws are enforced through state or local agencies with considerable discretion to decide what level of emission control will be required of an air or water polluter and when emission controls must be achieved. These become conditions for the permit that all air and water polluting firms must obtain to operate. In air pollution regulation, for instance, this discretion can arise from the regulator's authority under the Clean Air Act to decide which emission controls are technically and economically feasible and to issue "variances" that temporarily waive emission control deadlines or technology specifications.[14] Regulators seek voluntary compliance. They want to avoid penalties as a means of ensuring compliance if possible because they know that resort to administrative or judicial tribunals likely will involve a protracted, inflexible process with no assurances that the polluter will be compelled to control emissions speedily and efficiently at the conclusion. In fact polluters often provoke such action, hoping to avoid emission controls indefinitely by exploiting the complexities of the administrative or judicial procedures involved.

Regulated firms commonly balk at a regulatory agency's initial specification of acceptable control technologies and deadline dates for compliance with emission standards. The usual solution is bargaining between regulator and regulated, particularly when regulatory agencies confront an economically and politically influential firm, or group of firms, capable of creating political pressures upon the regulatory agency to reach some accommodation over required control technologies or compliance deadlines. Regulatory agencies typically will make some concession to firms concerning required control technologies or compliance deadlines. One form of these concessions is the frequently used variance that allows a firm some delay in achieving emission controls otherwise required under the law. A firm commonly is able to negotiate a variance permitting it to discharge on an interim basis at its existing emission levels and to obtain several additional variances that can significantly delay achievement of required emission controls.

Agencies also heavily depend upon firms monitoring and reporting their own pollution emissions. Most regulatory agencies lack the personnel and other resources to inspect routinely and monitor all emission controls within their jurisdictions. Thus voluntary compliance is almost a necessity in regulation. Quite often, as Paul B. Downing and James N. Kimball note in their careful review of enforcement studies, regulatory agencies accept the firm's own reports of its behavior under all but exceptional circumstances. "We find that the typical agency does not inspect frequently," they comment. "Furthermore, those inspections which do occur are usually pre-announced. Thus we find that the probability of being found in violation is virtually zero. There are two exceptions to this conclusion. One would be cases where a third party reports a violation. . . . The other occurs when a source self-reports a violation. Our case study did indicate that many violations were reported by the regulated companies." [15]

While administrative discretion and political pressure clearly do limit the vigor and strictness in enforcement of environmental regulations, these constraints are sometimes inevitable and may even be prudent. Often the use of administrative discretion to "make a deal" over pollution permits a regulatory agency to achieve more pollution abatement than would be the case if it insisted upon extremely stringent emission standards in full and immediate compliance with the law. This is true particularly when the regulated firm is either unable to comply fully and immediately with a strict interpretation of the law or willing to fight indefinitely in the courts or administrative hearing rooms to prevent any regulation. Many regulatory agencies, limited by staff and funding inadequate for their mandated responsibilities, have no practical alternative to reliance upon voluntary compliance and accommodation. Finally, regulatory agencies often confront regulated interests—including other governmental agencies subject to pollution control—too politically or economically powerful to be compelled to comply fully and immediately with the law. While this should be no excuse for exemption from full compliance with environmental regulation, it is often an immutable political reality with which regulatory agencies must make peace. In such circumstances agencies may logically conclude that it is better to bargain with the regulated interests in the hope of achieving some limited goals than to adopt what may well become an ultimately futile strategy of insisting upon stringent compliance with the law in spite of massive resistance from the polluter.

The existence of discretion in the enforcement of pollution regulation, however necessary or inevitable, also means that such discretion at times will be abused. It sometimes leads agencies to yield needlessly and negligently to political pressures preventing enforcement of essential pollution controls. Unfortunately these are among the unavoidable risks inherent in the exercise of discretionary authority without which environmental administration would be impossible.

The Clean Air Act

The Clean Air Act of 1970, together with its important 1977 amendments, constitutes one of the longest, most complex, and most technically detailed regulatory programs ever enacted in Washington. Generally it creates a standards-and-enforcement program in which the federal government establishes national air quality standards for major pollutants, the states assume primary responsibility for implementing the program within federal guidelines, and the two governments share enforcement responsibilities. In broad outline, the act mandates the following programs.

1. *National Air Quality Standards.* The act directed EPA to determine the maximum permissible ambient air concentrations for pollutants it found to be harmful to human health or the environment. EPA was instructed to establish such standards for at least seven pollutants: particulates, sulfur oxides, carbon monoxide, nitrogen oxide, ozone, hydrocarbons, and lead. The agency was to set two types of "national ambient air quality standards" (NAAQSs) without considering the cost of compliance:

   A. *Primary Standards.* These were supposed to protect human health with an adequate margin of safety to particularly vulnerable segments of the population, such as the elderly and infants. Originally all air quality control regions in the United States were required to meet primary standards by 1982; this deadline was extended.

   B. *Secondary Standards.* These were intended to maintain visibility and to protect buildings, crops, and water. No deadline was mandated for compliance with secondary standards.

2. *Stationary Source Regulations.* The EPA was to set maximum emission standards for new sources (plants and factories) called "new source performance standards" (NSPSs). In doing this, the following procedures were to be followed:

   A. Standards were to be set on an industry-by-industry basis; the states then were to enforce the standards.

   B. In setting NSPSs, EPA was to take into account the costs, energy requirements, and environmental effects of its guidelines.

   C. For existing sources (those dischargers active at the time the act was passed), the EPA was to issue control technique guidelines for the states' use.

3. *State Implementation Plans.* Each state was required to create a State Implementation Plan (SIP) indicating how it would achieve federal standards and guidelines to implement the act fully by 1982. The SIPs, which EPA was to approve no later than 1979, were to contain information relating to several important elements:

   A. The nation was divided into 247 "air quality control regions" (AQCRs) for which states were made responsible. The regions were classified as "attainment" or "nonattainment" regions for each of the regulated pollutants.

   B. States were also made responsible for enforcing special air quality standards in areas with especially clean air called Prevention of Significant Deterioration (PSD) regions.

C. States were required to order existing factories in nonattainment areas to retrofit their plants with control technologies representing "reasonably available control technology." Companies wanting to expand or build new plants in nonattainment areas had to install control equipment that limited pollutants to the least amount emitted by any similar factory anywhere in the United States. This technology was to be specified by the states without regard to the cost.

D. New factories in nonattainment areas also were required to purchase "offsets" from existing air polluters. This involved purchasing new pollution equipment for an existing polluter or paying an existing polluter to eliminate some of its pollution to the extent that the offset equalled the pollution the new source was expected to emit after it installed its own control technology.

E. States in nonattainment areas were given until 1987 to meet carbon monoxide and ozone standards if the state required an annual automobile inspection and maintenance of catalytic converters on newer automobiles.

F. In PSD areas, all new stationary emission sources were required to install the best available control technology.

4. *Mobile Source Emission Standards (for automobiles and trucks).* Title II of the act created a detailed but flexible timetable for achievement of auto and truck emission controls.

A. For autos there was to be a 90 percent reduction in hydrocarbon and carbon monoxide emissions by 1975 and a 90 percent reduction in nitrogen oxide emissions by 1976, when measured against 1970 emission levels.

B. The administrator of EPA was authorized to grant extensions of these deadlines for approximately one year. Considerable extensions were granted by EPA and others authorized by Congress:

(i) In 1973 the EPA granted a one-year extension of the 1975 deadline for hydrocarbons and carbon monoxide emissions and a one-year extension of the nitrogen oxide deadline.

(ii) In 1974 Congress granted an additional one-year extension for all emission deadlines.

(iii) In 1975 the EPA granted another one-year deadline extension for enforcement of hydrocarbon and carbon monoxide standards.

(iv) In 1977 compliance deadlines for all emissions were extended for two more years, to be followed by stricter standards for hydrocarbons and carbon monoxide in 1980 and further tightening of the hydrocarbon standard in 1981, together with higher nitrogen oxide standards.

Continuing Policy Conflicts

Any program determined to press technology in controlling previously unregulated pollution from virtually every major sector of the U.S. economy is bound to be controversial. Regulated interests have almost uniformly criticized the Clean Air Act for imposing excessive costs upon them when compared with the alleged benefits, for seeking unreasonable levels of pollution control, and for being excessively rigid, technical, and bureaucratic in its implementation. Many of these charges have been supported by economists, who believe much more effective and cheaper techniques could be used to control pollution without resorting to standards and enforcement. Much of this criticism is common to most regulatory programs. Leaving a general discussion of the merits of standards and enforcement compared with other approaches for a later chapter, we can examine some of the more specific conflicts spawned by the Clean Air Act.

Is the Act Too Costly?

Business consistently has asserted that the economic burden inflicted upon it for compliance with the act and the inhibiting effect these capital investments have upon U.S. economic growth are disproportionate to any alleged benefits that might be produced. Business spokespersons ordinarily assert that they are willing to accept "equitable" and "reasonable" costs for pollution abatement, but they find the act's statutory formulas for imposing regulatory costs neither reasonable nor equitable. More specifically, many business executives and economists believe the act imposes excessive regulatory costs because (1) it requires that primary ambient air quality standards be set to protect the most sensitive populations; (2) it explicitly requires the EPA to ignore cost considerations in establishing emission control standards for regulated interests; (3) it requires the EPA to establish industry-wide emission control standards instead of using a more economically efficient approach permitting variations and exceptions to the rule; and (4) its regulations are continually, and often unpredictably, changed.

The cost debate has littered the governmental arena with hundreds of competing, usually conflicting, cost estimates produced by public agencies, academic institutions, and economists for whom the job has become a cottage industry. Generally, business estimates of compliance costs tend to be higher, often hugely higher, than governmental estimates.

Projections of future costs often tend to vary widely according to differing assumptions about future political and economic trends made by the estimators. A further complication is the uncertainty in control costs introduced by industry challenges to every emission standard promulgated by EPA. Virtually all studies are open to the criticism that they have introduced, deliberately or not, some bias likely to work to the advantage of the sponsor. Thus, conclusions based on such data must always be treated with care, if not polite skepticism. Even so, some qualified conclusions seem reasonable.

Several recent national studies suggest that critics have exaggerated the negative national impacts of the act and that, on balance, its aggregate national benefits significantly exceed costs. The National Commission on Air Quality, required in 1980 to review the act and recommend amendments, concluded that the legislation created air quality benefits worth between $4.6 billion and $51.2 billion annually at a cost for installing, operating, and maintaining pollution controls of approximately $16.6 billion yearly.[16] Based on its cost-benefit data, the commission recommended that the provisions mandating that national air quality standards be established without consideration of cost be retained in the act. In a related matter the commission, like the EPA and the CEQ previously, found that air pollution control costs did not contribute significantly to annual inflation or inhibit economic growth, even in areas where energy production was expected to increase.[17] Other studies suggest that retrofitting control technologies on existing facilities has not produced the wave of plant closings and high unemployment predicted by some critics. Shortly before her involuntary departure from EPA, Administrator Anne Burford—no friend of the act—nonetheless released figures indicating that during the decade of the 1970s slightly fewer than 33,000 individuals had become unemployed as a result of all pollution control costs; about half the 154 plant closings were blamed on the Clean Air Act.[18]

Most major regulated industries do not accept these figures or their implications. The Business Roundtable, a major research and lobbying association representing the major U.S. corporations, has argued, for instance, that the act will cost $400 billion between 1980 and 1987, not the $261.6 billion estimated by the EPA or the somewhat larger figure used by the commission.[19] Critics of data favorable to the act note that much of it comes from federal agencies, such as the CEQ and EPA, with ideological commitments to environmental regulation. Then, too, controversy is inevitable—and probably perpetual—concerning how to assign monetary values to real but intangible benefits from pollution control such as improved public health, continued pristine air over the national parks, and reduced deterioration of buildings exposed to air pollutants.

Imbedded in these arguments are several issues that deserve continued study because they may shed light on economic problems with the future administration of the act. First, the economic costs of pollution controls may pose a particularly serious threat to several major American industries now economically fragile as a result of foreign competition, the domestic economic recession, and aging capital equipment. The steel and auto industries in particular may not be economically resilient enough to absorb the major air pollution abatement costs predicted in the 1980s without some relaxation of relevant standards or compliance deadlines. The steel industry has asserted that it will have to spend an additional $5.1 billion by 1989 to clean up an additional 5 percent of its emissions currently uncontrolled after having spent $5 billion to attain a 95 percent level of control. Environmentalists usually object vigorously to these claims for relief, largely because both industries have chronically complained about regulatory burdens in the best economic times and because the steel industry, in particular, has been among the most environmentally callous and reactionary of all the regulated industries.

In a broader perspective, the costs of compliance with the act are likely to increase very sharply throughout the 1980s, and consequently the negative economic impact may become greater if productivity, profits, new capital investment, and other indicators of healthy economic growth fail to expand significantly throughout the decade as well. EPA figures provide a rough, and conservative, estimate of these so-called incremental costs during the first half of the decade for major domestic industries; these data are presented in Table 4-5 below. These incremental costs are likely to be a source of continual debate throughout the 1980s particularly because, if past experience is instructive, the costs of pollution abatement generally rise above even careful initial predictions.

Finally, the inflexibility and complexity of the regulatory process along with the chronic unpredictability in the political climate of regulation continue to impose burdensome and needless costs upon many regulated interests. These stubborn problems are inherent in the regulatory process. While they may be unavoidable, the costs and delays they inflict are real and irritating to all regulated interests, including especially those struggling to comply in good faith with the law. Despite efforts to

Table 4-5 Estimated Costs of Compliance with the Clean Air Act: By Industry (billions of 1978 dollars)

Industry Group	1970-1977	1978-1986	Total
Energy	$10.7	$ 80.8	$ 91.5
Food processing	1.9	6.8	8.7
Chemicals	0.7	3.0	3.7
Construction	0.6	1.5	2.1
Metals	3.2	15.0	18.2
Soft goods	0.3	1.7	2.0
Electroplating	0.0	1.8	1.8
Dry cleaning	0.1	0.1	0.2
Waste disposal	4.8	15.1	19.9
Other industrials	1.5	5.6	7.1
Cars, trucks	38.2	92.1	130.0
Government	0.5	5.6	6.1
Total	$62.5	$229.1	$291.6

Source: Environmental Protection Agency (EPA), Office of Planning and Evaluation, *The Cost of Clean Air and Water: A Report to Congress,* chapter 1 (August 1980).

speed the process, it still takes an average of three years for major industries to obtain permits under the Clean Air Act. Many industries complain of "ratcheting"—the tendency of the EPA to change its regulatory standards continually—which often causes costly additional changes in emission control technologies already installed. Shifting party control of the White House and Congress, changes in public opinion, and other political factors create a constant uncertainty about the future course of regulation that makes economic planning difficult for regulated industries. American automakers, for instance, were continually unsure after 1978 whether they would have to reduce nitrogen oxide emissions from light trucks and heavy-duty engines by 75 percent no later than 1984 as the Clean Air Act currently requires. The Carter administration had failed to revise the deadline; the Reagan administration was trying unsuccessfully to do so.

Controversy will continue for some time over the benefits from the Clean Air Act and the validity of supporting data. It is apparent that a majority of Congress has chosen to accept economic arguments favoring the act and its stringent, cost-oblivious formula for setting ambient air standards. The Reagan administration's failure to achieve major changes in the act after making revision a high priority throughout the presidential election was an enormous disappointment to American business. But it was also evidence that Congress still regards the legislation as politically popular and symbolic of widely shared public sentiments for environmental preservation. Although further amendment is almost certain, most observers do not expect Congress to make major changes, particularly affecting the costs of the act, in the near future.

The Scrubber Wars

The conflict over scrubbers to control sulfur oxide emissions from utility stacks illustrates problems that typically arise when the EPA prescribes emission control technologies and declares which technologies must be used industry-wide as the Clean Air Act requires. At issue is the economic and technical justification for the agency's discretionary judgment and, in a larger context, the wisdom of requiring regulatory agencies to be the economic and scientific arbiters in deciding what emission controls are appropriate for regulated industries.

Control of utility emissions is especially important because public utilities currently emit more than half the annual load of sulfur oxides released in the United States. Scrubbers, which remove the sulfur oxides from flue gases as a solid or liquid precipitation, are ordinarily utilized after combustion of coal in the utility boilers. The scrubber controversy relates in part to utilities discharging sulfur oxide at the time the act was written—so-called existing sources. The act requires the EPA to issue to the states "control technique guidelines" for emissions from existing sources; based on these, the states are expected to prescribe to such sources the acceptable emission control judged to be "reasonably available." [20] These rules would apply to approximately 1,800 electric power plants qualifying as existing sources. The EPA consistently has pressed the states to require scrubbers for control of sulfur oxide from existing utility sources, although there are several alternative means for controlling these emissions including the burning of more expensive low-sulfur fuel, or chemically cleaning the coal to remove sulfur oxide before combustion— another costly process. As a result of the 1977 amendments, the EPA in 1979 issued a rule requiring the use of scrubbers in all new power plants built after 1978, a mandate consistent with the act's requirement that the agency create uniform emission standards for all new air pollution sources. Further, the regulations required utilities to achieve a 90 percent reduction in their sulfur oxide emissions with the scrubbers. Thus, more than 35 new or existing utilities by 1982 were apparently affected by the

EPA's scrubber requirement. The utilities, almost uniformly opposed to the scrubbers on technical and economic grounds, generally have managed to avoid compliance through litigation, deliberate delay, governmental lobbying, and other strategies.

Utilities complain that the scrubbers are excessively costly, complicated, and cranky. One major utility official has estimated that installing scrubbers may add between 15 percent and 20 percent to the cost of a new utility already costing hundreds of millions of dollars; retrofitting scrubbers on older facilities is even costlier. Utility officials are particularly critical of congressional amendments to the act that in effect require scrubbers on new installations even when burning low-sulfur coal alone might meet ambient air standards—a decision criticized by many economists and others as an unreasonable congressional capitulation to environmental pressure groups. The utilities also maintain that scrubbers are technically unreliable, extremely costly to operate, and often inefficient. The EPA continues to defend its scrubber policy on the grounds that the scrubbers have worked well in Japan, and often in the United States, when the utilities were willing to purchase high-quality equipment, train personnel adequately for servicing, and maintain service. Proponents of scrubbers also assert that the health and environmental effects of sulfur oxides are so dangerous that public welfare requires eliminating as much of them as possible. Moreover, they argue, the act requires technological controls because they are considerably easier to enforce, and air quality is more likely to be achieved, than by relying on low-sulfur coal in utility boilers alone.

The scrubber policy has had mixed results. Most new utilities coming on line in the 1980s will have flue gas scrubbers. But utilities also have frequently decided to keep in operation older plants without scrubbers rather than replace them with newer and far more costly scrubber-equipped facilities. Maintaining these older plants means the continuation of more polluting facilities. Many of these older facilities burn oil and natural gas. Most of the coal-fired older plants have evaded efforts to impose scrubbers upon them, in good part because state regulatory officials have permitted variances and exceptions to the scrubber rule. "As long as high-sulfur variances and delays in compliance schedules can be obtained," notes economist A. Myrick Freeman III, "they represent the cheapest option facing the dischargers. EPA has very limited authority to force the adoption of the scrubber technology on unwilling utilities...." [21] Currently, only about 10 percent of existing utilities are scrubber-equipped. This figure will rise slowly through the 1980s, but so will the reluctance of utilities to phase out their older, "dirtier" facilities so long as the current scrubber rule prevails.

How Valuable Is Really Clean Air?

The PSD conflict swirls about the complex and important issue of protecting unusually high-quality airsheds within the United States. It involves not only the predictable arguments over the relative costs and benefits of pollution control and the adequacy of the technological solutions but also regional conflicts over future economic development and matters of future energy availability.

As a result of a lawsuit by environmental groups in the early 1970s, the EPA was required by the federal courts to develop regulations to protect air quality in regions of the United States where the air was pristine (virtually unpolluted) or significantly above the national average—around national parks, deserts, and other largely undeveloped natural areas mostly in the West. In 1977 Congress, anxious to protect the EPA policy from modification and to reassure western interests that their economies would not stagnate under the new rules, largely wrote the EPA regulations into the act as amendments. These materials relating to high-quality airsheds are known as PSD regulations.

The 1977 amendments required that the states assign all airsheds within their jurisdictions meeting air quality standards into one of three PSD classes. Class I, the strictest, was a required category for national parks and large national wilderness areas, national memorial parks, and international parks; only very small increases in particulates and sulfur dioxide levels were permitted over these regions. All other airsheds were to be placed in Class II with opportunity for states to petition EPA to permit reclassification of some airsheds into Class III, the most pollution-permissive category. Class II and III areas permitted higher levels of all regulated pollutants and thus more opportunities for economic development; in no case, however, could air quality in the Class III regions be degraded until it fell below the U.S. primary or secondary standards. PSD standards, however, relate only to sulfur oxides and particulates, leaving other airshed pollutants uncontrolled.

The creation of the Class II and Class III areas was a response to strong political and economic pressure from western interests apprehensive that a strict nondegradation policy would seriously inhibit economic development in the West. At a time when the energy crisis had acquired political glamour, western interests were quick to emphasize that strict nondegradation regulations would surely discourage development of the West's abundant, untapped energy resources.

The PSD amendments were an attempt to reconcile a number of strongly held, and often strongly contradictory, views by politically powerful interest coalitions. Environmentalists, generally antagonistic to extensive economic development in high-quality airsheds, resisted concessions to the developers. Western states wanted generous latitude to decide for themselves how all but the Class I areas should be developed. Energy producers wanted the opportunity to get at the West's huge reserves of natural gas, coal, petroleum, and shale oil. Western farmers and ranchers did not want scarce water and valuable grazing or growing lands irreparably degraded by reckless development. While Congress and the EPA saw the three-class PSD arrangement as a way to give something to everybody, energy producers and other industries interested in moving into PSD areas have complained that the PSD regulations discriminate against them by imposing unfair costs when compared with comparable industries moving into non-PSD areas. Some western states also argue that the Class II and III areas are still so restrictive that they discourage desirable development.

One major complaint is that industries such as utilities, smelters, refineries, and others moving into Class II and III areas have to meet emission standards stricter than new sources in other areas; such industries have to use the best available control technology regardless of cost. Moreover, the PSD rules permit only slight pollution increments in Class II and III areas, leaving the areas still significantly below the national primary and secondary standards but imposing much higher control costs upon a facility than would be the case if it moved into a non-PSD area. For instance, national primary standards for sulfur dioxide average 80 micrograms per cubic meter per day. But in Class II PSD areas, an industry is permitted to add only 20 micrograms above existing levels. Thus, if a Class II area is very mildly polluted—say it has an average sulfur dioxide level of 40 micrograms—an industry seeking to locate there can only raise the sulfur dioxide levels to 60 instead of the 80 tolerated elsewhere.

Many industries, and those anxious to have them located in the West, have asserted that the practical impact of these regulations is to place the West at a competitive disadvantage with other regions in attracting new industry. Moreover, Congress mandated in the 1977 amendments to the Clean Air Act that in Class I areas any *existing* source emitting pollution affecting even visibility must retrofit the best available technology. This usually imposes very high costs upon electric-generating plants especially. Existing or prospective industries in PSD areas also commonly assert that the benefits to unusually high-quality air in Class II and III areas are seldom sufficient to offset the unusually high emission control costs imposed.

These views have not yet moved a majority of Congress. One reason is the almost implacable opposition among environmental groups to any measures that seem to be "selling out" air quality over or near national parks and other parts of the western public domain. Many environmentalists, particularly preservationist groups, hold with almost biblical intensity a conviction that "there is no right to pollute," which implies no right to contaminate clean air until it is just barely tolerable. Many other western interests fear any development that might diminish the quality of the national parks. Further, defenders of strict PSD rules deny that the nation has suffered a serious energy shortage or economic loss as a result of the regulations. Rather, critics often argue, industries wanting to move into PSD areas simply want to use a valuable public resource on the cheap when they can, in fact, afford to install efficient technologies to control their pollution and still make a reasonable profit. As often happens when political disputes are elevated to the level of principles, proponents of strict PSD regulations tend to regard most compromise as equivalent to moral surrender. Added to existing disagreements over the real economic burdens imposed upon industries locating in PSD areas, this makes any significant change in PSD regulations unlikely in the near future unless a reawakened national anxiety about energy resources creates enough political pressure to shift Congress toward accelerating western energy exploration.

An Issue for the Eighties: Acid Rain

In mid-1983 three scientific reports released almost simultaneously forced a reluctant Reagan administration to begin planning a national strategy for abating the sulfur and nitrogen oxide emissions, which appeared to be largely responsible for the growing acid rain problem discussed in chapter 1. Such a program would require amendment of the Clean Air Act or revision of EPA regulations implementing the act. It would also trigger a protracted, intensely fought political conflict in Congress, the White House, and state capitals where opponents of new acid rain regulations were certain to be active and outspoken. As the gravity of the acid rain problem magnifies with more research, the struggle to address the issue through the Clean Air Act grows in significance. The acid rain issue will become one of the major environmental issues of the 1980s.

The triple blow to White House inertia on acid rain began with a report by the Interagency Task Force on Acid Precipitation, appointed by Congress and representing 12 federal agencies, which asserted that man-made pollution from industrial stack gases was probably the major cause of the acid rain destroying fresh water in the Northeast.[22] Shortly thereafter, a report from scientists appointed by the White House Office for Science directly contradicted the administration's contention that further research was necessary prior to any federal action on acid rain. "If we take the conservative point of view that we must wait until scientific knowledge is definitive," concluded the panel, "the accumulated deposition and damaged environment may reach the point of irreversibility."[23] The panel's admonition for immediate action included an assertion that further reduction of sulfur oxide emissions would lead to reduced acid precipitation. Finally, the prestigious National Academy of Sciences released its report asserting that acid rain throughout the northeastern United States and southeastern Canada could be curbed by reducing the sulfur oxide emissions for coal burning power plants in the eastern half of the United States.

The reports were greeted with considerable appreciation not only by environmental groups and northeastern governors but by the Canadian government as well, which had been urging the United States with growing impatience to take more aggressive measures to deal with the problem.

Any federal efforts to address the acid rain issue place the states in the middle of a politically volatile confrontation between Washington and some of the nation's largest and most politically powerful industries. A major part of the controversy centers on tall stacks. Under the Clean Air Act, the states are ultimately responsible for prescribing the acceptable technologies for existing stationary sources of air pollution to bring Air Quality Control Regions (AQCRs) within national air quality standards. Most states have accepted "tall stacks" —stacks higher than 200 feet emitting hot flue gases—as an acceptable arrangement for achieving permitted sulfur oxide and nitrogen oxide levels in any particular AQCR. Unfortunately, tall stacks usually disperse the pollutants, primarily sulfur oxides, into the upper atmosphere where long-range transport carries them into another AQCR, "air mailing pollutants from some AQCRs to other areas where they are difficult to control," in the words of the CEQ. Since 1970, more than 429 tall stacks, many climbing above 800 feet, have been constructed by electric utilities, smelters, pulp and paper mills, steel factories, and petroleum refiners.

Air pollutants thus transported currently evade control by the Clean Air Act. Although section 126 of the act authorizes EPA to disapprove any SIP that allows a source within one state to contribute to air quality violations in another state, acid rain and snow are not as yet regulated pollutants. Further, it is often impossible to identify the source of pollution-tainted rain or snow transported hundreds or thousands of miles in the upper atmosphere. The high stacks are widely distributed throughout the United States (except in the Far West and Southwest), as Table 4-6 indicates. The largest volume of air pollutants contributing to acid precipitation in the Northeast and Canada, however, is assumed to originate in the Ohio River valley and Middle Atlantic states, the nation's industrial heartland. State regulatory agencies have been extremely reluctant to require, or even to suggest, that existing industries with tall stacks install other control technologies. The most commonly prescribed technology, moreover, would probably be scrubbers, thereby inflaming another scrubber war relating to existing air pollution sources. The political influence and economic importance of these industries within the states often effectively block any significant effort by state regulators to do more. This situation, common in regulatory politics, often explains why it is easier for environmental interests to persuade Congress to regulate specific pollutants than it is for them to persuade state legislatures to act: the political weight of the regulated interests can be more effectively counterbalanced by environmentalists on a national scale.

Industries liable to any new acid rain regulations, especially electric utilities that constitute more than half the total facilities involved, have argued that the sources of acid precipitation have not yet been proven or even strongly documented. Further—and scientists themselves readily admit this—it is almost impossible to assign a specific proportion of the acid precipitation in one region to some single distant source. How, ask the industries involved, can emission controls upon specific sources be assigned equitably under such conditions? All affected industries also point to the very large costs in retrofitting control technologies on existing

Table 4-6 Estimated Number of Tall Stacks Constructed in the United States, 1970-1979

Stack height (feet)	Electric utilities	Smelters	Pulp and paper	Steel	Oil, gas, and chemical	Total
$\geq$ 800	34	2	—	—	—	36
700-799	37	1	—	—	—	38
600-699	45	1	1	—	—	47
500-599	55	0	—	—	3	57
400-499	55	0	2	—	4	61
300-399	34	1	12	2	11	60
200-299	23	3	34	4	65	129
Total	283	8	49	6	83	429

Source: Council on Environmental Quality, *Environmental Quality 1979* (Washington, D.C.: Government Printing Office, 1980), 175.

facilities. Spokesmen for the steel industry have asserted that such a burden would further jeopardize the future of an industry already threatened gravely by foreign competition and sagging domestic sales. Midwestern utilities have asserted that some regulatory proposals considered by Congress might cost them $7 billion yearly and raise customer utility bills by 20 percent to 50 percent (utilities are especially prompt to convert any potential regulatory expense into customer costs on the often well-founded premise that public enthusiasm for regulation may thereby be dampened). All cost estimates still remain largely conjectural.

A variety of proposals will be considered by Congress in the next few years. Proposals under consideration in 1984 largely involved a mix of several general features:

1. A small tax on electricity consumed by all users of fossil-fuel fired electric plants in states largely east of the Mississippi River. The tax would create a trust fund to help utilities defray the cost of installing more effective emission controls.

2. An explicit schedule for emission reduction from all tall stacks specifying the amount of emission reduction and the compliance deadlines.

3. A requirement that utilities, and other industries using coal, switch when possible to low-sulfur coal or alternative fuels.

137

4. An accelerated federal program of research and development for new coal-burning utility boilers with much less sulfur oxide and nitrogen oxide emissions.

The major congressional battle sure to erupt in this decade over such regulation may eventually involve a different mix of substantive proposals, but the political alignments are in some ways already predictable. Midwestern industries and utilities, together with their local and congressional political spokesmen, will resist assuming the full burden for pollution abatement, as some legislation already proposes. The coal industry—fearing that regulation may mean a massive cutback in use of high-sulfur Appalachian coal, if not all coal—will seek to blunt the impact of regulation upon the industry as much as possible. State governments will generally insist upon a national set of standards for any control technologies or ambient air quality goals associated with acid precipitation, to avoid the politically and economically difficult problems they would inherit if too much enforcement discretion remained with them. Most environmental groups, long impatient at the pace of current efforts to control acid rain and snow, are largely committed to a strong national regulatory program. In this they are joined by the Canadian government, which asserts that two-thirds of the acid precipitation falling in its southeastern and midwestern provinces probably originates in the United States.

The Politics of Air Pollution

The emergence of the acid rain issue in the 1980s is further evidence that restoring the nation's air quality will require more decades, if not generations, to accomplish. Slowness in achieving the nation's air quality goals has been only partially the result of inadequate technologies and the complexity of air pollution itself. Cleaning up the air also has proven to be a difficult problem in social engineering. New governmental institutions, regulatory structures, and technical programs have to be integrated into the political process, and methods have to be discovered to create acceptance of technical and economic decisions made through these procedures. The Clean Air Act remains an unprecedented experiment for which the nation has no prior experience. If the political and economic structures essential to implementing the Clean Air Act largely fail, the nation will fail to restore air quality. Thus, the regulatory structures intended to implement the Clean Air Act appear essential to the restoration of air quality.

It should be equally apparent that many, if not most, crucial decisions affecting the regulation of air quality are shaped as much by political forces as by scientific or economic criteria. Indeed, we have repeatedly observed the extent to which scientific and economic processes end in a confusion of contradictory and inconclusive data when strategic decisions about implementing the act must be made. Issues relating to the acceptability of risks and costs from regulation, especially, are political determinations made through administrative discretion or congressional legislation. In this perspective, the direction of future air pollution regulation depends heavily upon the quality and balance of political forces in the governmental arena. It is very likely, in fact, that air pollution control will become more politicized as more decisions have to be made through administrative discretion and more problems arise in determining the acceptability of risks and benefits—the kinds of choices toward which political forces powerfully gravitate. In short, regulation is likely to become more politicized even as it appears to become more technical.

Substantial questions remain, to be fully addressed in the final chapter, concerning the adequacy of standards and enforcement as a means of dealing with the major problems we have defined in this chapter. Advocates of other solutions would assert that many of these problems are created by standards and enforcement. The persistence of enforcement issues in fact may compel a modification of the Clean Air Act in the direction of introducing other incentives to achieve greater compliance. This is another reminder of how early in the Environmental Era we still remain and how experimental the Clean Air Act and other legislation it inspired still remain.

Notes

1. Council on Environmental Quality (CEQ), *Environmental Quality 1981* (Washington, D.C.: Government Printing Office, 1982), 21.
2. *New York Times*, February 18, 1982.
3. *New York Times*, March 20, 1982.
4. *New York Times*, May 20, 1982.
5. CEQ, *Environmental Quality 1981*, 21.
6. CEQ, *Environmental Quality 1980*, 179ff.
7. CEQ, *Environmental Quality 1981*, 33.
8. CEQ, *Environmental Quality 1980*, 181.

9. A useful discussion of the distinction between the two approaches may be found in *Current Issues in U.S. Environmental Policy*, ed. Paul R. Portnoy (Baltimore: Johns Hopkins University Press, 1978), especially chapter 1; and *Federal Environmental Law*, ed. Erica L. Dolgin and Thomas G. P. Guilbert (St. Paul, Minn.: West Publishing, 1974), especially Robert Zener, "The Federal Law of Water Pollution Control," 682-791, and Thomas Jorling, "The Federal Law of Air Pollution Control," 1058-1148.

10. On this problem generally, see Allen V. Kneese and Charles L. Schultze, *Pollution, Prices and Public Policy* (Washington, D.C.: The Brookings Institution, 1975), chapter 2.

11. See section 112 of the Clean Air Act.

12. David D. Doniger, *The Law and Policy of Toxic Substances Control* (Baltimore: Johns Hopkins University Press, 1978), 67.

13. *Public Opinion*, February/March 1982, 36.

14. Paul B. Downing and James N. Kimball, "Enforcing Pollution Laws in the U.S.," *Policy Studies Journal*, vol. II, no. 1 (September 1982): 55-65.

15. Ibid., 58.

16. U.S. National Commission on Air Quality, *To Breathe Clean Air* (Washington, D.C.: Government Printing Office, 1981).

17. See CEQ, *Environmental Quality 1980*, 398ff.

18. *National Journal*, January 15, 1983, 132.

19. Lawrence Mosher, "The Clean Air That You're Breathing May Cost Hundreds of Billions of Dollars," *National Journal*, October 10, 1981, 1816-1820.

20. See Clean Air Act, section 110.

21. A. Myrick Freeman III, "Air and Water Pollution Policy," in *Current Issues in U.S. Environmental Policy*, 44.

22. *New York Times*, June 9, 1983.

23. *New York Times*, June 28, 1983.

For most of the compounds that frequently contaminate well water, EPA has not yet proposed maximum contaminant levels (MCLs). . . . For a few compounds the EPA . . . has prepared interim nonbinding guidelines, Suggested No Adverse Response Level (SNARL) documents. . . . EPA will replace the interim SNARLs with standards (MCLs) for trichloroethylene, 1,1,1-trichloroethane, tetrachloroethylene, carbon tetrachloride, 1,2-dichloroethane, and vinyl chloride in the near future.

—Environmental Quality 1980, *Council on Environmental Quality*

An Imperiled Abundance: The Nation's Water Supply

William B. Goldman, the city solicitor for Quincy, Massachusetts, doubtless could not distinguish a SNARL from an MCL when he decided to jog at dawn one day in early 1983 along the shore of Boston Harbor. According to a newspaper report, he saw what "he took to be a scattered gleaming of jellyfish, all down the beach." Upon more careful examination he reported, "They weren't jellyfish. They were little patties of human waste and patches of grease." Repelled and angered by the continuing contamination of Boston Harbor, Goldman initiated a suit on behalf of Quincy against Boston authorities responsible for the city's sewage system in an attempt to compel Boston to treat its raw sewage. Further investigation revealed that Boston, afflicted with a decaying sewer system more than a century old, was discharging annually 12 billion gallons of raw sewage into surrounding waters because the cost of upgrading the antique technology was a prohibitive $1.5 billion. Boston is only one of more than two hundred U.S. cities on the Atlantic and Pacific that continue to discharge raw sewage into marine waters.[1]

There is a direct and significant relationship between Boston's fouled harbor and the perpetual struggles of the Environmental Protection Agency (EPA) to turn SNARLs into MCLs. Untreated raw sewage is the oldest, most primitive, and most pervasive water quality problem known in the United States. Water contamination by hundreds of organic chemicals, most unknown a decade ago, is the most sophisticated new order of water contamination. That the EPA is currently struggling, with mixed success, to control both testifies to the persistence of the nation's

141

water quality problems. An essential resource with which the United States was extravagantly endowed, water remains dangerously degraded beyond the comprehension of most Americans. As with the nation's air, the full extent of water contamination and the technical, economic, and political complexity of the solution are only now becoming evident.

If volume alone were the measure of water quality, Americans would be prosperous indeed. Enough water falls upon the United States annually to provide every citizen with almost 6,000 gallons daily. Every day we each consume 65 gallons for personal use. Another 2,500 gallons go toward producing a day's food for each American. An additional 100,000 gallons per person are used to provide one day's industrial services (gasoline, electric power, newsprint, automobile materials, and so forth) to Americans. It is inconceivable that the American quality of life could endure long unless the nation could depend upon safely using a high proportion of its 449 trillion gallons of annual water runoff. Ninety percent of all water withdrawn from sources in the United States is used by industry or agriculture; almost three of every four gallons of water used in American industry cool the generators of electric power plants. Throughout most of U.S. history, water was treated as an inexhaustible resource, a natural bounty capable of assimilating unlimited human, commercial, and industrial pollution. Only in the last half century have we come to recognize that even the abundance of the nation's magnificent waterways and aquifers cannot withstand forever the onslaught of modern technology and pollution growth.

U.S. Water Systems

The nation's aquatic inheritance is not just water but different water systems, each essential to modern U.S. society and each currently threatened, or already severely degraded, by different combinations of pollutants. The full magnitude of the water quality problems can be appreciated if these different systems are considered individually.

Surface Waters

The nation's streams, rivers, and lakes are, together with the sea, the most visible of all water resources. Almost 99 percent of the population live within 50 miles of a publicly owned lake. Streams, rivers, and lakes account for a very high proportion of all recreation activities, commercial fishing grounds, and industrial water resources. Because surface waters are used so intensively and are highly visible, their rapidly accelerating degradation was the most immediate cause for congressional action in the 1960s and 1970s to arrest water pollution and restore the nation's once-high water quality. Indeed, to many Americans "water pollution" is surface water pollution. Most of the still fragmentary data available on national water quality during the last three decades come from monitoring surface water conditions.

Throughout the late 1970s and early 1980s, the Council on Environmental Quality (CEQ) consistently reported an ambiguous verdict on the nation's surface waters after a decade of new federal water pollution law. "Despite a growing population and increased gross national product," went a typical report in 1982, "there has been little or no change in water quality nationally in the last few years." [2] From one perspective, this might seem an impressive accomplishment because surface waters have been purged of the enormous volume of pollutants that might have been expected with growing population and economic activity over more than a decade.

Most environmentalists, however, regard this as cheerless news. First, they note that these statistics conceal the continued existence of more than 10,000 major U.S. lakes considered to have serious pollution problems. Moreover, federal agencies such as CEQ and EPA base their surface water quality indices largely on measurement of only six pollutants: fecal coliform bacteria, dissolved oxygen, total phosphorus, total mercury, total lead, and biochemical oxygen demand (BOD). These indices exclude important sources of water degradation such as other heavy metals, synthetic organic compounds, and dissolved solids. Existing surface water conditions, moreover, fall far short of the goals mandated by Congress in the early 1970s and, in the view of environmentalists, far below the quality that is technically and economically achievable. [3]

Measured by volume, about half the pollution dumped into surface waters originates from storm sewers, municipal sewage treatment plants, and industry. The remaining half originates from "nonpoint sources" such as agriculture activities, urban storm water runoff, mine runoff, silviculture areas, and construction sites. Nonpoint water pollution is an especially nettlesome problem for several reasons. Pollution originating from so many diffuse sources is not readily controlled technically or economically. And many pollutants are often involved. An estimated 68 percent of all river basins in the United States, for instance, are affected by agricultural runoff. This runoff can include many different pesticides, dissolved solids, organic nutrients from animal metabolic waste and synthetic fertilizers, sediment, and pathogenic organisms. Nonpoint pollution originating in agriculture and urban runoff is a major cause of the eutrophication, or "dying," of lakes; dissolved organic substances create such a high level of oxygen demand in the lakes that higher forms of plant and animal life gradually die from oxygen deprivation. Left uncontrolled, such eutrophication eventually will render most lakes lifeless; over time, they will disappear.[4]

Throughout the 1980s federal officials have given priority to controlling two of the most troublesome sources of surface water degradation: municipal treatment facilities and toxic substances—the latter, in fact, a major contaminant to all water systems. Toxic substances, including heavy metals as well as synthetic chemicals, have contaminated the nation's waters rapidly. By the mid-1980s, more than three quarters of the states were reporting to the EPA that their surface waters were significantly affected by toxics and heavy metals.[5] One major source of these pollutants is industrial discharges. Table 5-1 suggests the vast volume and diversity of these substances annually discharged into U.S. surface waters.

Other major sources of toxics are the pesticides, herbicides, and fungicides widely used in U.S. agriculture. The rising levels of toxic substances found in fish throughout the United States attest to the speed with which these pollutants disperse throughout the aquatic ecosystem. Recently, the EPA discovered that 22 percent of the hydrologic basins of the United States were at least partially inhabited by fish and shellfish whose tissues contained toxic substances. "Some toxic substances," reports the CEQ, "such as mercury, lead, and some chlorinated biphenyls (PCBs), can accumulate to high levels in living tissues. These toxic substances may reach concentrations much greater in aquatic organisms than in the water. In a number of areas, concentrations of mercury, PCBs, and pesticides in fish tissue have exceeded FDA action levels, and cadmium has been found in fish at levels exceeding the FDA interim guidelines."[6]

Toxics continue to flow into surface waters in high volume from abandoned or uncontrolled dump sites, from industry, and from municipal treatment facilities, which receive but often cannot eliminate many industrial pollutants. Incidents such as the following are not rare:

> More than 500 million gallons of water contaminated by hazardous substances are discharged daily into the Niagara River. Among the chemicals are known carcinogenic substances such as PCBs. Although more than 380,000 people

Table 5-1 Primary Industry Discharges of Toxic Priority Pollutants, 1979

	Organic chemicals		Metals	
Industry	Number of samples	Number of pollutants present	Number of samples	Number of pollutants present
Soaps and detergents	20	11	20	10
Adhesives and sealants	11	24	11	10
Leather tanning	81	38	72	10
Textile products	121	46	121	14
Gum and wood products	18	9	18	14
Pulp and paper	98	37	44	14
Timber	285	49	261	13
Printing and publishing	109	51	66	14
Paint and ink	94	42	149	13
Pesticides	147	80	104	14
Pharmaceuticals	95	49	77	12
Organics and plastics	723	106	557	14
Rubber	67	46	54	9
Coal mining	249	47	94	12
Ore mining	72	12	64	14
Paving and roofing	8	0	8	7
Steam electric power plants	84	29	82	9
Petroleum refining	76	58	346	12
Iron and steel	431	59	414	14
Foundries	54	46	54	14
Electroplating	18	17	18	9
Nonferrous metals	173	43	146	14
Batteries	3	8	0	NM
Coil coating	12	17	12	6
Photographic	25	42	0	NM
Inorganic chemicals	107	38	107	13
Electrical	35	36	2	14
Auto and other laundries	56	61	45	11
Phosphates	33	28	0	NM
Plastics processing	1	8	0	NM
Explosives	16	2	16	8
Porcelain and enameling	19	11	12	7
Landfill	7	17	NM	NM
Mechanical products	35	51	NM	NM

NM = No measurements taken.

Source: Council on Environmental Quality, *Environmental Quality 1980* (Washington, D.C.: Government Printing Office, 1981), 128.

drink from the river, cities using the river water are unequipped to filter out most of the dangerous pollutants. About 77 industrial dischargers produce 250,000 gallons of the contaminated water daily; about 310 million gallons more originate in municipalities.[7]

> When the U.S. Geological Survey tested a 39-year-old, 17-acre landfill at Islip, N.Y., it found the leachate plume extended a mile from the site and was 1,300-feet wide and 170-feet deep. The leachate had fouled about *1 billion gallons* of ground water (enough water to supply Washington, D.C., for a week).[8]

Despite a federal expenditure of more than $33 billion in the last decade to improve the quality of municipal waste treatment facilities, waste discharged from cities continues to be a major source of water pollution and a chronic obstacle to ambitious federal water quality goals. The federal waste treatment program has become a showcase for almost all the economic, political, and technical woes that can afflict environmental regulatory laws—an example of good intentions gone badly awry to receive attention later in this chapter. In practical terms, program failures have left a very substantial volume of municipally discharged wastes, including a large proportion of industrial pollutants, largely untreated.

Ground Water

Within the last decade, the quality of the nation's ground waters has become a major concern. Ground water lies beneath the earth's surface, between the porous upper layer and a lower layer of impermeable rock. Surface water percolates through the upper layer and collects until eventually it saturates subsurface soil and rock. Much of this water flows slowly to the sea through permeable layers of sand or gravel called aquifers. These aquifers sustain the life and vitality of communities throughout much of the United States. Indeed, ground water is as essential as surface water to the nation's existence, and it is far more abundant: the annual flow of ground water is 50 times the volume of surface flows, and most lies within a half mile of the earth's surface. About half of the U.S. population and 95 percent of its rural residents depend upon ground water for domestic uses; more than 40 percent of all agricultural irrigation originates from ground waters.[9] Because ground water filters slowly through many levels of fine soil as it percolates downward to the water table and flows onward through aquifers, it traditionally has been virtually free of harmful pollutants. In recent years, however, ground water has become often widely and dangerously degraded.

Ground water quality has been assaulted from many directions. The most important sources of such pollution include:

> 1. *Surface and Subsurface Waste Disposal Sites.* The EPA has identified more than 140,000 pools, ponds, lagoons, and pits used to treat, store, or dispose of

wastes. Most of these impoundments, usually unlined and uncontrolled, permit water contaminated by waste substances to leach into the earth, eventually reaching ground water supplies.

2. *Agricultural Runoff.* Water soluble pesticides, nitrates, other organic substances, and chemicals frequently infiltrate ground water systems from crop and animal production.

3. *Acid Mine Drainage.* Ground water in areas of intensive coal and other mineral mining is often polluted by high levels of iron, acid, and sulfate flowing into aquifers and water tables from mine runoff. More than 1,200 tons of acid are discharged daily from Pennsylvania mines alone.[10]

4. *Septic Tank Discharges.* Improperly maintained or spaced septic tanks are a major ground water pollutant in much of the United States. Organic chemicals used to clean septic tanks often contribute further to the problem.

5. *Road Salt.* Whenever salt is widely used to de-ice roadways, a very high increase—as much as tenfold—in the chloride concentration of ground water is likely. Since millions of tons of road salt are scattered annually throughout the Northeast in winter, salt contamination is a particularly significant problem there.

Subsurface water pollution is troublesome because ground water filters very slowly as it flows; an aquifer may move no more than 10 feet to 100 feet annually. Many toxic contaminants, in any case, are not captured or neutralized by filtering. Moreover, the extent of ground water pollution may be impossible to estimate adequately because the plume of pollution radiating outward through an aquifer from a pollution source can take a number of unpredictable directions; often, plumes will contaminate millions, or billions, of gallons of water. Some idea of the extent of toxic pollution in ground water is suggested by Table 5-2, which indicates the concentration of selected volatile chlorinated solvents, a major class of potentially toxic chemicals, in the raw and treated ground water used for drinking in 39 U.S. cities with populations between 10,000 and 1 million.[11]

Drinking Water

All ecosystems are subtly and intricately interrelated. Inevitably, the negligent dumping of contaminants into surface and ground waters eventually follows a circle of causality delivering the danger back to its sources. More than 80 percent of all the nation's community water systems depend upon ground water, and another 18 percent upon surface waters, for domestic use. About half the American population uses these

147

systems. Altogether, more than three in four Americans daily drink water drawn from surface or ground waters.

Recognizing that community drinking water was threatened by the rising volume of pollutants entering surface and ground waters, Congress passed in 1974 the Safe Drinking Water Act, intended to ensure that public water supplies achieved minimum health standards. In 1977 the EPA, following a mandate in the act, set National Primary Drinking Water Standards that established maximum contamination levels in drinking water for microbiological contaminants, turbidity, and chemical agents. Approximately 20 standards currently exist to which community water systems are expected to conform. The act left to the states most of the responsibility for enforcing its provisions on more than 215,000 public water systems.

Fragmentary evidence, such as the data in Table 5-3, suggests that many of the nation's largest water systems often have been infiltrated by dangerous concentrations of chemical and biological contaminants. However, information remains elusive largely because the act has been enforced so whimsically. A congressional staff study in the early 1980s found more than 4 out of 10 community water systems were either failing to meet water quality standards or neglecting to test the water at all. This widespread negligence usually is attributed to a lack of adequately trained state and local technicians, lack of enforcement personnel, and indifference. Among the worst offenders are many of the 100,000 small facilities serving limited populations. Consuming the local water in such communities often requires a certain boldness:

> During 1980 the Fredericksburg Water Association, serving 200 customers in Martinsburg, Pa., failed to test its water supply for coliform bacteria in ten of the twelve months the test was required. In one of the two months sampled, bacteria exceeded federal standards. An association official explained that the system operator was "a full-time truck driver and only works on the system part time," and, since he was absent much of the time, the tests were often ignored.[12]

> At the Bradley, Oklahoma, water system serving 150 customers, the operator explained that he took the required water samples when he had the time, which was not often. At the time inspectors visited the facility, the system's chlorinator was inoperative. "The operator manages a service station and said that he is generally too busy to devote much time to the water system. He further stated that he serves on the water board only to help the town. He receives no compensation for his work with the water system."[13]

While large systems are better maintained, they remain equally vulnerable to infiltration from hundreds of chemicals used industrially,

Table 5-2 Concentrations of Selected Organic Compounds in Raw and Finished (Treated) Ground Water (micrograms per liter = parts per billion)

Compound	Number of cities sampled		Percentage with chemical present		Concentration					
					Mean		Median		Range	
	Raw	Fin	Raw	Fin	Raw	Fin	Raw	Fin	Raw	Fin
Trichloroethylene	13	25	38.5	36.0	29.72	6.76	1.3	0.31	0.2–125.0	0.11–53.0
Carbon tetrachloride	27	39	7.4	28.2	11.5	3.8	11.5	2.0	3.0–20.0	0.2–13.0
Tetrachloroethylene	27	36	18.5	22.0	0.98	2.08	0.6	3.0	0.1–2.0	0.2–3.1
1,1,1-Trichloroethane	13	23	23.1	21.7	4.8	2.13	1.1	2.1	0.3–13.0	1.3–3.0
1,1-Dichloroethane	13	13	23.1	23.1	0.7	0.3	0.8	0.2	0.4–0.9	1.3–3.0
1,2-Dichloroethane	13	25	7.7	4.0	0.2	0.2	NA	NA	0.2–NA	0.2–NA
Trans-dichloroethylene	13	13	15.4	15.4	1.75	1.05	1.75	1.05	0.2–3.3	0.2–1.9
Cis-dichloroethylene	13	13	38.5	30.8	13.56	9.35	0.1	0.15	0.1–69.0	0.1–37.0
1,1-Dichloroethylene	13	13	15.4	7.7	0.5	0.2	0.5	NA	0.5–0.5	0.2–NA
Methylene chloride	27	38	3.7	2.6	4.0	7.0	NA	NA	4.0–NA	7.0–NA
Vinyl chloride	13	25	15.4	4.0	5.8	9.4	5.8	NA	2.2–9.4	9.4–NA

NA = Not applicable.

Source: Council on Environmental Quality, *Environmental Quality 1981* (Washington, D.C.: Government Printing Office, 1982), 93.

commercially, and domestically. Since even the most technologically advanced treatment facilities often cannot eliminate most of these chemicals, particularly those in extremely small concentrations, the nation's drinking water appears in continuing jeopardy of chemical contamination until more effective control is achieved.

Just as the surface, ground, and drinking water systems are physically related, so pollution of one source eventually pollutes them all. In the next chapter we shall examine in greater detail the problem of regulating toxic substances, which contributes so substantially to water pollution.

A Neglected Association: Water Quality and Quantity

Many of the nation's water pollution problems are created, or exacerbated, by the widespread failure of the country's governments to recognize the strong association between water quantity and water quality when planning water use within their jurisdictions. Even when the association is recognized, coherent water use planning sensitive to both water quality and quantity is very difficult in a nation where authority over water bodies is fragmented vertically among federal, regional, state, and local governments and internally among different institutions of the same government. Jurisdictional rivalries and competing constituencies often aggravate the differences in these governmental units.

The recognition that policies affecting water availability also affect water quality has come slowly and belatedly to the nation's governments. In the West and Midwest, for instance, federal subsidies intended to ensure farmers abundant water for irrigation have severely affected water quality in many regions. In Colorado's Grand Valley, for instance, subsidized federal irrigation water is so cheap that farmers use the highly wasteful technique of "flood irrigation" to cover farmlands with approximately six times the necessary volume of water. The resulting runoff, loading the Colorado River with 300,000 tons of mineral salts annually, creates serious problems in the Los Angeles basin, 700 miles to the south. There another federal agency, the Agriculture Department, subsidizes farmers for 75 percent to 90 percent of the cost for installing pipelines, automated irrigation systems, and other equipment to prevent the saline damage created by this upstream salt runoff.[14]

State and local governments, eager to promote the economic development of southern Florida, subsidized the construction of an

Table 5-3 Organic Compounds Found in Ground Water as Reported by the States (micrograms per liter = parts per billion)

State	Number of wells tested	Percentage of wells with chemical present								
		Trichloro-ethylene	Carbon tetra-chloride	Tetra-chloro-ethylene	1,1,1-Trichloro-ethane	1,2-Dichloro-ethane	1,1-Dichloro-ethane	Dichloro-ethylenes	Methylene chloride	Vinyl chloride
Alabama	80	10%	0%	4%	10%	3%	8%	10%	0%	1%
Connecticut	1,200	2	NM	NM	NM	NM	NM	NM	NM	NM
Delaware	19	79	NM	NM	NM	73	NM	NM	56	NM
Florida	329	NM	50	20	15	15	36	38	1	16
Idaho	9	11	NM	11	11	NM	NM	NM	NM	NM
Kentucky	22	0	5	0	0	0	0	0	NM	0
Maine	89	0	0	0	18	0	0	0	0	0
Massachusetts	163	36	0	19	21	3	1	8	2	NM
New Hampshire	6	17	0	0	0	NM	NM	NM	NM	NM
New Jersey	411	27	23	11	48	2	NM	NM	NM	0
New York	372	13	5	15	9	NM	NM	NM	NM	NM
North Carolina	44	18	0	5	2	7	14	45	18	34
Rhode Island	88	22	0	NM	NM	NM	NM	NM	NM	NM
South Carolina	4	0	0	0	0	25	0	50	0	0
South Dakota	1	0	0	0	NM	0	NM	NM	NM	NM
Tennessee	50	14	8	2	26	8	26	26	8	6
Virginia	1	100	NM	NM	NM	NM	NM	NM	NM	NM
Washington	6	33	NM	33	66	0	0	NM	0	0
Maximum concentration	NM	35,000	379	50	2,250	400	11,330	860	3,600	380

NM = No measurements taken.

Source: Council on Environmental Quality, *Environmental Quality 1980* (Washington, D.C.: Government Printing Office, 1981), 94.

elaborate, multimillion-dollar water management system to divert abundant surface and subsurface waters to agricultural irrigation and to drain wetlands for urban development. That region's explosive growth in the last two decades, sustained by constantly mounting use of underground aquifers for drinking water, further depleted the region's once luxuriant aquatic resources. The result was predictable: the gradual and growing degradation of surface and subsurface waters through salt-water intrusion, agricultural runoff, deep-well injection of hazardous substances, and other sources, all exacerbated by the greatly diminished volume of water available for competing uses. Few states recognize the relationship between surface and subsurface water quality in their water use planning.

Divided authority over water management often obstructs recognition of these interrelated issues and frustrates coherent planning to make water quality and quantity goals compatible. In Congress, 12 House committees, 29 House subcommittees, 10 Senate committees, and 21 Senate subcommittees all have some authority over national water planning. Four different federal agencies, the Bureau of Reclamation (Interior Department), the Soil Conservation Service (Agriculture Department), the Army Corps of Engineers (Defense Department), and the Tennessee Valley Authority, have major responsibilities for water management. Regulation of water pollution, in contrast, is handled for the most part by a different array of agencies, of which EPA is most important. State and federal agencies often do not coordinate their own water quality and supply planning.

Although efforts have been made in recent decades to achieve some coordination in state and federal water planning, it remains a difficult task. State and local governments, anxious to keep decisions over water use responsive to local interests, usually are reluctant to yield voluntarily much of their own water authority to regional or national planning agencies. Federal agencies, with their own set of clientele and congressional patrons, have different and conflicting policy priorities for water use. And congressional committees, no less than administrative agencies, have their own jurisdictional "turf" to protect. Thus, federalism and checks and balances often work against prudent environmental planning.

Among the most significant efforts to create better water quality planning is the Federal Water Pollution Control Act (FWPCA). In this chapter we shall concentrate on this ambitious effort to control the most widespread sources of pollution: municipal and industrial wastes. The

FWPCA and its 1972 and 1977 amendments have become the statutory centerpiece in America's water pollution legislation. They also illustrate some of the economic, technical, and political difficulties entailed in the congressional determination to "press technology" in restoring environmental quality.

Water Pollution Legislation

The federal government's major water pollution regulatory program, embodied in the FWPCA, began in 1948 but changed drastically in 1972. A series of complex and broad amendments, collectively known as the Federal Water Pollution Control Act Amendments of 1972, completely changed the substance of the older legislation and established the regulatory framework prevailing ever since then. In 96 pages of fine print, the amendments mandated the following regulatory program for the nation's waterways.

1. *Goals.* The amendments established two broad goals whose achievement, if possible, assumed an unprecedented regulatory structure and unusually rapid technological innovation:

A. "... the discharge of pollutants into navigable waters of the United States be eliminated by 1985."

B. "... wherever attainable, an interim goal of water quality which provides for the protection and propagation of fish, shellfish and wildlife and provides for recreation in and on the water be achieved by 1 July 1983."

2. *Regulatory Provisions for Existing Dischargers.* The legislation required that all direct dischargers into navigable waterways satisfy two different standards, one relating to water quality, the other to effluent limits. The water quality standards, established by the states according to EPA guidelines, were to identify the use for a body of water into which a polluter was discharging (such as recreation, fishing, boating, waste disposal, irrigation, etc.) and to establish limits on discharges in order to ensure that use. Effluent standards, established by EPA, were to identify what technologies any discharger had to use to control its effluents. In meeting these dual requirements, the polluter was required to achieve whichever standard was the more strict. A different set of standards was established for publicly owned waste treatment facilities.

A. *Effluent Limits for Existing Nonmunicipal Sources.* Except for city waste treatment plants, all existing dischargers were required to have technological controls, prescribed by EPA, which were to meet the following criteria:

153

    a. The "best practicable control technology currently available" by 1 July 1979.

    b. The "best available technology economically achievable" by 1 July 1983.

B. *Effluent Limits for Municipal Treatment Plants.* All treatment plants in existence on 1 July 1977 were required to have "secondary-treatment" levels. All facilities, regardless of age, were required to have "the best practicable treatment technology" by 1 July 1983.

C. *Effluent Limits for New Nonmunicipal Sources.* All new sources of discharge, except municipal treatment plants, were required to use control technologies based on "the best available demonstrated control technology, operating methods or other alternatives."

D. *Toxic Effluent Standards.* The EPA was required to establish special standards for any discharge determined to be toxic.

3. *Regulatory Provisions for Indirect Dischargers.* Many pollutants, including chemical toxics, are released into municipal waste water systems by industrial and commercial sources and later enter waterways through city sewage treatment plants unable to eliminate them. The law required the EPA to establish "pre-treatment" standards, which were to prevent the discharge of any pollutant through a public sewer that "interferes with, passes through or otherwise is incompatible with such works." The purpose of this provision was to compel such "indirect dischargers" to treat their effluent before it reached the city system.

4. *Federal and State Enforcement.* The EPA was authorized to delegate responsibility for enforcing most regulatory provisions to qualified states who would issue permits to all polluters specifying the conditions for their effluent discharges.

5. *Waste Treatment Grants.* The act authorized the expenditure of $18 billion between 1973 and 1975 to assist local communities in building necessary waste water treatment facilities. The federal government assumed 75 percent of the capital cost for constructing the facilities.

The 1972 amendments to the FWPCA were written by a Congress largely unchastened by the political, economic, and technological obstacles to pressing technology in pollution regulation. The legislation, as originally written, is the purest example of "technology forcing" in the federal regulatory code. The use of effluent standards in addition to water quality standards for dischargers was based on the premise that "all pollution was undesirable and should be reduced to the maximum extent that technology will permit." [15] Compliance deadlines were almost imperiously ordained for the total elimination of national water pollution in a decade. The administrative and technical complexities of making the legislation work seemed surmountable. It serves as an enduring monument to the American politician's belief in the possibilities of social engineering and to the political muscle of the environmental movement in the early 1970s.

In at least one respect, however, the newly amended act made concessions to the states that Congress had been unwilling to make in the Clean Air Act of 1970 and that environmentalists generally opposed. The FWPCA permitted the states to decide upon the designated use for a body of water. In contrast, the Clean Air Act vested final authority for the designation of airsheds into Class I, II, or III with the EPA and, consequently, left the final determination of an airshed's use with Washington. Generally, state regulatory agencies are more vulnerable to pressure from local water polluters to designate uses for bodies of water that will permit moderate to heavy pollution than Washington is. This greater propensity of local regulatory agencies to accommodate regulated interests extends, as well, to enforcement of designated water uses and the associated emission controls. Thus, regulated interests often are likely to press vigorously for a major state role in the administration of water quality standards and their enforcement, believing that this works more to their advantage than implementation largely through EPA regional and national offices.

Politics of the Unattainable

Even among the most ardent of the act's advocates, few were confident that the rigorous deadlines for compliance with its effluent discharge provisions and waste treatment facility plans would be attained. They were certainly convinced that pressing technology would work ultimately—eliminating all pollutants from the nation's waters hardly seemed unattainable for a people who could launch satellites carrying their language a billion light years into a black void. But the likelihood of some short-term failures at least was tacitly recognized. Advocates of the legislation were convinced, however, that only by pressing fiercely for rapid compliance with regulations could they sustain the sense of urgency and bring sufficient weight of federal authority to bear among polluters to achieve their long-term objectives. Thus, from the beginning, the implementation of the FWPCA was a struggle on the part of its congressional, administrative, and environmental proponents to force compliance with its provisions while simultaneously recognizing that some compromise and defeat were inevitable. Controversies surrounding the FWPCA have focused on which provisions are economically, technically, or politically attainable and which are not, and on which provisions can, or cannot, be sacrificed without defeating the ultimate purposes of the legislation.[16]

The Political Setting

The political struggle over the FWPCA has been shaped by several factors. First, the implementation of the legislation is largely federalized: state governments were given an opportunity, which most have accepted, to assume major responsibilities such as issuing and enforcing permits for effluent dischargers, initiating requests for federal grants to build new municipal waste treatment facilities, and supervising the administration of the grant programs in their jurisdiction. The states thus exercise considerable influence upon the implementation of the program directly through their own participation—and their pursuit of their own interests in the program—and through their congressional delegations, who remain, like all members of Congress, ever vigilant to protect the interests of the folks back home in federal programs. Conflict arising from differing state and federal viewpoints on program implementation, moreover, becomes interjected immediately into the daily administrative implementation of the law.

The political character of the program also depends upon the enormous administrative discretion left to the EPA in prescribing the multitude of different technologies that must be used by effluent dischargers to meet the many different standards established in the law. At the time the FWPCA was amended in 1972, for instance, about 20,000 industrial dischargers were pouring pollutants into more than 2,500 municipal waste treatment facilities. The EPA was charged with identifying the pretreatment standards to be used by each major class of industrial discharger. This might eventually require standards for several hundred different classes and modified standards for subclasses. The final standards issued by EPA in 1976 for industries producing "canned and preserved fruits and vegetables" alone contained specifications for 51 different subcategories.[17] Administrators also are limited by the state of the art in treatment technologies and by dependence upon the regulated interests for information concerning the character of the discharger's production processes and technical capacities. We already have noted that administrative discretion invites political pressure and conflict. The technical determinations required in setting effluent standards also invite controversy and litigation.

Finally, the program's implementation has been continually affected by the active, if not always welcome, intervention of the White House, Congress, and the federal courts in the program development. Federal and state regulatory agencies have had to conduct the program in a highly political environment, where all major actions have been subject to continual scrutiny, debate, and assessment by elective public officials and judges. This is hardly surprising for a program involving so many billions of dollars and so many politically and economically sensitive interests. But, as we shall observe, the economic and environmental costs of such politicized administration are high.

Failed Deadlines

The nation will not have eliminated all pollution discharges into its waters by 1985, nor will it have made all, or even most, waterways "fishable and swimmable" by mid-1983 as the FWPCA intended. More significantly, the major regulatory programs established by the legislation—the truly operational elements in the law—frequently failed to achieve their compliance deadlines, which had to be extended. Generally, almost all phases of the program created by the 1972 amendments have been laggard. Although few of these regulatory programs have clearly failed, few have attained the impact intended when the law was written. The reasons for these failures are legion, but among them several political factors are significant: the halting pace at which the EPA has implemented many program elements, the delays imposed by constant litigation over program regulations and enforcement, difficulties in achieving vigorous state implementation of the programs, and the unpredictability of congressional and White House support for various program elements.

Of the major programs in the FWPCA, that which seems the most successful is the permit system for all direct dischargers into navigable waterways, the National Pollution Discharge Elimination System (NPDES). In the mid-1980s, 33 states were issuing permits under the NPDES structure (the EPA issues permits in the remaining states). More than 64,000 permits, affecting more than 90 percent of the major pollution dischargers and more than 75 percent of all dischargers, had been issued.[18] Yet in many respects, this is a counterfeit success. In the mid-1980s approximately one out of five industrial dischargers had failed to meet the conditions of permits that called for the installation of the best practicable control technology on their effluents. A great many dischargers, industrial and municipal, were failing to report regularly, as required by the law, the amount and nature of their discharges. (The FWPCA, like other pollution laws, depends heavily upon voluntary reporting to ensure compliance with permit conditions. Federal and state agencies base their judgments about the law's impact largely on the basis of these voluntary reports.) It is also evident that many, and probably most, states are not aggressively monitoring the dischargers to ensure that they conform to permit conditions. Perhaps as many as one-third of all permit holders in fact are not complying with some significant condition of their permit.[19]

Other regulatory programs of the FWPCA, continually embattled politically and legally, have moved at a slow pace. Not until 1978, several years later than the law had mandated, did the EPA issue the important general regulations prescribing the acceptable pretreatment standards for water pollutants discharged by industry into municipal treatment systems. By the end of that year, implementation of the standards had been smothered by litigation; more than 200 cases had been initiated in state and federal courts challenging the new standards. The EPA revised its pretreatment standards in response to these challenges and reissued them in 1981, but further enforcement of the new regulations was delayed because the Reagan administration objected that the new regulations were too inflexible and costly. By early 1984 the EPA's final pretreatment regulations, whose issue was essential before state enforcement agencies and the regulated industries could act upon them, had yet to appear. While many industries affected by pretreatment regulations have taken steps to eliminate pollutants in anticipation of new regulations, many have not and will not until compelled by final regulations yet to be issued.

The EPA's difficulty in creating regulations to define what treatment technologies had to be installed by polluters to conform with the law has meant continuing congressional or EPA extensions of deadlines for compliance with these different mandates. For example:

1. The requirement that all municipal waste treatment facilities had to achieve at least secondary treatment levels by 1977 was extended until 1983 or beyond.

2. The requirement that industrial dischargers install the best-available treatment technologies has been extended from a deadline of 1983 to 1984 or beyond.

3. Controls on nonpoint pollution sources originally mandated for 1983 have been postponed indefinitely.

The waste treatment grant program, shortly to be examined, remains a deeply controversial undertaking whose long-term environmental impact and economic burden have been a continuing source of conflict even among those committed to its broad philosophy.

Despite the continuing slippage of compliance deadlines within the law, some significant achievements are apparent. The quality of the Great Lakes, and particularly severely polluted Lake Erie, has improved conspicuously since the law's enactment. Major rivers such as the Mississippi, Cuyahoga, Willamette, and Hudson have been purged of dangerous concentrations of numerous organic and chemical pollutants. However, the magnitude and rate of water quality improvement throughout the United States continues to lag behind the goals assumed in the FWPCA.

EPA Guidance: Late, Changing, and Confusing

The FWPCA, like other standards-and-enforcement programs, moves on a path papered with federal regulations and guidelines. State and local governments, regulated polluters, judges, and other affected interests depend upon this federal guidance to define in detail how EPA expects the law to be implemented. Indeed, EPA regulations and guidelines are, for all practical purposes, the law for those who must implement the FWPCA programs. The FWPCA has been afflicted with massive delays, confusion, contradiction, and inconsistencies in its program regulations. Delay above breeds indecision below. Uncertainties and contradictions in regulations from Washington spawn inertia and frustration among state agencies and their regulated interests. Time has eased only some of these early problems. The EPA's difficulties with regulation writing still seriously obstruct program implementation.

EPA's problems are attributable far less to bureaucratic incompetence than to the political, economic, and administrative context in which the agency must implement the law. The law created an avalanche of requirements for new regulations to accompany a multitude of new programs, all of which had to be done in a decade or less. EPA, operational only in 1972 and chronically understaffed throughout the 1970s and early 1980s, attempted to solve its problems by setting priorities for program implementation—an arrangement that deliberately destined some programs to benign neglect in order to concentrate limited resources on other, presumably more important ones.

Such a strategy depends heavily upon the cooperation of environmental groups and other proponents of the legislation; in effect, an informal agreement must be negotiated in which those likely to go to court to compel the agency to fulfill its statutory duties to enforce all the law agree not to do so in the interest of ensuring that some provisions are implemented in the required time. Environmental groups, however, have been extremely wary of such arrangements. They often see an agency's plea for "realistic" program planning as a pretense to delay important programs. Using litigation initiated by specialized legal groups such as the Environmental Defense Fund and the Natural Resources Defense Council, environmentalists frequently forced the EPA to reformulate its own internal planning, to attempt to implement more programs simultaneously than it intended, and generally to undertake more than it was able to accomplish. Delays were also created by litigation initiated by regulated firms to challenge almost all the major treatment and emission standards promulgated by the EPA.

Congress, however unintentionally, has been a talented collaborator in delaying and complicating essential regulations and guidelines. Throughout the 1970s and early 1980s, legislators continued to thrust upon the agency massive new environmental regulatory programs without concurrently providing the necessary organizational and financial resources to discharge the responsibilities. After creating the FWPCA amendments in 1972, for instance, Congress further charged EPA with enforcing the new Clean Water Act of 1974 with its multiple regulatory schemes. In 1976 Congress added to the agency's mission the enforcement of the Toxic Substances Control Act (TSCA) and the Resource Conservation and Recovery Act (RCRA); the list of additional new programs continues through the early 1980s.

In many instances, as we have observed, legislators deliberately left crucial provisions of such laws vague or contradictory, sometimes to avoid an unresolved political conflict. The result was a steady flow of political "hot potatoes" to the bureaucracy. EPA and the courts were left to settle the meaning and impact of such provisions. The EPA thus has been enmeshed in protracted litigation and political bargaining; program regulations often become hostages to such procedures. Moreover, many regulations can be competently formulated only after research that may take years or decades to accomplish. Congressional insensitivity to these administrative realities, however, is evident in the criticism vented upon the EPA by legislators who underestimate, if indeed they comprehend at all, the technical and administrative complexities of the laws they mandate.

Major disruptions of FWPCA programs were also caused in the early 1980s by the Reagan administration. Two broad approaches to "regulatory relief" by the president and his appointees to leadership positions in EPA have produced confusion and delay in program guidance from Washington. First, the Reagan administration substantially reduced the budgets and personnel necessary to provide this guidance. In the fiscal 1983 EPA budget, the Reagan administration reduced funding for water quality protection by almost 40 percent. Other substantial reductions were proposed and later implemented in the agency's research activities crucial to providing data needed for writing regulations on control technologies for water pollutants. Second, the EPA's new leadership ordered a comprehensive review of most proposed new regulations and a second look at older ones to discover which could be rewritten or eliminated because they were excessively costly or inefficient.[20] While the White House passion for "regulatory relief" might have been cooled by the controversies it triggered, the delays and confusion in program guidance produced in the early 1980s would set back many programs by years. Nor could anyone be confident that the White House, whether controlled by Democrats or Republicans, might not be inspired again to attempt massive and disruptive new changes in EPA regulations.

Finally, regulation writing is as much politics as science or administration. EPA cannot issue regulations like papal encyclicals. Useful regulations require prolonged negotiation and bargaining among the affected parties, with opportunity for experts and technicians to provide needed scientific data. Regulation writers need experience to temper their often excessive ambitions and to sharpen their appreciation for the practical and achievable approaches to regulation. This takes time, and, when technical information is fragmentary or absent, regulations often languish while the necessary research is obtained. It took many EPA offices a long time to accept these facts of administrative life. The obituary delivered by EPA in 1978 to explain the initial failure of its "areawide waste planning" regulations lists problems that have haunted many other regulation writers:

> Policy was often developed late, had changing objectives, and
> confused the ongoing planning efforts. There was a belated recogni-

tion that the program was a political process, and public participation was under-emphasized. Ill-defined and shifting relationships existed between States and areawide [planning agencies] as to responsibilities. Most importantly, an overly ambitious attempt was made to cover all water quality and waste treatment problems in the initial two-year process.[21]

Eventually—usually—these hard lessons are learned.

The States and Implementation

The responsibility for implementing the FWPCA and most other federal water pollution regulations rests heavily upon the states. The states have an especially critical role because, unlike the Clean Air Act, the FWPCA permits each state to designate the primary use for waters within its jurisdiction; in effect, this means substantial authority to establish rigorous or lenient water pollution standards. Thirty-three states were also qualified in 1984 to enforce the National Pollution Discharge Elimination System—to write the permits and monitor compliance with effluent limits for water polluters. This means that regulation of water pollution is federalized not only administratively but also politically. The state governments, and the constellation of interests that organize around state political structures, regard the states' position in the regulatory framework as a political leverage point, a place where states and their associated pressure groups can articulate and defend their regulatory interests. Federal and state viewpoints on regulatory matters rarely coincide. Differences must be articulated and reconciled through a continual process of negotiation and bargaining within the flow of administration decisions linking Washington and the states when implementing the FWPCA. Difficulties in implementing the act are often problems of federal-state relations.

Washington's enormous visibility in water pollution regulation often obscures the very substantial stake that most states have in the policy implementation. Since 1972 the states have invested more than $11 billion as their share in the construction of new municipal treatment facilities. The interests the states regulate are likely to constitute a vital—and sometimes the sole—component in their economic base. Regulation, moreover, is costly in scarce state resources: public funds, personnel, and administrative time. Regulatory policies also contribute to what public officials commonly regard among the most sensitive of all environments, the "business climate." For all these reasons the states often differ from

Washington, and among themselves, in their perspective on water pollution issues.

From the inception of the FWPCA, a chronic problem has been widespread understaffing and underfunding of state agencies responsible for the act's implementation. Although federal grants contributed substantially before 1981 to reducing state costs of implementing air and water pollution programs (about $209 million in the 1979 fiscal year, for instance), most states still complained of understaffing and pressured Washington for more. Data gathered by the congressional General Accounting Office in the early 1980s lend credibility to these assertions. A survey of state regulatory agencies revealed that vacancy rates in staff responsible for enforcing pollution regulations ranged from 7 percent to 20 percent. Just prior to the Reagan administration, when environmental programs were a Carter administration priority, the average state agency implementing the FWPCA nonetheless had a 10 percent staff vacancy.[22]

The Reagan administration's fiscal and regulatory policies aggravated these problems. Efforts to reduce the general level of federal support for all state programs squeezed state budgets and made additional support for regulatory activities more difficult. Many states also were suffering a prolonged decline in tax revenues as a result of the national recession. At the same time, the Reagan administration was determined to delegate increasing responsibility for administering federal pollution programs to the states as part of the president's avowed intention to reduce what he alleged to be unreasonable federal authority over the states. Thus the states were hit with the double shock of declining federal support and increasing regulatory responsibilities. "We simply don't have the resources to pick up the slack when federal grants are cut," complained Connecticut's deputy commissioner of environmental protection. "If the federal government is thinking of turning over more programs to the states without funding, they will find the states are already spread too thin." [23] By 1982 Iowa had been forced to abandon its municipal water monitoring program as required by the Safe Drinking Water Act; when EPA assumed the job, it could only do about 15 percent of the work previously done.

This increasing responsibility for the FWPCA almost ensured flagging enforcement in numerous states. Many, such as West Virginia, had used the threat of EPA lawsuits as a potent weapon against polluters resisting regulation. Many states lacked, or asserted they lacked, the resources to initiate aggressively their own litigation. Environmentalists were quick to note that the administration's programs, ostensibly intended to give greater authority to the states, often weakened state authority instead, particularly in environmental regulation. In a broader perspective, the president was using his traditional administrative and budgetary powers to alter drastically the scope and impact of congressionally mandated water pollution regulations. The implications often were obscured, however, because the alterations were discussed in the language of administrative organization and fiscal policy and conducted through routine procedures of executive management largely, or wholly, in White House control. Congress, environmentalists, and others critical of the present's program had considerable difficulty in discovering when such presidential acts were undertaken and what their environmental implications might be. In short, Ronald Reagan, like other previous presidents, was playing politics through administration.

State regulators, however, are not passive pieces in a political game managed from Washington. Even with more generous federal support state regulatory agencies often would choose to approach many regulatory responsibilities at a crabwise pace. In many states local water polluters have economic and political weight quite disproportionate to their national stature. Often a handful of industries constitutes practically the whole of a state's economic base. Intense and effective political pressure often can be exerted by such interests to impede implementation of the law. Regulating local governments—counties and cities—is an especially nettlesome task to many state regulatory agencies because state legislatures are bastions of political strength for the counties and cities that make up the legislative constituency. Local governments are quick to take complaints about regulation to the legislature, or the governor, and to press elective officials to represent local interests in the regulatory process. State regulators often find themselves embattled and frustrated by elective officials who have risen to defend local governments against the state or federal authorities. Thus cities have often appealed successfully to governors or state legislators to force delay in state requirements that they construct, or modify, sewage treatment facilities to comply with federal standards. A variation on this use of legislative influence by local governments is found, as we shall shortly note, in Washington as well.

The Congressional and Presidential Presence

Federal regulators, like all administrative officials, always look with a wary eye toward Congress and the White House. In a Madisonian government of separated institutions sharing powers, both the Congress and the president have a multiplicity of formal and informal means of influencing the implementation of environmental regulations. And both exploit such opportunities.

Congressional influence over the implementation of water pollution law, like that of any other law, takes several forms. Congress may amend or rescind the law. It can use the budget as a policy-making tool by altering levels of support for various elements in a regulatory program; it can punish or reward an agency such as the EPA for its regulatory decisions when the agency's budget is annually reviewed and reauthorized. Congressional committees may use inherent power to exercise "oversight" of the administrative branch to investigate the conduct of agencies responsible for environmental management. Members of the congressional committees with authority over a regulatory agency's budget and programs enjoy particular influence within the agency. Moreover, members of Congress regard themselves as Washington representatives of their state or local constituencies—ambassadors, in effect, looking after the local interests in federal programs including pollution regulation. For these reasons and more, Congress collectively and legislators individually become directly and continually involved in the daily implementation of pollution programs.[24]

In several respects, this congressional involvement has been a rich source of the delay and confusion about which Congress often complains in federal water pollution programs. Congressional support for various elements in the program is often highly volatile, waxing and waning according to changing public moods, emerging environmental crises, or economic circumstances; it is often difficult for regulators and the regulated to anticipate enough continuity in the programs to plan effectively. Congress easily falls into the "pollution-of-the-year" mentality, mandating changes in regulatory priorities according to what pollutant, or pollution issue, seems currently most critical. One example was the sudden congressional decision in 1977—dignified as a "midcourse correction"—to switch emphasis in the FWPCA away from controlling conventional industrial pollutants such as suspended solids or oxygen-demanding materials toward controlling toxic pollutants whose dangers were then becoming obvious. However persuasive the need for such changes may seem, they are highly disruptive in the daily implementation of water pollution programs. It is an illustration of the congressional tendency to be highly responsible to short-term political forces in environmental regulation, often at the expense of prudent long-term planning.

In a political culture where members of Congress are expected to be eternally vigilant to represent the interest of their own constituencies in national matters, members of Congress are quick to intervene in regulatory affairs when local interests are involved. Industries and municipalities habitually appeal to their local congressional delegations for assistance in dealing with EPA or state water pollution regulators when problems arise. Most commonly, members of Congress receive appeals from local governments or industries to persuade EPA or the states to modify permit conditions, to extend compliance deadlines for pollution control, or to make numerous other modifications in regulatory decisions. This continual legislative intervention does not necessarily mean an obstruction of program implementation or special privileges for polluters with powerful congressional friends. More often it means extending the time for implementation of permit programs, greater difficulty in agreeing upon permit conditions, and greater reluctance of regulatory agencies to be aggressive with some influential polluters, public or private. Even if legislators do not actively seek to influence regulatory decisions, administrators know that legislative intervention is possible. Possibilities can be as persuasive as certainties. Acting in anticipation of legislative reactions, regulators can become far more conservative than they might otherwise be in implementing the daily details of program enforcement.

We have already observed that presidents habitually attempt to affect implementation of water and air pollution legislation. The greatest short-term impacts on program implementation are achieved through the president's appointment of the EPA administrator and other upper- and middle-level agency managers and through the agency's annual budget request submitted by the president to Congress. Proposals to amend existing legislation or write new laws can be included in the president's annual legislative program. Also the president may encourage other White House officials and agencies to influence EPA or state regulatory agencies in whatever policy direction he prefers.

While Reagan has been severely criticized by environmentalists for his efforts to influence EPA's water pollution policies, all recent presidents have sought in some manner to bring its programs more in line with their goals. President Jimmy Carter's Regulatory Analysis Review Group, created in the White House to review proposed new federal regulations, put considerable pressure upon the EPA to delay its implementation of controls on nonpoint water pollution sources because they were allegedly too costly.[25] The Reagan administration has been distinguished by its determination to retard most major water pollution control agencies through presidential action. Advocates of Reagan's approach have asserted that his intention has been only to make the programs more cost efficient, simpler, and responsive to the need for more national resource exploration and use. Nonetheless, the widespread perception among many public and private water polluters that the Reagan White House would not vigorously enforce major water pollution programs, together with its cutbacks in fiscal support for state regulatory agencies, significantly delayed the implementation of water pollution legislation in the early 1980s.[26]

Many political problems with enforcing water pollution controls can be sharply focused by examining the nation's experience with the FWPCA's waste treatment grant program. This hugely expensive undertaking, whose cost is exceeded in the history of U.S. public works only by the federal interstate highway system, illustrates particularly well the opportunities and problems inherent in the political management of an ambitious but necessary pollution abatement effort.

Political Pork and Municipal Waste

When the water pollution control amendments were written in 1972, it was obvious that the nation's municipal waste treatment systems had to be substantially improved. Municipal waste water was the largest source of BOD, coliform bacteria, phosphorus, and several other pollutants widely contaminating surface and subsurface waters across the United States. In the early 1970s, more than 21,000 municipal treatment plants were pouring wastes into the nation's waterways, yet only 16 percent were achieving even secondary treatment levels needed to control the most commonly recognized of these pollutants.[27] More than 1,500 rural communities had no treatment facilities whatsoever. Uncounted communities too tiny to qualify as municipalities had yet to be identified as important sources of water pollution requiring regulation.

The $18-Billion Carrot

The FWPCA required in effect that virtually all U.S. municipalities have waste treatment facilities that could achieve at least secondary

167

treatment by 1977. To facilitate compliance with these new waste treatment provisions, Congress authorized in the 1972 legislation a construction grant program of $18 billion to assist state and local governments in building new waste treatment facilities. This huge new public works program was inspired by sound fiscal logic and some practical political calculation. Many states, and probably most local governments, would be hard pressed to raise from their own tax resources the millions of dollars required to build treatment plants in the relatively short time required, even if the projects were popular. Many among the thousands of small communities affected by the regulations lacked even a city engineer to comprehend the meaning of a waste treatment facility. Many state and local governments, in any event, would consider any stringent new treatment requirements inequitable, unreasonably sudden, and premature; they were inclined to fight. Since Congress is, in effect, a convention of delegates from state and local governments, it would be difficult for legislators to support the program unless incentives for compliance could be written into the act.

The $18-billion grant program was the budgetary carrot that Congress so often combines with the regulatory stick to make federal regulatory programs palatable to state and local governments.[28] The congressional tendency to "sweeten" regulatory programs with federal subsidies to encourage compliance was made the more defensible, in this instance, because there clearly existed a need for massive fiscal assistance to local governments in constructing new treatment facilities. Then, too, so large a program ensured virtually every state, and thousands of local governments, millions of federal dollars in subsidized waste treatment facilities. Moreover, these facilities are both labor- and capital-intensive; the local economic impact of construction activity would be considerable. And the plants are splendidly visible. "Even a fiscal conservative is a fiscal liberal at home," remarked a freshman conservative representative recently. The construction grants converted nearly all members of Congress into hometown liberals.

Like most other major federal grant programs, the waste treatment program also nurtured a well organized, vigorous coalition of interests with a stake in the program and a zeal to keep it growing. This large, diverse aggregation included the Association of Metropolitan Sewage Agencies, the National Utility Contractors Association, the Association of State and Interstate Water Pollution Control Administrators, and many potential contractors for facility materials. This coalition of professional waste treatment officials, facility contractors, equipment manufacturers, professional engineers (often the consultants in designing the facilities), and others became part of the program's permanent political infrastructure.

By the early 1980s about 4,000 waste treatment plants had been constructed with federal subsidies, and the EPA was predicting that 6,000 more would be on line by 1985. EPA surveys indicated that about two-thirds of the new facilities were achieving secondary treatment or better. Yet controversy has grown about the effectiveness of the program and especially about runaway facility costs and the continually inflating estimates of future subsidies.[29]

Subsidies Ad Infinitum

Congress originally authorized $18 billion to finance the program between 1972 and 1975 and committed Washington to paying 75 percent of the facility costs (state and local governments were to provide the rest). By the mid-1970s it was evident that Congress had grossly underestimated the need for new facilities, the actual cost of facility construction, and the rapid cost inflation for all aspects of the program. Congress certainly had not anticipated the demand for new facilities (which was not necessarily the same as a need for them) among state and local governments. Under continuing pressure to provide more money, Congress by the mid-1980s had authorized more than $39 billion and had appropriated more than $33 billion. All this, however, would become little more than a down payment on the total program if Congress accepted the EPA's estimate that further program costs would approach $120 billion.[30]

This rapid cost escalation was driven by several factors. The need to replace "combined sewers" in the nation's older cities—sewers mostly constructed in the nineteenth century to move both storm runoff and sanitary wastes through the same pipes—had not been adequately appreciated nor the huge costs anticipated. Additionally, many cities requested federal support to build new facilities with a designed capacity far exceeding what seemed necessary in the near future. In fact, many communities were deliberately designing treatment facilities with very generous "excess capacity" in order to stimulate rapid local growth in the next decade. By a perverse logic, the federal subsidies were enticing many communities to accelerate their population growth, thereby increasing the volume of waste waters flowing into the nation's waterways and hastening the time when yet additional sewage treatment facilities would be required. Many plants often were poorly designed and managed, partially because neither the EPA nor the states were carefully reviewing most proposed plans. Federal and state officials protested that they lacked the personnel or money necessary to make thorough reviews, especially when pressures for program implementation were so intense. One federal review of more than 200 completed treatment plants in 10 states revealed that 8 in 10 of the facilities were violating some effluent standard.[31]

Operational Problems

Many newly constructed facilities failed to achieve design standards because they were improperly operated, sometimes by unqualified personnel. Many smaller communities discovered that the cost of operating a sophisticated new treatment facility—a cost they were expected to assume fully upon the plant's completion—exceeded their expectations or abilities to underwrite. By the mid-1980s average construction time for new facilities had stretched to more than eight years, in part because design errors constantly had to be corrected at many plants. Moreover, graft and corruption in the planning and construction of some facilities annually drained millions of dollars from the program.

Many problems in maintaining the facilities might be attributed to state or local governments, but it was difficult, as a practical matter, for the EPA to apply strong sanctions against them. Almost never, for instance, did the EPA withdraw a grant or otherwise severely punish state or local governments for failures in program implementation. EPA's aversion to tough sanctions was motivated at least partially by a reluctance to draw congressional representatives of local governments into conflict with the agency. But the agency also recognized realistically that sanctions probably would invite prolonged litigation, require cumbersome administrative procedures, and entail a host of other delays; it would take less time, and probably accomplish more, to negotiate a settlement with the errant governments.[32]

Is the Solution the Problem?

Whether the thousands of new treatment facilities coming on line are significantly contributing to the goals of the FWPCA is a continuing controversy. Many facilities are not technologically capable of removing a variety of toxic substances poured into waste water largely by industrial sources; instead, the toxics must be eliminated through industrial pretreatment before they reach the public facilities. Some communities are not capable of managing the treatment plants efficiently; the technology fails to perform to design specifications. Some facilities have been criticized for wasting millions of dollars in a technological overkill. Since the FWPCA required that virtually all new treatment facilities be high-technology plants capable of eliminating all pollution discharges by 1985, some communities were discharging highly (and expensively) treated effluent into relatively clean, or largely undegraded, water already meeting national water quality standards. Conversely, some other communities were discharging high quality water into receiving waters so polluted that the treatment made little difference in water quality.[33]

In some instances it also seemed reasonable that communities might find a less costly solution to their waste treatment problems than a high-tech new sewage plant. In some smaller communities, for instance, water pollutants might be better removed by "land treatment," which involves evaporating waste waters on open land where the solid matter, or "sludges," can be collected as fertilizer or treated for other uses. There was no doubt, however, that in many instances the large treatment facilities had contributed significantly to a marked, and sometimes remarkable, improvement in surface and subsurface waters, particularly in the Great Lakes, the Hudson River valley, and several other large river systems. Some problems also might disappear as EPA gains more program experience. But Congress also has recognized that the program needs substantial changes.

Reform

By 1977 Congress recognized that municipalities would not meet the FWPCA's goal of secondary treatment for all facilities in that year; the deadline was extended to 1983. New financial incentives were added to the act to encourage communities to create less costly, and perhaps more efficient, innovative alternatives to traditional treatment plants. The states were given more responsibility for reviewing new plant proposals, and other efforts were made to make the program more fiscally lean and administratively flexible.

In the early 1980s the Reagan administration, in collaboration with Congress, took actions intended to reduce future program costs drastically while adding more flexibility to the program. Congress passed the president's proposal to limit future program funding to no more than $10 billion annually. New restrictions were added to the act preventing municipalities from adding excessive capacity to their plant designs. The federal subsidy for new plants was reduced to 55 percent from 75 percent. The administration asserted, with fingers crossed, that the new measures would limit further federal contributions to approximately $36 billion by the end of the century. Many environmentalists supported the president's insistence that cities design facilities primarily to reduce pollution and not to accommodate a future population explosion.

Construction Grants and Construction Politics

The nation's experience with the federal waste treatment grants illuminates some of the trade-offs between benefits and costs inherent in most of the new regulatory programs designed to press technology in environmental management. It is also a reminder that all strategies for environmental protection inevitably will involve some trade-offs between benefits and costs.

The construction grant program clearly forced many laggard communities finally to accept responsibility for improving the treatment of badly degraded water supplies. Smaller cities and rural communities, especially, often were able for the first time to construct treatment plants long needed to control what had been largely an uncontrolled release of pollution into surface and subsurface waters across the nation. Several of the nation's great waterways and lakes, including long segments of the Mississippi River, are gradually returning to an ecological vitality that earlier generations had never witnessed. The huge infusion of federal dollars into waste treatment technology also produced some significant technological innovations. These considerable achievements would proba- bly not exist without the grants program.

Less fortunately, program costs no doubt have been buoyed contin- ually upward, far beyond reasonable expenses, by the tendency of Congress to treat the construction grants just like any other federal distributive program such as the interstate highways or water resource projects. Total grant authorizations have grown relentlessly, partially because Congress continually expands program resources to satisfy its desire to make spending programs widely available to members of both chambers. Moreover, Congress cannot easily relieve the pressure from state and local governments to keep the program expanding; political pork is addictive. Various "allocation formulas" have been devised by

Congress to ensure that most local governments can qualify for some federal subsidies, although actual need may be at best dubious. Any multibillion-dollar public works program is likely to invite fraud and corruption; the task of responsibly implementing so ambitious and expensive a program in a short time defies the ability of even conscientious administrators. And, as we have observed, any program that categorically mandates the use of specific pollution control technologies in a great diversity of different settings is likely to require inadvertently economic waste and technical inefficiency in some, perhaps many, instances.

Congressional experience with the construction grants, as with other major elements of the FWPCA, may be producing a legislative learning curve; if so, it would be among the most valuable unintended consequences of such legislation. The willingness of Congress and the White House to make substantial changes in the construction grant program in 1977 and the early 1980s suggests that federal officials may be educated by the difficulties encountered in implementing the FWPCA enough to produce greater flexibility in their future approach to water pollution regulation. Educating Congress, to be sure, has been exceedingly expensive. Congress was prompted to reform the grant program only when costs threatened to become not merely an embarrassment but unsupportable. Nonetheless, program transformations resulting from greater governmental experience with implementation can mean that in the long term the program may well become more efficient and effective. In this perspective, the governmental learning curve may be an expensive, yet essential and perhaps inevitable, component of all the ambitious environmental programs of the 1970s and 1980s. If governments do in fact profit from their mistakes, the future of the construction grant program, like other elements in the FWPCA, may well be more promising than the past. In any event, the construction grant program remains in the mid-1980s an ambitious and promising program whose quality has yet to be convincingly demonstrated and whose achievements remain in substantial dispute.

Conclusion

The nation's polluted waters remain among the highest priorities on the unfinished agenda for environmental action in the 1980s. Despite the enactment of the ambitious Clean Water Act of 1970 and its rigorous

173

amendments in 1972, Congress's intention to remove all major pollutants from U.S. waters by the mid-1980s may well remain unachieved at the turn of the century. While new federal and state water pollution regulations have contributed to reducing the rate of water quality degradation in the United States—on the basis of preliminary data the nation's waters do not appear to be significantly more degraded than a decade ago—the larger objective of improving national water quality still remains elusive. The apparently arrested pace at which federal water pollution programs are progressing is not necessarily an indication that higher water quality is unattainable. Rather, this slowness probably should be considered almost inevitable in light of the complexity of water pollution problems, the necessity of working through a federalized regulatory structure, and the lack of governmental experience with the new laws. In this perspective, the decision to press technology by creating largely visionary goals for the program, such as the elimination of all significant pollution discharges in the nation's waters by the mid-1980s, created an unrealistic and finally unattainable program goal. Given more time and the possibility of a learning curve for governmental regulators, it is likely that a marked improvement in national water quality will be attained within several more decades rather than several additional years.

Equally important, many of the problems encountered in current water pollution regulation are created, or aggravated, by two unpredictable factors that haunt all environmental planners: technological innovation and data inadequacies. We have observed that the continual multiplication of new potentially toxic substances and their dissemination throughout the ecosystem is an instance of technological invention continually outdistancing governmental innovation. The nation's waters never will be securely purged of pollutants until public policy succeeds in controlling the creation and proliferation of these toxic substances by regulation before they are released for national use. Moreover, many current difficulties in water pollution control, such as contaminated ground waters and drinking water, represent a heightened concern created by the availability of new data forcing attention on these issues. Undoubtedly even now new data are becoming available that indicate yet other water quality problems previously ignored. In short, water pollution regulation, like all environmental regulation, is partially a process of continually adjusting regulatory structures and laws to technological change and the growing sophistication of scientific information. No regulation program can operate wholly free of these impediments.

Responsibility for some serious delays in implementing the water pollution programs must also rest with the Reagan administration. The Reagan agenda for "regulatory relief," its controversial and disruptive appointments to management positions in the EPA, and other attempts to reform federal water pollution programs generally have produced considerable confusion and demoralization among many federal regulatory officials. The administration's continuing destruction of federal support for state enforcement of water pollution regulations has further enfeebled an already weak process in many states.

Among the most serious political problems in water quality management have been the political and jurisdictional conflicts between state and federal regulatory agencies that obstruct the essential collaboration required between them, the erratic and unpredictable program enforcement at the state level due to limited resources and political pressures against enforcement, and bloated program costs, particularly in the construction grants program. We have previously observed that the political management of regulatory programs will almost always involve some substantial social costs of this kind. Experience with federal water pollution programs in the 1970s and 1980s raises serious questions about the desirability of alternative regulatory strategies for water pollution that rely less on pressing technology, an elaborate standards-and-enforcement process, and all the other familiar attributes of federal regulatory programs. Certainly program reform and the exploration of imaginative alternative procedures for eliminating some of the worst management problems would seem worth serious consideration. Indeed, one of the major issues affecting water pollution regulation in the 1980s concerns the desirability of alternative regulatory strategies. We shall consider these further in the final chapter.

Notes

1. On the problem of municipal discharges generally, see Council on Environmental Quality (CEQ), *Environmental Quality 1979* (Washington, D.C.: Government Printing Office, 1980), 112-148.
2. CEQ, *Environmental Quality 1981* (Washington, D.C.: Government Printing Office, 1982), 52.
3. Ibid., chapter 3.
4. A useful summary of the major issues in nonpoint source control is found in U.S. General Accounting Office, "National Water Quality Goals Cannot Be Attained Without More Attention to Pollution from Diffused or Nonpoint Sources," Report No. CED 78-6 (December 20, 1977).

5. CEQ, *Environmental Quality 1981*, 53.
6. Ibid., 55.
7. *New York Times*, October 11, 1981.
8. CEQ, *Environmental Quality 1981*, 182.
9. Current ground water conditions are usefully summarized in U.S. General Accounting Office, "Ground Water Overdrafting Must Be Controlled," Report No. CED-80-96 (September 12, 1980).
10. CEQ, *Environmental Quality 1981*, 110-111.
11. Problems of ground water contamination by toxics are discussed in Samuel S. Epstein, Lester O. Brown, and Carl Pope, *Hazardous Waste in America* (San Francisco: Sierra Club Books, 1982), chapter 11.
12. U.S. General Accounting Office, "States' Compliance Lacking in Meeting Safe Drinking Water Regulations," Report No. CED-82-43 (March 3, 1982), 6.
13. Ibid., 7.
14. *New York Times*, August 8, 1981. On the problem more generally, see the useful summary in J. Clarence Davies III and Charles F. Lettow, "The Impact of Federal Institutional Arrangements," in *Federal Environmental Law*, ed. Erica L. Dolgin and Thomas G. P. Guilbert (St. Paul, Minn.: West Publishing Co., 1974), 126-191.
15. Robert Zener, "The Federal Law of Water Pollution Control," in *Federal Environmental Law*, 694.
16. Most of these arguments are summarized in Allen V. Kneese and Charles L. Schultze, *Pollution, Prices and Public Policy* (Washington, D.C.: The Brookings Institution, 1975). A summary of more recent critiques is found in Jerome W. Milliman, "Can Water Pollution Policy Be Efficient?" *Cato Journal*, vol. 2, no. 1 (Spring 1982): 165-196.
17. CEQ, *Environmental Quality 1978* (Washington, D.C.: Government Printing Office, 1979), 104.
18. CEQ, *Environmental Quality 1981*, 81-82.
19. On compliance data, see CEQ, *Environmental Quality 1981*, 138. The literature on state enforcement problems is summarized in Paul B. Downing and James N. Kimball, "Enforcing Pollution Control Laws in the U.S.," *Policy Studies Journal*, vol. 11, no. 1 (September 1982): 55-65.
20. The Reagan program is examined in Conservation Foundation, *State of the Environment 1982* (Washington, D.C.: Government Printing Office, 1983), chapter 9.
21. U.S. General Accounting Office, "Federal-State Environmental Programs—the State Perspective," Report No. CED-80-106 (August 1980), 37.
22. Ibid., iii. See also Lawrence Mosher, "Reagan's Environmental Federalism—Are the States Up to the Challenge?" *National Journal*, January 30, 1982, 184-188.
23. Ibid., 184.
24. The political connection is emphasized in Barbara S. Davies and J. Clarence Davies III, *Politics of Pollution* (Indianapolis: Bobbs-Merrill, 1976).
25. Most of the Carter administration's actions in this respect are summarized in U.S. Congress, Senate Committee on Environment and Public Works, Subcommittee on Environmental Pollution, *Hearings on Executive Branch Review of Environmental Regulations*, 96th Congress, 1st sess., 1979.

26. Mosher, "Reagan's Environmental Federalism."
27. Lawrence Mosher, "Clean Water Requirements Will Remain Even if the Federal Spigot Is Closed," *National Journal*, May 16, 1981, 874-878.
28. This carrot-and-stick approach is critiqued in Kneese and Schultze, *Pollution, Prices and Public Policy*, chapters 1 and 2.
29. See, for example, U.S. General Accounting Office, "Large Construction Projects to Correct Combined Sewer Overflows Are Too Costly," Report No. CED-80-40 (December 28, 1979); "Better Planning Can Reduce Size of Wastewater Treatment Facilities, Saving Millions in Construction Costs," Report No. GAO/CED-82-82 (July 8, 1982); and "Costly Wastewater Treatment Plants Fail to Perform as Expected," Report No. CED-81-9 (November 14, 1980).
30. *New York Times*, December 30, 1981.
31. Mosher, "Clean Water Requirements Will Remain."
32. This, of course, is the same enforcement strategy used in other pollution programs. The political logic is summarized in Lettie McSpadden Wenner, *One Environment Under Law* (Pacific Palisades, Calif.: Goodyear Publishing, 1976), chapter 4.
33. U.S. General Accounting Office, "Costly Wastewater Treatment Plants."

Outdated birth control pills, 96,000 drums of chemicals, hospital wastes including extracted tumors and tapeworms, carcinogenic solvents, toxic metals, radioactive substances, dioxin, 28 million pounds of contaminated soil and ash, phosgene nerve gas, 500 pounds of TNT, nitroglycerin, and picric acid.

—Partial inventory of Chemical Control
Company's Elizabeth (N.J.) site shortly
before it exploded on April 21, 1980

A Chemical Plague: Toxic and Hazardous Wastes

In late 1983 the Environmental Protection Agency (EPA) announced that the amount of hazardous waste currently generated in the United States was four times the previous estimate. Preliminary figures suggested that 150 million metric tons of hazardous substances, including toxic chemicals, solvents, corrosive agents, and other materials, were produced annually—enough to fill Houston's Astrodome more than twice daily for a year. This figure did not include the unregulated wastes of "small manufacturers" generating less than 2,000 pounds of materials yearly.[1] Remarkable as the magnitude of acknowledged error was the depth of uncertainty revealed that the new estimate might still be too conservative. After almost a decade of new federal regulation, the fragmentary data available about the production, distribution, and disposal of hazardous substances indicate that the scale of the regulatory problem and the character of risks involved in the widespread use of these substances are still incompletely understood and greatly underestimated.

The nation's hazardous substance problem is partially a composite of biochemical dangers: thousands of abandoned hazardous waste sites, widespread worker exposure to potentially hazardous chemicals, and widely disseminated substances whose danger to man and the environment may reach across many generations and infiltrate all levels of the biological hierarchy. In the mid-1980s controlling these known or suspected dangers was itself another problem compounded by governmental confusion, delay, and complexity born of political conflict and scientific controversies within the governmental agencies newly entrusted

179

with the regulation of such hazards. Despite new federal programs intended to regulate these materials "from the cradle to the grave," this legislation often remains a fabric of paper promises with many programs unimplemented and others barely enforced. Despite some significant accomplishments, the governmental regulation of the nation's hazardous and toxic substances still falls gravely short of its objectives. In this chapter we shall examine briefly the character of the nation's toxic and hazardous wastes, the major regulatory policies intended to deal with them, and the serious, perhaps intractable political and technical obstacles to more effective regulation.

An Ambiguous Inheritance

The nation's difficulties with toxic and hazardous substances are the inheritance of a worldwide technological revolution that was initiated in this century and that expanded explosively after World War II. It began with the creation and manufacture of synthetic chemicals on a rapidly increasing scale by the world's industrialized nations after the turn of the century. By the end of World War II the United States, leader among industrialized countries in producing new chemicals, began three decades of uninterrupted discovery and marketing of many thousands of new chemical substances.[2] By 1965 the American Chemical Society had registered more than 4 million chemicals, an increasing proportion of which were synthetics created by American chemists since 1945.

Most chemicals are not dangerous to man or the environment when properly used. Many have vastly increased human longevity, improved public health, stimulated economic development, or otherwise improved the quality of life in the United States and elsewhere. But a relatively small proportion of all these substances, those currently identified as hazardous or toxic, does pose risks, and a greater number are suspected of risks to man or the ecosystem. While numerous federal laws before 1970 attacked the most obvious risks from chemicals, such as dangers in food additives and cosmetics, only in the last two decades has science begun to suggest the full scope and subtlety of the risks associated with a great many of these substances.

Hazardous and Toxic Substances

Governmentally regulated substances are usually classified, not always with precise distinction, as "hazardous" or "toxic." Generally, hazardous substances are toxic, corrosive, ignitable, or chemically reactive materials posing a threat to humans; in the last several decades, the term sometimes has been expanded in federal law to include threats to the ecosystem.[3] Toxic substances, a smaller category, includes only those materials that produce "detrimental effects in living organisms." Usually, these effects are further differentiated into the following categories:

> *Acute Toxicity:* an effect from short-term exposure to a chemical substance. The most important effects include neurological damage, injury to the lungs, liver, kidney, or immune functions, and acute effects upon the offspring during gestation.
>
> *Subchronic Toxicity:* an effect resulting from prolonged but time-limited exposure. Effects studied are the same as those identified under acute toxicity.
>
> *Chronic Toxicity:* effects produced by prolonged, continuing exposure. These include delayed toxic reactions, progressive degenerative tissue damage, reproductive toxicity, and cancer.
>
> *Environmental Toxicity:* a toxic effect upon fish, birds, or other organisms in the ecosystem.[4]

A substance's degree of toxicity is often difficult to describe with scientific precision yet important economically and politically. Magnitudes of toxicity become important in calculating the benefits to be expected from regulating a substance and, hence, a consideration when public officials must decide what forms of regulation, and what costs, ought to be accepted. The dangers associated with a substance—or, at least, the public's beliefs about the dangers—become a major factor in governmental decisions to initiate regulation itself. And regulated interests liable to bear high costs in money and administrative work from regulation usually will attack the evidence establishing the toxicity of a substance as one strategy for eliminating or reducing the regulatory burden upon themselves.

Where They Originate

About 98 percent of the 55,000 chemical substances widely used in the United States generally are considered harmless to man or the ecosystem. In 1980 less than 7 percent of approximately 1,000 new chemicals proposed for manufacture and reviewed by the EPA aroused any concern among the scientific review panels.[5] However, the traditionally rapid development of new chemicals in the United States has been further accelerating in recent years. With the chemical industry's

181

continual growth into a major economic sector, the capacity to produce and distribute yet more new substances rises. The American Chemical Society's list of distinct chemical compounds has been growing at a rate of more than 5,000 new substances weekly; in 1983 about 50,000 chemical substances were in commercial production in the United States. About 120,000 establishments in the United States, whose production represents about 8 percent of the Gross National Product, create and distribute chemicals. As new chemicals continue to multiply and the long-term risks associated with older chemicals are more clearly understood, the need to protect man and the environment from the relatively small but still enormously diverse set of hazardous or toxic substances grows more imperative.

While many chemicals have been tested to determine their hazardousness—it is often relatively easy to decide if a chemical is corrosive, or ignitable, or otherwise clearly dangerous when handled or abandoned in the environment—few have been rigorously tested to determine their toxicity. Testing is particularly difficult and expensive when the long-term effects of a chemical are being investigated. Studies may require decades: moreover, many substances currently suspected of toxic effects have not been in existence long enough for long-term impacts to become apparent. Today's middle-aged American blue-collar workers, for example, may be the first generation of U.S. laborers to reveal the chronic effects of workplace exposure to new chemicals introduced in American industry during World War II. If testing deals with the chronic effects of exposure to very small quantities of chemicals—doses as small as several parts per billion or trillion in water, for instance—the difficulties in identifying the presence of the substance and the rate of exposure among affected populations may be formidable. For all these reasons, a major problem in regulating dangerous substances has been to obtain, or to create, the essential test data upon which determinations of toxicity depend.

Cancer is the gravest and most widely feared of all toxic impacts from hazardous substances. In the mid-1980s perhaps 1,500 to 2,000 of all chemical substances, a small proportion of all suspected carcinogenic chemicals produced in the United States, had been tested sufficiently to determine their carcinogenicity. Among those tested, between 600 and 800 have shown substantial evidence of carcinogenicity.[6] The substances, or industrial processes, most strongly linked to human cancer are identified in Table 6-1. The list of chemicals convincingly associated with acute or chronic human cancer is slowly growing with additional research. Currently, more than 24 federal laws and a dozen Washington agencies are concerned with regulating the manufacture, distribution, and disposal of carcinogenic substances; yet, as the data indicate, their work is seriously impeded by a chronic lack of accurate information on a multitude of chemicals within their jurisdiction.

Hazardous Wastes

Hazardous and toxic substances can be found not only in the workplace but also widely distributed throughout the ecosystem in air, water, soil, and biological life, bridging the whole food chain from microbes to man. The human and ecological dangers of exposure to small doses of such substances often remain controversial. In the last decade, however, the widespread distribution of hazardous and toxic waste in the ecosystem has become an acute governmental concern. Such waste is often the major, and unsuspected, source of persistent human exposure to toxics and the origin of toxics later discovered to have been dispersed throughout the ecosystem. In the number of individuals affected, the variety of ecosystems at risk, and the persistence of the danger, toxic wastes may pose a threat to human and ecological health far greater than the more obvious risks from toxics used in the workplace or at home. Toxics may become the nation's chemical plague. About a ton of hazardous waste for every American is created annually in the United States. Among more than 14,000 regulated producers of this waste, the overwhelming majority are chemical manufacturers or allied industries, as Table 6-2 indicates.[7] Hundreds of potentially dangerous substances can be found in hazardous waste, but, as Table 6-3 reveals, the most common are few in number.

America's chemical junkyards are growing in volume by 3 percent to 10 percent annually; figures are always very tentative. At best, no more than 10 percent of this waste has been properly disposed. Accidents and investigations have disclosed that more than 50,000 hazardous waste sites, the legacy of a century's irresponsible but widely tolerated dumping of chemicals by virtually all segments of U.S. industry, permeate America's earth. No accurate count of the abandoned sites posing acute threats to public health is yet available in the United States. In 1982 the EPA released its first list of the nation's most dangerous hazardous waste dumps as required by the 1980 "Superfund" legislation. Experts widely believe that these priority sites for remedial cleanup, listed in Table 6-4,

183

Table 6-1 Chemicals or Industrial Processes Associated with Cancer Induction in Humans

Chemical or Industrial Process	Main Type of Exposure[a]	Target Organs in Humans	Main Source of Exposure[b]
Aflatoxins	Environmental, occupational[c]	Liver	Oral, inhalation[c]
4-Aminobiphenyl	Occupational	Bladder	Inhalation, skin, oral
Arsenic compounds	Occupational, medicinal, environmental	Skin, lung, liver[c]	Inhalation, skin, oral
Asbestos	Occupational	Lung, pleural cavity, G.I. tract	Inhalation, oral
Auramine manufacturing	Occupational	Bladder	Inhalation, skin, oral
Benzene	Occupational	Hemopoietic system	Inhalation, skin
Benzidine	Occupational	Bladder	Inhalation, skin, oral
Bis(chloromethyl)-ether	Occupational	Lung	Inhalation
Cadmium-using industries (possibly cadmium oxides)	Occupational	Prostate, lung	Inhalation, oral
Chloramphenicol	Medicinal	Hemopoietic system	Oral, injection
Chloromethyl ether [possibly associated with bis(chloromethyl)-ether]	Occupational	Lung	Inhalation
Chromate-producing industries	Occupational	Lung, nasal cavities[c]	Inhalation

Cyclophosphamide	Medicinal	Bladder	Oral, injection
Diethylstilbestrol (DES)	Medicinal	Uterus, vagina	Oral
Hematite mining	Occupational	Lung	Inhalation
Isopropyl oil	Occupational	Nasal cavity, larynx	Inhalation
Melphalan	Medicinal	Hemopoietic system	Oral, injection
Mustard gas	Occupational	Lung, larynx	Inhalation
2-Naphthylamine	Occupational	Bladder	Inhalation, skin, oral
Nickel refining	Occupational	Nasal cavity, lung	Inhalation
N,N-bis(2-chloroethyl)-2-naphthylamine (chlornaphazine)	Medicinal	Bladder	Oral
Oxymetholone	Medicinal	Liver	Oral
Phenacetin	Medicinal	Kidney	Oral
Phenytoin	Medicinal	Lymphoreticular tissues	Oral, injection
Soot, tars, and oils	Occupational, environmental	Lung, skin, scrotum	Inhalation, skin
Vinyl chloride	Occupational	Liver, brain,[c] lung[c]	Inhalation, skin

[a] The main types of exposure mentioned are those by which the association has been demonstrated.
[b] The main routes of exposure given may not be the only ones by which such effects could occur.
[c] Denotes indicative evidence.

Source: Council on Environmental Quality, *Environmental Quality 1979* (Washington, D.C.: Government Printing Office, 1980), 199-200.

185

Table 6-2 Total U.S. Industrial Hazardous Wastes

Source	Percentage of total
Chemical and allied products	60
Machinery (except electrical)	10
Primary metals	8
Paper and allied products	6
Fabricated metal products	4
Stone, clay, and glass products	3
All others	9

Source: Council on Environmental Quality, *Environmental Quality 1980* (Washington, D.C.: Government Printing Office, 1981), 217.

represent a very small proportion of the national sites that eventually will qualify as acutely dangerous.

Public apprehension about hazardous waste has been heightened by repeated discoveries, often sudden and dramatic, that citizens have been exposed unknowingly to toxic substances that had originated in previously undiscovered or neglected waste sites or transported through the ecosystem through careless chemical use. While Love Canal has become a national synonym for chemical contamination, incidents of real or suspected community exposure to hazardous waste are now commonplace. Nonetheless, relatively few communities are mobilized to control such waste until emergencies, or possible tragedies, compel attention to the problem. Thus, a chemical explosion akin to a sideshow in Hell was necessary to awaken a civic consciousness of waste problems in Elizabeth, New Jersey. The fiery maelstrom that incinerated Chemical Control Company's Elizabeth site was widely suspected of consuming a far greater variety of toxic substances than the preliminary inventory that introduced this chapter suggests.[8] Hundreds, perhaps thousands, of sites containing similar volumes of toxic and volatile chemicals are distributed widely throughout the nation's industrial centers.

More subtle is the quiet, gradual accumulation of hazardous wastes in soil, air, or water through normal industrial, commercial, or agricultural use. Such waste rarely accumulates in quantities sufficient to attract public attention. Its existence is often revealed only through deliberate monitoring by public or private organizations, sometimes only after sophisticated and lengthy testing. The following incidents testify to the speed with which these wastes can disperse throughout the ecosystem:

> The powerful nerve toxin aldicarb, the active ingredient in the pesticide Temik, was found in at least eight wells in central Florida, including drinking wells. In high doses, aldicarb can kill on skin contact or by ingestion, but little is known about its effect on animal or human life in small doses. In one well the concentration reached 315 parts per billion. EPA's recommended safety threshold is 10 parts per billion in drinking water.[9]

> The Mt. Sinai School of Medicine released a study indicating that 97 percent of Michigan's residents have retained residual levels of the toxic chemical PBB after 2,000 pounds of the fire retardent were accidentally substituted for feed additive on a Michigan farm in 1973.[10]

Table 6-3   Common Hazardous Wastes

Chemical	Use	Manufacturing Hazard
C-56	Bug and insect killer	Acutely toxic, suspected carcinogen
Trichloroethylene (TCE)	Degreaser	Suspected carcinogen
Benzidene	Dye industry	Known human carcinogen
Curene 442	Plastics industry	Suspected carcinogen
Polychlorinated biphenyls (PCBs)	Insulators, paints, and electrical circuitry	Acutely toxic, suspected carcinogen
Benzene	Solvent	Suspected carcinogen
Tris	Fire retardant	Suspected carcinogen
DDT	Bug and insect killer	Acutely toxic
Vinyl chloride	Plastics industry	Known human carcinogen
Mercury	Multiple uses	Acutely toxic
Lead	Multiple uses	Acutely toxic, suspected carcinogen
Carbon tetrachloride	Solvent	Acutely toxic, suspected carcinogen
Polybrominated biphenyls (PBBs)	Fire retardant	Effects unknown

Source: Council on Environmental Quality, *Environmental Quality 1980* (Washington, D.C.: Government Printing Office, 1981), 217.

187

Table 6-4 The Nation's Most Dangerous Hazardous Waste Sites: The EPA "Priority" List

City/County	Site Name (Priority Group)	City/County	Site Name (Priority Group)
Alabama		Redding	Iron Mountain Mine (2)
Limestone and Morgan	Triana, Tennessee River (1)	Ukiah	Coast Wood Preserving (4)
Greenville	Mowbray Engineering (3)	Fresno	Purity Oil Sales, Inc. (5)
Perdido	Perdido Groundwater Contamination (8)	Fresno	Selma Pressure Treating (5)
		Fullerton	McColl (5)
American Samoa		Richmond	Liquid Gold (5)
American Samoa	Taputimu Farms (2)	Cloverdale	MGM Brakes (7)
		Hoopa	Celtor Chemical (8)
Arizona		Sacramento	Jibbom Junkyard (9)
Globe	Mt. View Mobile Home (2)		
Phoenix	19th Avenue Landfill (2)	**Colorado**	
Tucson	Tucson International Airport (2)	Boulder	Marshal Landfill (2)
Goodyear	Litchfield Airport Area (4)	Leadville	California Gulch (3)
Kingman	Kingman Airport Industrial Area (6)	Commerce City	Woodbury Chemical (4)
Scottsdale	Indian Bend Wash Area (6)	Denver	Denver Radium Site (4)
		Idaho Springs	Central City, Clear Creek (4)
Arkansas		Commerce City	Sand Creek (6)
Jacksonville	Vertac, Inc. (1)		
Mena	Mid-South (4)	**Connecticut**	
Edmondsen	Gurley Pit (6)	Naugatuck	Laurel Park Inc. (2)
Ft. Smith	Industrial Waste Control (6)	Beacon Falls	Beacon Heights (4)
Walnut Ridge	Fritt Industries (6)	Southington	Solvents Recovery System (6)
Newport	Cecil Lindsey (7)	Canterbury	Yaworski (7)
Marion	Crittendon Company Landfill (8)		
		Delaware	
California		New Castle	Army Creek (1)
Glen Avon Heights	Stringfellow (1)	New Castle County	Tybouts Corner (1)
Rancho Cordova	Aerojet (2)	New Castle	Delaware Sand and Gravel (4)

Table 6-4 (Continued)

City/County	Site Name (Priority Group)	City/County	Site Name (Priority Group)
Indiana (Cont.)		Sorento	Cleve Reber (3)
Lebanon	Wedzeb Inc. (8)	Bayou Sorrel	Bayou Sorrel (6)
Allen County	Parrot Road (9)	Slidell	Bayou Bonfouca (7)
Iowa		**Maine**	
Charles City	Labounty Site (1)	Gray	McKin Company (1)
Council Bluffs	Aidex Corporation (2)	Winthrop	Winthrop Landfill (2)
Des Moines	Dico (9)	Washburn	Pinette's Salvage Yard (6)
		Augusta	O'Connor Site (8)
Kansas		Saco	Saco Tanning (8)
Cherokee County	Tar Creek, Cherokee Co. (1)		
Arkansas City	Arkansas City Dump (2)	**Maryland**	
Holiday	Doepke Disposal, Holiday (4)	Elkton	Sand, Gravel, and Stone (5)
Wichita	John's Sludge Pond (7)	Annapolis	Middletown Road Dump (6)
		Cumberland	Limestone Road Site (8)
Kentucky			
Brooks	A. L. Taylor (2)	**Massachusetts**	
Louisville	Lee's Lane Landfill (6)	Acton	W. R. Grace (1)
Newport	Newport Dump (6)	Ashland	Nyanza Chemical (1)
West Point	Distler Brickyard (6)	East Woburn	Wells G and H (1)
Calvert City	Airco (7)	Holbrook	Baird and McGuire (1)
Jefferson County	Distler Farm (7)	Woburn	Industri-Plex (1)
Calvert City	B. F. Goodrich (8)	New Bedford	New Bedford (2)
		Plymouth	Plymouth Harbor/Cordage (2)
Louisiana		Dartmouth	Re-Solve (4)
Darrow	Old Inger (2)		

191

Table 6-4 (Continued)

City/County	Site Name (Priority Group)	City/County	Site Name (Priority Group)
Minnesota (Cont.)		Dover	Dover Landfill (6)
Andover	South Andover Site (7)	Londonderry	Auburn Road Landfill (7)
Mississippi		**New Jersey**	
Gulfport	Plastifax (2)	Bridgeport	Bridgeport Rent. and Oil (1)
Missouri		Fairfield	Caldwell Trucking (1)
Ellisville	Ellisville Site (2)	Freehold	Lone Pine Landfill (1)
Springfield	Fulbright Landfill (5)	Gloucester Township	Gems Landfill (1)
Verona	Syntex Facility (5)	Mantua	Helen Kramer Landfill (1)
Imperial	Arena 2: Fills 1 and 2 (7)	Marlboro Township	Burnt Fly Bog (1)
Moscow Mills	Arena 1 (Dioxin) (8)	Old Bridge Township	CPS/Madison Industries (1)
Montana		Pittman	Lipari Landfill (1)
Anaconda	Anaconda-Anaconda (1)	Pleasantville	Price Landfill (1)
Silver Bow/Deer Lodge	Silver Bow Creek (1)	Brick Township	Brick Township Landfill (2)
Milltown	Milltown (4)	Carlstadt	Scientific Chemical Processing (2)
Libby	Libby Ground Water (6)	East Rutherford	Universal Oil Products (2)
Nebraska		Hamilton Township	D'Imperio Property (2)
Beatrice	Phillips Chemical (9)	Hillsborough	Krystowaty Farm (2)
New Hampshire		Bound Brook	American Cyanamid (3)
Epping	Kes-Epping (1)	Dover Township	Reich Farms (3)
Nashua	Sylvester, Nashua (1)	Edison	Kin-Buc Landfill (3)
Somersworth	Somersworth Landfill (1)	Franklin Township	Myers Property (3)
Kingston	Ottati and Goss (3)	Maywood & Rochelle Pk.	Maywood Chemical Sites (3)
Londonderry	Tinkham Site (5)	Parsipanny, Troy Hls	Sharkey Landfill (3)
		Pedricktown	N. L. Industries (3)
		Pemberton Township	Lang Property (3)
		Ringwood	Ringwood Mines/Landfill (3)
		South Brunswick	South Brunswick Landfill (3)

Table 6-4 (Continued)

City/County	Site Name (Priority Group)	City/County	Site Name (Priority Group)
New York (Cont.)		Deerfield	Summit National (3)
Vestal	Vestal Water Supply (5)	Ironton	Allied Chemical (4)
Brewster	Brewster Well Field (6)	Salem	Nease Chemical (4)
Horseheads	Kentucky Ave. Wellfield (6)	Ironton	E. H. Schilling Landfill (5)
Wheatfield	Niagara County Refuse (6)	Byesville	Fultz Landfill (6)
Clayville	Ludlow Sand and Gravel (7)	Coshocton	Coshocton City Landfill (6)
Fulton	Fulton Terminals (7)	Dodgeville	New Lyme Landfill (7)
Lincklaen	Solvent Savers (7l)	Jefferson	Poplar Oil (7)
Niagara Falls	Hooker-Hyde Park (7)	Kingsville	Big D Campgrounds (7)
Cold Springs	Marathon Battery (8)	Reading	Pristine (7)
Niagara Falls	Hooker-102nd Street (8)	Rock Creek	Rock Creek/Jack Webb (7)
		St. Clairsville	Buckeye Reclamation (7)
North Carolina		West Chester	Skinner Landfill (8)
210 miles of roads	PCB Spills (2)	Marietta	Van Dale Junkyard (9)
Charlotte	Martin Marietta, Sodyeco (3)	Zanesville	Zanesville Well Field (9)
Swannanoa	Chemtronics, Inc. (8)		
		Oklahoma	
North Dakota		Ottawa County	Tar Creek (1)
Southeastern	Arsenic Trioxide Site (2)	Criner	Criner/Hardage (3)
Northern Marianas		**Oregon**	
North Marianas	PCB Warehouse (2)	Albany	Teledyne Wah Chang (4)
		Portland	Gould, Inc. (8)
Ohio			
Arcanum	Arcanum Iron and Metal (1)	**Pennsylvania**	
Hamilton	Chem Dyne (2)	Bruin Boro	Bruin Lagoon (1)
Ashtabula	Fields Brook (3)	Grove City	Osborne (1)
Circleville	Bowers Landfill (3)		

194

Pennsylvania (Cont.)

Location	Facility
McAdoo	McAdoo (1)
Douglasville	Douglasville Disposal (2)
Buffalo	Hranica (3)
Harrison Township	Lindane Dump (3)
Malvern	Malvern TCE Site (4)
Palmerton	Palmerton Zinc Pile (4)
Philadelphia	Enterprise Avenue (5)
West Ormond	Heleva Landfill (5)
Erie	Presque Isle (6)
Girard Township	Lord Shope (6)
Haverford	Havertown PCB Site (6)
Jefferson	Resin Disposal (6)
Lock Haven	Drake Chemical Inc. (6)
Lower Providence Township	Moyers Landfill (6)
State College	Centre County Kepone (6)
Chester	Wade (ABM) (7)
King of Prussia	Stanley Kessler (7)
Old Forge	Lackawanna Refuse (7)
Seven Valleys	Old City of York Landfill (7)
Old Forge	Lehigh Electric (8)
Philadelphia	Metal Banks (8)
Stroudsburg	Brodhead Creek (8)
West Chester Township	Blosenski Landfill (8)
Westline	Westline (8)
Kimberton	Kimberton (9)
Parker	Craig Farm Drum Site (9)
Upper Saucon Township	Voortman (9)
Warminster	Fischer and Porter (9)

Puerto Rico

Location	Facility
Florida Afuera	Barceloneta Landfill (5)
Juana Diaz	GE Wiring Devices (5)
Rio Abajo	Frontera Creek (5)
Barceloneta	RCA Del Caribe (8)
Juncos	Juncos Landfill (8)

Rhode Island

Location	Facility
Coventry	Picillo Coventry (1)
Burrillville	Western Sand and Gravel (3)
North Smithfield	L and RR-N. Smithfield (3)
Smithfield	Davis Liquid (4)
Cumberland	Peterson/Puritan (5)
North Smithfield	Forestdale (7)

South Carolina

Location	Facility
Columbia	SCRDI Bluff Road (2)
Cayce	SCRDI Dixiana (5)
Fort Lawn	Carolawn, Inc. (8)

South Dakota

Location	Facility
Whitewood	Whitewood Creek (1)

Tennessee

Location	Facility
Memphis	North Hollywood Dump (2)
Lawrenceburg	Murray Ohio Dump (4)
Toone	Velsicol Chemical (4)
Chattanooga	Amnicola Dump (8)
Galloway	Galloway Ponds (8)
Lewisburg	Lewisburg Dump (8)

Texas

Location	Facility
Crosby	French, Ltd. (1)
Crosby	Sikes Disposal Pits (1)
Houston	Crystal Chemical (1)

Table 6-4 (Continued)

City/County	Site Name (Priority Group)	City/County	Site Name (Priority Group)
Texas (Cont.)		**Washington**	
La Marque	Motco (1)	Tacoma	Commencement Bay, S. Tacoma Channel (2)
Highlands	Highlands Acid Pit (6)	Vancouver	Frontier Hard Chrome (2)
Grand Prairie	Bio-Ecology (7)	Mead	Kaiser Mead (5)
Houston	Harris (Farley Street) (7)	Seattle	Harbor Island Lead (5)
Orange County	Triangle Chemical (9)	Tacoma	Commencement Bay, near Shore Tide Flat (5)
Trust Territories		Spokane	Colbert Landfill (6)
Pacific Trust Terr.	PCB Waste (2)	Kent	Western Processing (7)
		Yakima	FMC Yakima (8)
Utah		Yakima	Pesticide Pit, Yakima (8)
Salt Lake City	Rose Park Sludge Pit (2)	Lakewood	Lakewood (9)
Vermont		**West Virginia**	
Burlington	Pine Street Canal (2)	Point Pleasant	West Virginia Ordnance (2)
Springfield	Old Springfield Landfill (7)	Leetown	Leetown Pesticide Pile (7)
		Nitro	Fike Chemical (7)
Virginia		Follansbee	Follansbee Sludge Fill (8)
Roanoke County	Matthews (2)	**Wyoming**	
Saltville	Saltville Waste Disposal (3)	Laramie	Baxter/Union Pacific (6)
York County	Chisman (4)		
Piney River	U.S. Titanium (7)		

Source: Environmental Protection Agency, "Proposed National Priorities List: As provided for in Section 105 (8) (B) of CERCLA" (Washington, D.C.: Environmental Protection Agency, December 20, 1982).

196

The toxic pesticide toxaphene, used widely in the South to protect cotton crops, has been detected recently in fish from the Great Lakes, leading scientists to conclude that winds were sweeping the pesticide northward.[11]

Contributing to the problem is the deep burial, or underground injection, commonly used in the United States to dispose of such substances. Little more than a third of all current hazardous waste is stored in landfills or other surface receptacles. About 57 percent of the hazardous waste is flushed into deep underground cavities, or water systems, where it is presumed to disperse too deeply to contaminate water or soil to which humans are exposed. However, such disposal has seldom been carefully monitored or regulated. Often assurances of the safety in such procedures were bland promises unsupported by credible evidence. Experts suspect that many hazardous materials thus buried migrate through subsurface water flows until they contaminate drinking-water wells, aquifers used for irrigation, lakes, rivers, other water bodies, or soil used by humans. Compared with the variety of treatment technologies currently available, both surface and underground disposal are primitive, dangerous, and ultimately inefficient. For these reasons, the National Academy of Sciences recently suggested that the federal government recommend incinerating, chemical processing, or other more modern procedures for hazardous waste disposal.[12]

Risks Certain and Uncertain

David Doniger has observed that there are "boundaries of analysis" that prevent government agencies from making exact, objective, and uncontroversial decisions in regulating a suspected toxic material.[13] Of these, notes Doniger, the most important is that all decisions must be made under substantial uncertainty about the medical and ecological risks associated with varying levels of chemical exposure.[14] Here, as we have observed in other domains of environmental regulation, the limits of scientific data again introduce an issue that readily becomes politicized in the regulatory process.

Generally, it is difficult to establish definitive proof that a suspected toxic chemical will cause a given number of deaths, or other harmful effects, in a given dose over a specified period of time. Thus, experts often must rely upon estimates, usually in the form of probability statements, when predicting the magnitude of toxic effects to man or the environment from a chemical substance. Even after known levels of exposure to suspected toxics can be identified, tracing the consequences to

197

humans can be enormously complex and controversial, particularly when chronic exposure has been to small doses.

Consider the continuing controversy over the effects upon the neighborhood adjacent to the Love Canal dump site, widely regarded since 1978 as the epitome of lethal abandoned waste pits.[15] In late 1982 the EPA released the results of a massive inquiry it had made, along with the U.S. Public Health Service, into the health effects of the Love Canal site. Contrary to earlier studies by the state of New York, the EPA asserted that it had found the neighborhood near Love Canal no less safe for residents than any other part of Niagara Falls, N.Y. The evidence seemed formidable. More than 6,000 samples of human and environmental materials near the site were collected and subjected to 150,000 analytical measurements to determine what contaminants they contained. This evidence suggested that only a ring of houses a block or less from the waste site had been significantly affected. But the study was challenged immediately because 90 percent of the samples were free of any chemicals. This, asserted experts, could mean either an absence of chemicals or insufficient sensitivity among the measuring procedures. Although the assistant secretary for health and the deputy EPA administrator for New York testified to congressional committees that they were confident the undetected chemicals could not be present in more than minute quantities, the Environmental Defense Fund's own scientific expert asserted that so much variance existed in the competence of the many laboratories conducting the tests and so many sources of error could exist in some tests that chemicals could indeed have been present. Officials at the National Bureau of Standards also questioned the sensitivity of the test procedures. Less than a year later, the federal Centers for Disease Control released their own study of former Love Canal area residents, indicating that they were no more likely to suffer chromosome damage than residents elsewhere in Niagara Falls. Even if such damage were present, noted the study, it was impossible to know if it was linked to the later occurrence of illnesses.[16]

Accurately describing the risks from exposure to the Love Canal site may require decades, or generations; it may never happen. Uncertainties about risk must almost be assumed to be a constant in regulating hazardous substances, and consequently errors of judgment leading to excessively strict regulation or perhaps to dangerously negligent control of chemical substances are probably inevitable. Generally, Congress and the regulatory agencies implementing congressional hazardous waste programs have been risk averse, preferring to reduce severely or to eliminate the assumed risks from toxic materials. In effect, regulators have chosen to err, if err they must, in the direction of stricter control and more willingness to accept pessimistic estimates of risk from toxic substances. However, beginning with the later years of the Carter administration and continuing with greater vigor under the Reagan presidency, federal agencies have moved toward greater attention to costs and regulatory complexity in setting standards of exposure and control.

Costs and Complexity

It is doubtful that either friend or foe of the federal regulatory programs enacted in the mid-1970s realistically understood the enormous expense that would be involved in the new hazardous substance legislation. New regulatory agencies would have to be created, or existing ones expanded. An inventory of many thousands of chemicals would have to be created, existing literature on the health effects of chemicals searched, new research initiated, new regulations promulgated, litigation involving the legality of new regulatory standards conducted, and so forth. Only as regulatory agencies began the first tentative steps in assembling data on the human and environmental effects of chemical substances did the vast vacuum of relevant information become obvious. A major reason for the protracted delays in implementing the new laws has been the tedious but essential work of building a foundation of necessary technical data upon which regulatory standards could be erected. The collective costs to the 14,000 regulated chemical manufacturers will add additional billions of dollars to the regulatory total.

A small sampler of direct and indirect costs associated with recent hazardous substance legislation can only suggest the scale upon which such regulatory programs must operate:

> The average priority abandoned waste site cleaned up by the EPA under Superfund legislation has cost $6.5 million; the aggregate expense for eliminating all the nation's worst abandoned waste sites is expected to be three or four times the initial Superfund authorization of $1.6 billion.[17]

> The EPA's regulations for disposal of hazardous waste on land sites exceeded 500 pages in the *Federal Register*. EPA officials say the costs of compliance for the affected industries will exceed $1 billion yearly.[18]

> The state of New York requested a grant of $20 million from the federal government to remove from the Hudson River the 25-year accumulation of the toxic chemical polychlorinated biphenyl (PCB) dumped into the Hudson by the General Electric Company.[19]

When massive costs are projected against the fragmentary scientific data on the effects of many chemicals and the often tenuous evidence relating to chronic impacts from extremely low levels of exposure, arguments over the acceptability of the costs in light of the benefits inevitably ensue. Critics, especially of federal regulatory programs enacted in the 1970s, have asserted that such programs impose not only unacceptable costs for the regulation of acknowledged hazards but also staggering costs for the stringent control of substances with unproven effects. Some critics, including the leadership of the Reagan administration, have argued that costs and benefits should become a routinely important—though not necessarily the most important—factor in determining whether a substance should be regulated.

Criticism of regulatory costs often feeds upon the disparity between the timing and character of the costs and the timing and character of the benefits from regulation. The costs tend to be tangible, immediate, and massive: dollars must be spent, agencies created, rules promulgated, and other expensive actions initiated. In contrast, years or decades may pass before any apparent benefits accrue. The benefits may be in intangible terms—such as deaths and illnesses prevented, public costs of future regulation avoided, and public safety enhanced—that tend to be discounted in the present by those who must pay for regulation. Examples exist that show how the future benefits of regulation can be enormous. The number of U.S. deaths from exposure as much as 40 years ago to asbestos will grow to between 8,000 and 10,000 annually by the century's end. More than 20,000 claims outstanding against major asbestos manufacturers in 1984 must be settled. With an average settlement in the mid-1980s of $350,000, the current value of these future claims has been estimated conservatively at $40 billion.[20] But few regulated chemicals have demonstrated such deadliness that the benefits of regulation become indisputable. Regulators rarely have the sure knowledge that a given chemical, if left unregulated, ever would manifest its long-term effects as unambiguously as asbestos did.

From the Cradle to the Grave

Among the two dozen federal laws that relate to hazardous or toxic substances, three that were passed in the 1970s have defined the fundamental framework of existing regulation: the Toxic Substances Control Act of 1976, the Resource Conservation and Recovery Act of

1976, and the Comprehensive Environmental Response, Compensation and Liability Act of 1980 (usually known as Superfund). These laws represent a congressional effort to create a comprehensive regulatory program for all chemical substances from their initial development to their final disposal—the cradle-to-grave control that seemed so essential to achieving for the first time responsible public management of chemical products. Few laws, even by the standards of recent environmental legislation, mandate a more complex and technically formidable administrative process than do these programs. A brief review of the major provisions will suggest the enormous regulatory tasks involved.

TSCA: Regulating Chemical Manufacture and Distribution

The major purpose of the Toxic Substances Control Act (TSCA) is to regulate the creation, manufacture, and distribution of chemical substances so that those hazardous to man or the environment can be identified early and then controlled properly before they become fugitive throughout the ecosystem. TSCA required EPA to achieve four broad objectives.[21]

1. *Gather Information.* EPA was required to issue rules asking chemical manufacturers and processors to submit to the administrator information about their use of important chemicals. The information was to include the chemical's name, its formula, uses, estimates of production levels, description of byproducts, data on adverse health and environmental effects, and the number of workers exposed to the chemical. In achieving these goals the administrator also was to:

A. Publish a list of all existing chemicals.

B. See that all persons manufacturing, processing, or distributing chemicals in commerce keep records on adverse health reactions, submit to EPA required health and safety studies, and report to EPA information suggesting that a chemical represents a previously undetected significant risk to health or the environment.

2. *Screen New Chemicals.* Manufacturers of new chemicals were to notify EPA at least 90 days before producing the chemical commercially. Information similar to that required for existing chemicals was required for new chemicals also. The EPA was allowed to suspend temporarily the manufacture of any new chemical in the absence of adequate information as required under the law and to suspend permanently a new chemical if it found a "reasonable basis to conclude that the chemical presents or will present an unreasonable risk of injury to health or the environment."

3. *Test Chemicals.* The EPA was given the authority to require manufacturers or processors of potentially harmful chemicals to test them. An Interagency

Testing Committee, composed of representatives from eight federal agencies, was created to recommend to EPA priorities for chemical testing. As many as 50 chemicals were allowed to be recommended for testing within one year.

4. *Control Chemicals.* EPA was required to take action against chemical substances or mixtures for which a reasonable basis existed to conclude that the manufacture, processing, distribution, use, or disposal presented an unreasonable risk of injury to health or the environment. Permitted actions ranged from a labelling requirement to a complete ban. The control requirements were not to "place an undue burden on industry," yet at the same time they were to provide an adequate margin of protection against unreasonable risk. TSCA specifically required regulation and eventual elimination of PCBs.

The breadth of regulation mandated by TSCA indicates Congress's intent to make it the most comprehensive of all federal hazardous waste laws, spanning the whole cycle of chemical use from the creation of chemical feedstocks to the disposal of industrial and consumer wastes. However, it was apparent to Congress that TSCA alone was inadequate for regulating the nation's rapidly mounting volume of solid waste, of which discarded chemicals were one major component. In the same year Congress wrote the Resource Conservation and Recovery Act, hoping that their combined effect finally would bring solid wastes under effective management.

RCRA: Regulating Solid Waste

The major purposes of the Resource Conservation and Recovery Act (RCRA) were to control solid waste management practices that could endanger public health or the environment and to promote resource conservation and recovery. Solid wastes were defined in the act to include waste solids, sludges, liquids, and contained gases—all forms in which discarded hazardous or toxic substances might be found. In addition to providing federal assistance to state and local governments in developing comprehensive solid waste management programs, RCRA also mandated:

1. *Criteria for Environmentally Safe Disposal Sites.* The EPA was required to issue regulations defining the minimum criteria for solid waste disposal sites considered environmentally safe. EPA was further required to publish an inventory of all U.S. facilities failing to meet these criteria.

2. *Regulating Hazardous Waste.* EPA was required to develop criteria for identifying hazardous waste, to publish the characteristics of hazardous wastes and lists of particular hazardous wastes, and to create a "manifest system" that tracks hazardous wastes from their point of origin to their final disposal. EPA also was to create a permit system that would require all individuals or industries generating hazardous waste to obtain a permit before managing such

waste. Permits would be issued only to waste managers meeting the safe disposal criteria created by EPA.

3. *Resource Recovery and Waste Reduction.* The act required the Commerce Department to promote commercialization of waste recovery, to encourage markets for recovered wastes, and to promote waste recovery technologies and research into waste conservation.

4. *State Implementation.* The act provided for state implementation of regulations affecting solid waste management and disposal if state programs met federal standards. EPA will enforce these provisions in states that do not, or cannot, comply with federal regulations for the program's enforcement.

While RCRA attempted to provide for the first time a comprehensive federal program to control future hazardous waste disposal, it gave little attention to the thousands of abandoned hazardous waste sites across the nation. These abandoned dumps, constituting a vast chemical wasteland whose ominous proportions finally emerged to public recognition in the late 1970s, required immediate comprehensive control or elimination. In the wake of Love Canal and other abandoned waste emergencies, Congress passed in 1980 the Comprehensive Environmental Response, Compensation and Liability Act, known as Superfund, to eliminate the threat of abandoned or uncontrolled hazardous waste sites.

Superfund

When Superfund was enacted, the nation's abandoned and uncontrolled hazardous waste dumps were largely an uncharted wasteland. The nation's governments knew little about the location or composition of many waste sites, some abandoned longer than memory of their existence. The law seldom clearly placed financial responsibility for the management or removal of these wastes with their creators; liability for damage or injury to individuals or communities from such wastes often was difficult, or impossible, to assign or to enforce. Often, procedures for cleaning up waste sites were unknown, or local officials were ignorant of them. The financial burden upon state and local governments to control or remove these wastes seemed overwhelming. Because a comprehensive, collaborative program among the nation's governments seemed essential, Congress attempted to address these and other major abandoned waste problems through four major Superfund programs:[22]

1. *Information Gathering and Analysis.* Owners of hazardous waste sites were required to notify EPA by June 1981 about the character of buried wastes. Using this information, the EPA would create a list of national sites.

2. *Federal Response to Emergencies.* The act authorized the EPA to respond to hazardous substance emergencies and to clean up leaking chemical dump sites if the responsible parties failed to take appropriate action or could not be located.

3. *The Hazardous Substance Response Fund.* The act created an initial trust fund of $1.6 billion to finance the removal, cleanup, or remedy of hazardous waste sites. About 86 percent of the fund was to be financed from a tax on manufacturers of petrochemical feedstocks and organic chemicals and on crude oil importers. The remainder was to come from general federal revenues.

4. *Liability for Cleanup.* The act placed liability for cleaning up waste sites and for other restitution upon those responsible for release of the hazardous substances.

Insofar as it was feasible, the intent of Congress was to make the creators of hazardous waste sites bear as much financial responsibility as possible for ensuring the safety of the sites. With Superfund Congress finished its attempt to create within less than a decade the first truly comprehensive federal regulation of virtually all hazardous or toxic materials existing in the United States. With TSCA, RCRA, and Superfund, Congress in effect was ordering the federal government, in collaboration with state and local authorities, to become the primary manager of all dangerous chemical substances currently used or planned for production.

A Trinity of Tribulations

These regulatory programs, each a thicket of administrative and technical complexity, all were passed within a period of less than four years. The EPA and other responsible governmental agencies thus were confronted with an avalanche of new regulatory mandates, bristling with insistent compliance deadlines, for which they were expected to be rapidly prepared. It is doubtful that the agencies could have satisfactorily discharged these responsibilities under the most benign circumstances. From their inception, moreover, all the programs were afflicted in varying degree by technical, administrative, and political problems impeding their development. By the mid-1980s most TSCA and RCRA programs, mired in administrative and technical complications, were running years behind statutory schedules. The nation was still at serious risk from the hazardous and toxic waste ills Congress intended to remedy through TSCA, RCRA, and Superfund.

Despite differences in their intent and substantive details, the three regulatory programs illuminate the interplay between political, technical, and administrative issues inherent in all environmental regulation. Arising in different contexts among regulatory programs, this interplay is the common source of the delay, conflict, and volatility of program regulations and interpretations that so frequently impede policy implementation. These problems are largely inherent in environmental regulation.

Technical and Scientific Difficulties

TSCA, RCRA, and Superfund all have been burdened by delays and complications arising from the difficulty in obtaining technical information and resolving scientific conflicts over the program objectives. One formidable problem is that each law requires the EPA to assume the initiative for creating and interpreting a vast volume of integrated technical information. Obtaining the data often requires that chemical manufacturers, processors, consumers, and waste disposers provide information previously guarded jealously. Inevitably, program administrators have discretionary choices even in the apparently routine task of information gathering. We have often observed the tendency of organized interests to seek access to administrators and influence over them wherever in the administrative process there are discretionary judgments affecting them. Not surprisingly, all those interests with real or potential stakes in the guidelines for information gathering have gravitated toward the EPA and state regulatory agencies responsible for implementing these laws in an effort to sway administrative discretion to their advantage. In this way basic technical determinations are politicized, and the settlement of technical problems is greatly delayed.

The politicizing of information gathering can be observed in many ways. TSCA's requirements that EPA create an inventory of existing chemical substances and screen new chemicals provide one example. The tasks themselves are formidable. The agency's initial inventory of existing substances, when published more than a year after its mandated deadline, included 43,000 unique formulations reported by 7,400 manufacturers. From the outset EPA's efforts to enforce TSCA requirements that chemical manufacturers maintain health and safety records relating to all these chemicals have met with indifference and noncompliance among many manufacturers. Even more difficult has been enforcement of TSCA regulations requiring notice from manufacturers prior to their production of new chemicals. Chemical manufacturers frequently have objected that the formula for a new substance constitutes a legally protected "trade secret" unlikely to remain confidential in EPA hands. Dow Chemical, the largest producer of commercial chemical wastes in the United States, so jealously guards its trade secrets that it has refused to permit government officials to examine effluents released on the plant grounds, lest proprietary information be obtained. Disputes over what constitutes a sufficient "Premanufacture Notice" between the agency and regulated manufacturers continue to arise.

Discharging another major responsibility—the required testing of potentially harmful chemicals—has become an exercise in frustration for the EPA, as economic interests become implicated in the technical issues. Consider, for instance, the agency's attempt to create test rules for a whole category of chemicals.[23] Some chemical groups are quite small, but others are voluminous; the aryl phosphates, for instance, include about 300 existing chemicals with more to be manufactured. The chemical industry asserts that testing by broad categories will involve very high costs, will stigmatize many "innocent" chemicals along with dangerous ones in the same group, and will prevent introduction of new chemicals until all existing chemicals in a category are tested. Small wonder that EPA explained its delay in establishing chemical testing guidelines by citing "gross underestimation of the number and complexity of the issues, and time spent in resolving one-time issues."[24]

Like TSCA, the Resource Conservation and Recovery Act has proceeded at a glacial pace because technical problems, including a number of surprises, continually have arisen. For example, EPA's regulations for RCRA exclude from control any combustible liquid wastes with a "beneficial reuse" as boiler fuel. In fact, a much larger volume of industrial hazardous waste than had been supposed is combined with petroleum or other combustible materials and burned in boilers—in effect, "grandfathered" out of the law. Unfortunately, the furnaces in which these waste-spiked fuels are burned usually are not designed to control the hazardous chemicals in the fuel, and consequently many hazardous substances are released into the atmosphere contrary to the law's intent.

Misadministration and Nonadministration

Considering the complexity of TSCA, RCRA, and Superfund, administrative problems were predictable. Congress and the White House have compounded administrative problems, however, by only erratically providing the resources essential for proper program imple-

Table 6-5 Changes in EPA Expenditures for Hazardous Waste and Toxic Substances Control Programs (millions of dollars)

	1980	*1981*	*1982*	*1983*	*1984 (est.)*
Hazardous Wastes	$ 77.5	$141.3	$110.5	$118.4	$128.8
Toxic Substances	59.2	93.9	81.6	69.9	68.6
Total:	$136.7	$235.2	$192.7	$188.3	$197.4

Source: Executive Office of the President, Office of Management and Budget, *The Budget of the United States: Appendix.*

mentation and by suddenly changing program priorities. While fitful support and scrambled priorities may sometimes be good politics, they produce bad administration, which Congress or the president, perversely enough, often blame on the afflicted agencies.

One major problem in all three programs has been the lack of funding levels sufficient to provide the EPA with the technical personnel, program facilities, and other resources necessary to carry out the program mandates in the time constraints ordained by Congress. During the early 1980s, particularly, the EPA was confronted simultaneously with growing responsibilities for all three programs and shrinking financial support from Congress and the White House. The extent of this squeeze is suggested by Table 6-5, which identifies changes in EPA's expenditures in fiscal years 1980 through 1984 on hazardous and toxic waste programs, adjusted for inflation.

Particularly hard hit by these budget constraints were EPA's in-house research program and its contracting for outside research support—activities considered essential by many EPA professionals.

While environmentalists largely attributed the EPA's shrinking budget in the early 1980s to the Reagan administration, the continual scrambling of program priorities through changes in program budgets and additional legislation was often a congressional achievement. Congress has been prone to a pollutant-of-the-year mentality, a tendency to order the responsible executive agencies to attend to whatever environmental hazard may seem most publicly visible and disturbing at the moment. Thus, the congressional response to Love Canal was enactment of Superfund to demonstrate the legislators' alertness to the menace of abandoned waste sites. When writing annual appropriations for environmental agencies or considering new legislation on environmental issues, congressional committees often write into the law a mandate that regulatory agencies attend to specific environmental issues then dominating the news. While this is understandable, perhaps even healthy in a representative institution, the effect has been to prevent agencies from developing continuity of programs and marshalling their resources predictably for long-range program goals. Moreover, the cumulative effect of all these mandates has been to overwhelm the responsible agencies with work.

Even without Reaganomics and irresolute congressional support, the EPA and state agencies responsible for implementing TSCA, RCRA, and Superfund still would be underfunded and understaffed. The magnitude of work required to regulate hazardous substances in the manner contemplated by these laws far exceeds what Congress had anticipated; the costs have become equally disproportionate to expectations. This problem can be solved only by a very substantial absolute increase in funding levels for all three programs. Without such absolute funding increases or a reduction in the regulatory responsibilities assigned to EPA, failure to meet the program objectives will become almost routine.

The laggard implementation of TSCA's requirements for the regulation of PCBs, among the most widely distributed and hazardous of all commercial substances, illustrates this problem. Section 6e of TSCA requires that EPA develop regulations for marking materials containing PCBs and for prescribing acceptable techniques for disposing of the materials. By early 1984 the agency was able to inspect only a small fraction of the facilities where PCBs were used or dumped to ensure that the chemical was being handled according to agency regulations. Indeed, the agency still lacked a complete list of major facilities where PCBs were to be examined. The U.S. comptroller general's review of EPA's enforcement activities in 1982 was bleak:

> EPA averages 750 inspections a year. At the current rate of inspection, it would take over 60 years to inspect just the approximately 45,000 facilities listed in EPA's strategy and over 450 years if public buildings were included. As a result, a PCB user's likelihood of inspection in the next 5 years is small.[25]

While the report cited numerous reasons for this situation, a major cause was a lack of enforcement personnel to do the job. The size of the job itself apparently is growing. Recently, experts have suggested that there may be as many as 1.8 million electric capacitors and 100,000 electrical transformers insulated with PCBs in U.S. office buildings that may require inspection to ensure worker safety in the buildings.[26] In this respect, PCBs are not unique. The discovery of new, unanticipated costs has become routine in all three programs.

Politics Administrative Style

It is impossible to insulate completely environmental policy from the influence of political party partisans or from zealots determined to bend policy to the shape of their ideological prejudices. Furthermore, government in a democracy assumes that policy makers and administrators will be reasonably sensitive to changing public opinion and electoral majorities whose will may be expressed by changes in public policy. Thus, environmental policy formulation and implementation normally proceed in a politicized environment. It is ritual in American politics for political opponents of the president and his party to stigmatize many disagreeable changes in administrative policy as "politics." In short, a certain amount of real or alleged political influence in the implementation of environmental policy is normal and is not necessarily subversive of the law or of good environmental management.

Politics assume a more ominous aspect when they subvert good environmental management or disrupt programs intended to achieve desirable environmental goals. It is seldom easy to define precisely where the line ought to be drawn between tolerable and intolerable political interference in environmental administration. In the early 1980s, however, a pervasive effort was evident within the Reagan administration to impose certain political tests on regulatory policies that clearly seemed to impede the implementation of hazardous substance controls and sometimes to approach deliberate subversion of congressional intent. This seemed to many critics of the president to constitute an excessive and unethical, if not illegal, interference in environmental administration. The controversies prompted by this White House strategy became a fertile source of disruption and delay in hazardous substance control during the early 1980s.

After Ronald Reagan's 1980 election victory, controversy over political interference in hazardous waste management focused upon the EPA. Congressional critics of the president's environmental program—a coalition made up primarily of Democrats, Republican environmentalists, and almost all environmental interest groups—identified several procedures through which important program elements in TSCA, RCRA, and

Superfund were exposed to highly partisan influence intended to turn policy decisions upon largely political considerations. While EPA's administrator, Anne Burford, and her subordinates were the immediate targets of this criticism, their actions were, in a broader perspective, a primer on strategies any partisan administration might attempt in order to impose a political viewpoint on the policy implementation process.

One procedure widely criticized was the repeated use by EPA administrators of irregular or secret meetings with representatives of regulated industries to decide regulatory policies affecting them. These meetings, lacking public notice, public comment, or other procedural arrangements normally required for such agency deliberations, seemed highly irregular and suspiciously biased. Critics charged that the meetings were cloistered caucuses where the agency's administrators resolved sensitive issues in close consultation with interests to which they were strongly sympathetic and without interference from environmentalists or other groups. On at least three occasions, charged the AFL-CIO and the Natural Resources Defense Council, the EPA used such an arrangement to determine whether it should restrict the use of the pesticide permethrin and the herbicide picloram, both suspected human carcinogens.[27] Administrators responsible for implementing Superfund also were accused by several congressional committees of holding similarly sequestered conversations with businesses responsible for cleaning up abandoned hazardous waste sites, a practice that critics charged often produced lenient conditions for dump rehabilitation.

Another action suggesting strong partisan bias was the use of political criteria, rather than technical and statutory standards, for determining how to award federal grants to clean up priority dump sites under Superfund. The insinuation of political tests into the program became a cause célèbre when it was revealed that the director of the office of toxic substances had ordered, apparently with approval from the administrator, awards to be withheld in hope of influencing the 1982 gubernatorial and congressional elections. The most blatant instance involved EPA's decision to delay a large award to clean up one of the nation's most dangerous waste sites—California's Stringfellow Pit, a lethal earthen reservoir of many thousand barrels of chemicals—lest the award favorably reflect upon Governor Jerry Brown, then a Democratic candidate for the U.S. Senate from California. Similarly, EPA administrators frequently were accused of selectively using or suppressing technical information on the dangers of suspected hazardous chemicals according to how the information squared with their own prejudices about the merits of regulation.[28]

Pressure also fell upon EPA from above. Using the Office of Management and Budget (OMB), the White House encouraged the agency to revise existing regulations or to write new ones, where possible, to make policies more sensitive to cost-benefit criteria and other principles at the core of the president's "regulatory relief" program. OMB provides the president with an important means for reviewing new or existing regulations and other decisions of federal agencies. Yet under the Reagan administration OMB became a primary means for exerting backdoor influence on EPA regulatory decisions without formally or publicly becoming part of the regulatory decision-making process, as is usually required of participants in regulatory rule making. In addition to giving the White House a channel of influence into EPA that was largely insulated from public review, using OMB as a policy advocate also could permit the president and his collaborators at EPA to alter the impact of TSCA, RCRA, and Superfund through changes in regulations that might violate the law's congressional intent without formally altering the legislation itself. Thus, by skillfully using the "administrative presidency," Reagan—or any other president sufficiently adept and willful—could apply partisan pressure in the regulatory process despite congressional attempts to reduce such pressures through various public and formal policy-making procedures required by law.

Many EPA efforts in the early 1980s to rewrite existing TSCA, RCRA, or Superfund regulations were widely suspected by critics to be evidence of such backdoor political manipulation. The attempts, although often futile, still exacted a price in program delay and confusion. Writing and retracting regulations became, for a time, the house style for EPA, reflecting political manipulation and conflict within. The record for regulation reversal was probably achieved by EPA in 1982 when it announced its intention to increase the amount of liquid hazardous chemicals permitted at waste sites in February, only to retract it in March when a fierce protest arose from Congress and environmental critics. It was usually difficult for the public, or most members of Congress, to appreciate the larger policy implications of these many proposed changes because they were framed in technicalities. Nor was it possible for even alert and informed environmental groups to keep abreast of all the changes being simultaneously proposed. However, the agency was thrown sharply on the defensive by environmentalist attacks on several of its major proposals. Congressional investigations began to reveal the underlying political process prompting many regulation changes. As a result, by the time that William D. Ruckelshaus replaced Anne Burford as EPA's administrator, the politicizing of regulation writing was substantially diminished.

The controversies spawned by real and alleged political interference exacted a heavy toll from TSCA and Superfund especially. Many technicians and other professionals essential to program implementation resigned or were fired from the agency. Agency administrators and personnel had to spend weeks away from their jobs, testifying before congressional committees, defending themselves through the media, and attempting to overcome the confusion in regional offices and state agencies also responsible for the programs. The credibility of the EPA's scientific and administrative judgment was diminished. The internal conflicts created by political disagreements among agency officials produced continual squabbling, widespread demoralization, and mutual suspicion that dragged upon the program schedules. The costs had to be reckoned not only in dollars but also in months and years lost in program enforcement.

The NIMBY Problem

Another sort of politics also impedes the implementation of RCRA and Superfund, which in different ways attempt to create safe siting of hazardous waste. Administrators attempting to implement state programs for permitting hazardous waste sites as required by RCRA frequently encounter widespread and intense public resistance to the location of hazardous waste sites—no matter how allegedly safe—near inhabited areas. Also, citizen organizations and local governmental officials often express deep skepticism of federal assertions that abandoned hazardous waste sites can be rendered safe through Superfund. They often prefer that abandoned sites be permanently removed. This growing citizen resistance is recognized—with no particular amusement—among public officials as the Not in My Back Yard, or NIMBY, problem.

Behind the NIMBY phenomenon are several political forces. One is the rapid proliferation in recent years of national and statewide organizations committed specifically to educating Americans about hazardous waste and to helping local communities organize politically to deal with local hazardous waste problems. One of these new organizations is the national Citizen's Clearing House for Hazardous Waste, created in 1981 by Lois Gibbs, a housewife whose experiences with the Love Canal waste crisis of 1978 convinced her of the need to educate other communities about hazardous wastes and related issues. These organizations often mobilize local residents and public officials to deal with community hazardous waste problems and provide technical and political advice on specific issues. There also has been an explosion of ad hoc state and local groups organizing to deal with specific hazardous waste issues, ranging from the closing of a city waste dump to a state policy for transportation of hazardous waste. In 11 of the 13 states with the largest number of priority abandoned waste sites listed by EPA, officials noted a significant growth in the number and activism of these groups.[29]

A great many existing national and state environmental organizations also are beginning to give major attention to hazardous waste issues and in the process are acquiring specialized resources for the task. The Environmental Defense Fund and Natural Resources Defense Council, for instance, have greatly increased their technical staffs and their litigation on hazardous and toxic substance matters. These national, state, and local organizations are gradually forming a complex network for the communication of political and technical information, the mobilization of public officials and citizens for political action, and the litigation of hazardous waste issues.

Most of the state and national groups heavily involved in hazardous waste policy regard their work as providing technical assistance and education for concerned citizens. Indeed, most leaders of such groups believe they are ultimately contributing to better implementation and enforcement of RCRA and Superfund by ensuring greater citizen understanding and acceptance of waste policy decisions eventually made by local, state, and federal officials. Quite often, however, this group activism in local communities arouses or strengthens citizen resistance to permits for local hazardous waste sites. Public officials, chemical industry spokesmen, and others commonly complain that organized citizen groups are too often agitators rather than educators in community waste issues.[30]

The Love Canal tragedy, and other widely publicized chemical horror stories, haunt all public discussions of hazardous waste policy. The public seems to fear close proximity to hazardous materials and to reject the prospect of a hazardous waste site appearing, or remaining, nearby a community. Regardless of the actual risks involved, many people are disinclined to believe reassurances of their safety, no matter the source. Well-conceived education campaigns intended to familiarize citizens with the technology of waste disposal, the character of hazardous chemicals, and the options available to communities in dealing with waste issues often fail to blunt the edge of this deep public antipathy. As early as 1981 EPA consultants warned that the agency would have to adopt special new strategies to avoid a massive community backlash against proposed hazardous waste sites to be permitted by the states:

> Should present approaches to siting facilities continue, the data from this [study of 21 siting controversies] indicate that the prospects for successful sitings in most regions of the country are dubious at best, and grim at worst. National publicity concerning abandoned sites has made citizens and local officials increasingly aware of hazardous waste problems. They are also likely to be increasingly aware of actions taken by others to stop siting. Opposition will, in all likelihood, become more widespread and sophisticated.[31]

Pennsylvania's early experience in issuing permits for waste sites under RCRA suggests the intensity of this citizen involvement. During the first year of the program, more than 75 percent of the state's proposed permits were challenged by organized groups; significantly, more than a third of these protests were led by municipal officials or other governmental officers. Equally important, almost half (46 percent) of these protests led to permit rejections, withdrawals, or delays. The high visibility of local public officials in Pennsylvania characterizes hazardous waste politics nationally; local and state officials often lead the coalitions fighting waste permits. One way that state governments have interposed themselves between Washington and local communities being considered for hazardous waste sites under RCRA or Superfund has been to write siting regulations stricter than the federal code and consequently more restrictive to proposed local waste dumps. Elected state and local officials, in any case, are quite commonly wary of the political risks from public advocacy of local hazardous waste siting, and thus administrators responsible for implementing RCRA and Superfund often lack any organized local constituency for their programs.

The continuing public resistance to hazardous waste sites under RCRA and Superfund is one of the most serious and unsolved political problems affecting both programs. Coupled with the use of litigation, the many political and administrative strategies available to citizen groups determined to prevent or delay the issuing of permits for local hazardous waste dumps could delay program implementation for years or decades. More plausibly, continued widespread resistance might result in rewriting of the law and its regulations to give federal officials greater authority to issue permits over the objections of local, and perhaps state, officials. The existing situation amounts to a sharp and troubling conflict between the government's attempt to be responsive to the interests and opinions of citizens affected by federal programs and the need to protect public health and safety by creating secure storage sites for a constantly mounting volume of hazardous substances.

Regulation at a Crippling Pace

In no other major area of environmental policy is progress measured in such small increments as the regulation of toxic and hazardous wastes. The slow pace at which TSCA, RCRA, and Superfund have so far been implemented has produced a quality of regulation so tenuous and variable that a serious question exists whether regulation in any significant sense has yet been achieved. The nation remains seriously at risk from hazardous waste in abandoned or deliberately uncontrolled landfills numbering in the tens of thousands. Federal and state governments have yet to approve and implement on the appropriate scale the required strategies for ameliorating hazardous waste problems. The risks already associated with hazardous substances, and the many others to become apparent with continuing research throughout the 1980s, are unlikely to diminish within the decade without a massive and continuing federal commitment of resources to implement the programs as intended by Congress—a commitment of resources and will on a scale lacking so far in this decade.

Even with sufficient resources, the implementation of TSCA, RCRA, and Superfund is likely to be slow because these laws raise technical, legal, and political problems on an order seldom matched in other environmental policy domains. First, no other environmental programs attempt to regulate so many discrete, pervasive substances; we have observed that the hazardous substances that may lie within the ambit of these laws number in the tens of thousands. Second, regulation is delayed by the need to acquire technical information never previously obtained by government, to conduct research on the hazardousness of new chemicals, or to secure from corporations highly guarded trade secrets. Third, almost every major regulatory action intended to limit the production, distribution, or disposal of chemical substances deemed toxic or hazardous by government is open to technical controversy, litigation, and other challenges concerning the degree of risk associated with such substances and their suitability for regulation under the laws. Fourth, opponents of regulatory actions under TSCA, RCRA, and Superfund have been able to utilize to good advantage all the opportunities provided by requirements for administrative due process and the federalized structure of regulation to challenge administrative acts politically and judicially. Finally, in many instances the states responsible for implementing the programs have been unable, or unwilling, to provide from their own resources the means necessary to ensure proper implementation. None of these problems are unique to hazardous substance regulation, but few other environmental policies raise all these problems so persistently and acutely.

In a broader perspective, the enormous difficulties in controlling hazardous substances once they are released into the ecosystem, together with the problems of controlling their disposal, emphasize the crucial role that production controls must play in hazardous substance management. Indeed, it may be that the human and environmental risks from hazardous chemicals may never be satisfactorily constrained once these substances are let loose in the environment. American technology development has proceeded largely with an implicit confidence that whatever human or environmental risks may be engendered in the process can be adequately contained by the same genius that inspired technology's development—a faith, in effect, that science always will cure what ills it creates. The risk to man and his environment from now pervasive chemical substances created within the last half century ought to prompt some thoughtful reservation about the efficacy of technological solutions to technological problems. Toxic and hazardous substances pose for the nation a formidable technological challenge: how to reckon the human and environmental costs of technology development while technologies are yet evolving and, then, how to prudently control dangerous technologies without depriving the nation of their benefits.

Notes

1. *New York Times*, August 31, 1983.
2. On the proliferation of these chemicals and the ecological effects generally, see Michael Brown, *Laying Waste: The Poisoning of America by Toxic Chemicals* (New York: Pantheon Books, 1980); and Erik P. Eckholm, *The Picture of Health: Environmental Sources of Disease* (New York: W. W. Norton, 1977).

3. Council on Environmental Quality, *Environmental Quality 1979* (Washington, D.C.: Government Printing Office, 1980), 181.
4. Ibid.
5. CEQ, *Environmental Quality 1981*, 115.
6. Ibid.
7. Congressional Quarterly, *Environment and Health* (Washington, D.C.: Congressional Quarterly, 1981), 35.
8. *New York Times*, April 23, 1980.
9. *New York Times*, June 20, 1983.
10. *New York Times*, June 13, 1982.
11. *New York Times*, October 10, 1982.
12. National Research Council, *Management of Hazardous Industrial Wastes* (Washington, D.C.: National Academy of Sciences, 1982).
13. David D. Doniger, *The Law and Policy of Toxic Substances Control* (Baltimore: Johns Hopkins University Press, 1978), 9.
14. Ibid.
15. *New York Times*, August 10, 1982.
16. Ibid.
17. *New York Times*, July 8, 1983.
18. *New York Times*, July 14, 1982.
19. *New York Times*, January 3, 1983. Other useful cost estimates may be found in U.S. Environmental Protection Agency, *Administration of the Toxic Substances Control Act 1980* (Washington, D.C.: Government Printing Office, 1981).
20. Estimates by Paul MacAvoy, *New York Times*, February 14, 1982. See also U.S. Library of Congress, Congressional Reference Service, *Six Case Studies of Compensation for Toxic Substances Pollution*. Report to the Committee on Environment and Public Works, U.S. Senate, Ser. No. 96-13 (Washington, D.C., 1980).
21. The full text may be found in P.L. 94-469, 90 Stat. 2003, 15 U.S.C. 2601 (1976).
22. See 42 U.S.C. 9601-9657 (1980).
23. CEQ, *Environmental Quality 1980*, 217.
24. Ibid., 219.
25. U.S. General Accounting Office, "EPA Slow in Controlling PCBs," Report No. CED-82-21 (December 30, 1981), 11.
26. Ibid.
27. *Environment*, vol. 25, no. 7 (September 1983): 5.
28. *New York Times*, March 20, 1983.
29. Walter A. Rosenbaum, "The Politics of Public Participation in Hazardous Waste Management," in *The Politics of Hazardous Waste Management*, ed. James P. Lester and Ann O'M. Bowman (Durham, N.C.: Duke University Press, 1983), 191.
30. On the problems of public involvement generally, see James P. Lester, "The Process of Hazardous Waste Regulation," in *The Politics of Hazardous Waste Management*, 3-23.
31. Centaur Associates, *Siting of Hazardous Waste Management Facilities and Public Opposition* (Washington, D.C.: U.S. Environmental Protection Agency, 1979), Doc. No. SW-809, iv.

I have seen moonscapes on mine sites.

—Official, U.S. Office of Surface
Mining Reclamation and Enforcement,
after visiting a Tennessee mine site.

Pump, Dig, and Boil:
Energy and Ecology in the 1980s

Energy policy is environmental policy. Most forms of energy production upon which the United States depends create significant and often adverse environmental impacts. Any change in the amount, variety, or duration of U.S. energy production or consumption will produce corresponding alterations in environmental quality. Consider, for example, the environmental impact of fossil fuels. About 93 percent of all energy currently consumed in the United States comes from petroleum, natural gas, and coal.[1] The important ecological consequences of this combustion include the following:

> Transportation and fossil-fuel fired electric generating plants produce annually 36 percent of the particulates, 37 percent of the hydrocarbons, 83 percent of the carbon monoxide, 84 percent of the sulfur oxides, and 95 percent of the nitrogen oxides emitted into the atmosphere as pollutants.

> The total land area disturbed by coal surface mining in the United States by 1984 had reached more than 5.7 million acres, an area equal in size to the state of New Hampshire. Of this total more than 3 million acres remained "unclaimed," creating abandoned and sterile wasteland.

> In 1984 steam electric utilities consumed about 45 percent of all the water withdrawn from surface and subsurface sources, a proportion far greater than was used by all of U.S. agriculture for irrigation.[2]

This intimate association between energy and environment means that the nation's current energy policies will have profound and enduring environmental implications throughout the 1980s. So often are environmental issues grounded in the development of energy technol-

219

ogies that the nation's energy policies will be, in a very significant measure, its environmental policies for the 1980s. Thus, the current patterns of U.S. energy use and current public energy policies are crucial to understanding how environmental quality is likely to change throughout the decade.

Energy Use in the 1980s

In the mid-1980s the United States was poised insecurely between an Energy Crisis it had momentarily averted and an energy future it could not confidently predict. The Energy Crisis that lasted from 1973 to 1978 was triggered by a sudden but brief Arab embargo upon petroleum exported to the United States, quickly followed by several years of sharply rising world petroleum prices. The United States was forced to recognize that it had become heavily dependent upon imported petroleum and could no longer satisfy its own rapidly rising energy demands from its existing domestic energy production. More ominously, it appeared that the United States might face a worldwide shortage of petroleum within a few decades and eventually might be forced to accelerate rapidly, at severe environmental risk, the mining of its huge domestic coal reserves. At the very least, years of sharply rising energy prices, with all the attendant domestic economic shocks, seemed certain. By the mid-1980s, however, most of these predictions had failed to materialize. Yet experts remained divided and uncertain about the future. The ecological and economic adversities of another domestic energy crisis could not be dismissed as mere speculation.

One certainty in the mid-1980s was that the United States continued to follow patterns of energy consumption and to promote public energy policies placing enormous stress upon the environment and making the nation vulnerable to an ecologically devastating raid on resources should another energy crisis emerge. Thus, energy policy remained among the most ecologically risky public issues of the 1980s.

Dependence on Fossil Fuels

One major cause of environmental stress in U.S. energy use is the nation's continued heavy dependence upon nonrenewable fossil fuels as its major energy source. As Table 7-1 indicates, the United States in the early 1980s was as dependent upon fossil fuels for energy as it had been when

Table 7-1 U.S. Energy Consumption, 1974 and 1980 (quadrillion BTUs of energy)

	Coal	Natural Gas	Petroleum	Hydro-electric	Nuclear	Geo-thermal	Wood	TOTAL
1974	12.88	21.73	33.45	3.31	1.27	.05	°	73.9
	(17.6%)	(26.9%)	(45.8%)	(.05%)	(.02%)	—		(100.0%)
1980	15.67	20.44	34.25	3.13	2.7	.11	°	76.3
	(20.6%)	(26.7%)	(44.9%)	(.04%)	—	—		(100.0%)

° Less than .01 quads.

Source: Council on Environmental Quality, *Environmental Quality 1981* (Washington, D.C.: Government Printing Office, 1982), 235.

the Energy Crisis first shocked Americans in 1973 and 1974. This continued reliance means not only dependence upon environmentally damaging fuel production but an inability to displace it quickly and safely with more environmentally benign alternatives.

It is not unthinkable that the United States might experience another petroleum embargo and a sharp rise in energy prices such as characterized the Energy Crisis of the 1970s. Should this happen the nation's current dependence upon fossil fuels could powerfully impel the United States toward another raid on its domestic fossil fuel resources—especially coal—that would accelerate environmental stress and force difficult choices between energy supply and environmental protection. Americans have done relatively little in the last decade to promote a more environmentally benign response to another energy crisis or to give themselves significant options to fossil fuel dependence in the near future.

Another factor strongly affecting U.S. energy policies in the 1980s was the virtual disappearance of public concern about energy availability, costs, and conservation. Energy had become a nonissue in American public opinion, less than a decade after "Energy Crisis" had entered the public vocabulary. In 1974, with memories of the economic shocks following the Arab oil embargo fresh, the public's sharp awareness of national energy problems was reflected in the Gallup poll's report that energy was among the three national issues considered most important by the public. Thereafter, energy rapidly disappeared from public awareness. By 1984 less than 5 percent of the public spontaneously listed energy among important national problems.[3]

Many factors hastened energy from public attention. The deep economic recession of the early 1980s dampened U.S. energy demand, creating a decline in most energy prices and an unexpected rise in energy reserves. Government and public turned toward problems of unemployment and industrial recovery. Moreover, the nation was able to moderate somewhat its ravenous energy appetite; energy conservation precluded, at least temporarily, some of the worst energy price and supply problems once anticipated. This was not a political environment congenial to discussion of a continuing energy crisis. As political pollster Daniel Yankelovich observed, there was no public or governmental consensus upon either the existence of an energy crisis or the means to alleviate it.[4] The public received no clear and compelling message from Washington, or from anywhere else, leading to public reappraisal of current energy practices.

Uncertain Conservation

In the early 1980s some gain in energy conservation, together with a sluggish national economy, temporarily dampened the growth rate for energy demand in the United States, produced a domestic surplus of petroleum, and seemed to suggest that energy supply problems and soaring energy prices would be less serious than had been expected a few years earlier. This further contributed to public apathy about energy issues, discouraged a searching debate about current energy policies, and eliminated a sense of urgency in discussing the environmental risks of future energy development. However, all this could be only temporary with new pressures on domestic energy resources to follow.

Sharply rising energy prices have been a major incentive for domestic energy conservation. In early 1973 a barrel of imported petroleum had cost less than $5; by the mid-1980s it was more than $32. This steep rise, together with the gradual deregulation of domestic petroleum and natural gas prices, encouraged all major U.S. economic sectors to conserve energy. The amount of energy needed to produce a dollar's worth of the Gross National Product (GNP), a standard measure of energy efficiency, was declining from 30,000 British thermal units (BTUs) in 1971 to less than 25,000 BTUs by the mid-1980s. The fuel efficiency of automobiles, electric appliances, and heavy industry showed significant improvement by 1984. Energy economist Daniel Yergin has estimated that most of the energy efficiency achieved by industrialized nations during the years since 1973 is largely the result of conservation.[5]

Despite conservation gains, the United States remains vulnerable to another energy crisis with the resulting pressure to increase domestic energy production quickly. More than a third of all U.S. current oil consumption still originates from imports. Although the Persian Gulf now provides only 5 percent of the national oil consumption, the domestic economy still would be affected adversely by a sudden and sustained shortfall of Middle Eastern oil, particularly if the blockade extended concurrently to U.S. allies. The nation is bound by treaty with the International Energy Agency to share its petroleum oil resources. Although the U.S. Strategic Petroleum Reserve currently contains enough oil for three year's domestic consumption, it cannot be expected to last this long nor buffer the domestic economic shocks of an import shortfall nearly so well if it must also offset lost oil imports to Europe and Japan.

Moreover, the United States has no excess oil production capacity and few alternatives to substitute for oil used in most economic sectors if it has to find a replacement. Federal promotion of nonfossil fuel energy technologies, as we shall shortly elaborate, has virtually ceased. Synthetic fuels technologies, promoted by President Jimmy Carter and Congress in the late 1970s as an alternative to petroleum, had bleak prospects as federal support for synthetic fuel research and development steadily dwindled.[6] The nuclear fuel industry, once expected to be a major producer of electric power, is too burdened by technical and economic problems to fulfill such a role. While the United States apparently has large natural gas reserves, they will not readily replace petroleum if the need arises. Thus, in the event of a severe new petroleum shortfall, the United States would have to depend on rapid, enforced energy conservation or on its abundant coal reserves as a short-term solution to energy needs.

Even without a new oil blockade, a sharply increasing demand for energy may occur as the United States and other industrial nations recover from the severe economic recession of 1979 to 1983. Many economists believe that the recent moderating trend in U.S. energy consumption, and some conservation gains, resulted from this temporary economic slowdown. Many energy-intensive industries had been operating at reduced capacity; the American steel industry and Japanese aluminum manufacturers, for instance, were working at only 40 percent capacity in 1983. The decline in the historic growth rate for new electric power appeared to have ended by 1983; from 2.5 percent in 1982, new domestic demand jumped to 5.5 percent in 1983, leading many governmental and electric utility experts to predict further increases throughout the decade.[7] If current U.S. energy conservation is largely the result of cyclical influences such as recession, rather than a result of more enduring "structural" transformations in the economy, the reviving U.S. economy will create a strong surge of new energy consumption within this decade. This would place considerable pressure on domestic energy resources, perhaps quickly eliminating the existing excess U.S. energy production capacity in coal and natural gas and triggering a new raid on resources with environmental risks involved.

The Politics of Pump, Dig, and Boil

The 1982 annual report of the Council on Environmental Quality (CEQ), the first published under the Reagan administration, produced a novel solution for the nation's energy problems: it single-handedly eliminated them. For the first time since the 1973 Arab oil embargo, the CEQ report contained no chapter on energy and no comprehensive examination of energy issues.

Unlike Carter, President Ronald Reagan's administration resolutely refused to treat energy issues, or their environmental implications, as a major national problem. Rather than proposing a coherent, high-priority energy program that accepted the need for better energy management and conservation, the Reagan administration relied upon a few inconsistently promoted strategies for energy production. First, the president and his advisers maintained that the nation's future energy needs could be adequately met by an aggressive program of greatly increased domestic energy production. Refusing to believe that a significant future domestic energy shortage was inevitable, the administration insisted that future energy needs, including any new energy crisis, could be resolved by ambitious new coal production on federal land, vastly expanded leasing of oil and natural gas exploration rights on the Outer Continental Shelf (OCS) and Alaska, and increased production of electricity by nuclear power.

This heavy tilt in the direction of new energy production became the driving force behind the Interior Department's determination to lease more than a million acres of new federal coal reserves for surface mining and to open the OCS off the California, Alaska, and Atlantic coasts to oil and gas exploration. It also became a major reason for the administration's desire to amend the Clean Air Act and other air pollution controls so that fossil fuel combustion could be greatly increased during the decade.

This enthusiasm for pumping oil, digging coal, and boiling generator water with nuclear power also involved an aversion to enforced energy conservation. Instead, the Reagan administration was confident that the economic market, acting through rising energy prices, would force energy conservation. Consequently, virtually all federal programs to promote energy conservation and to encourage the development of solar energy technologies or other environmentally benign measures were almost eliminated from the federal budget. Within the first three years of the Reagan administration federal expenditures for research and development of solar energy, energy conservation, and conservation information were cut by more than 90 percent. Significantly, only the nuclear energy research programs among all Energy Department research and development activities were increased during this period. Yet mineral exploration at the Interior Department was prospering. There programs for mineral exploration, for development of new mineral extraction technologies, and for mineral information were increasing between 30 percent and 80 percent during the same period.[8]

To many observers this one-strategy reliance upon the marketplace to create energy conservation amounted to an implicit proclamation that conservation was no longer an important national priority. According to economist Yergin, "Whatever the exact shape of the final outcome of the Reagan Administration's energy policy, it became clear that financial incentives for conservation and new energy sources would drop substantially, excessive energy consumption would still be encouraged by market imperfections, and the public would continue to be given the message that the nation's energy problems were over."[9]

This indifference to conservation through governmental incentives also turned the United States away from what many experts considered the most economically attractive and ecologically benign approach to meeting future energy needs. Through governmental programs promoting cogeneration (the simultaneous production of electricity and heat by industry and utilities), better home insulation, the use of solar heating and cooling for homes or businesses, the development of other solar technologies, and more, the United States could, according to some studies, save enormously on energy consumption. "If the United States were to make a serious commitment to conservation," asserts economist Yergin, "it might well consume perhaps 30 percent less energy than it now does, and still enjoy the same or an even higher standard of living. That saving would not hinge on a major technological breakthrough, and it would require only modest adjustment in the way people live."[10] Such conservation, moreover, could be accomplished largely without environmental pollution or depletion of nonrenewable energy sources.

This conservation, however, would require governmental encouragement for the development of solar technology, new tax incentives for homes, businesses, and industries to use cogeneration, and other governmental actions to which the Reagan administration was philosophically opposed. Also, whatever its intrinsic merits, conservation was not publicly popular or attractive to elective officials when no sense of crisis about energy supply existed. Partially because many government officials and citizens also assume that conservation means doing without something considered essential to the American lifestyle, conservation proposals must overcome strong public and official resistance.

Thus, the United States was committed to relying largely upon nonrenewable fossil fuels and nuclear power for its continuing energy needs. This meant reliance upon the most environmentally polluting energy sources and continual risk of a crisis-induced raid on such resources if the United States should experience another petroleum blockade. The ecological risks of the existing pattern of energy consumption can be better appreciated by examining the environmental implications to current coal and nuclear power development.

Twilight of the Nuclear Dream

Behind current conflicts over the environmental safety of nuclear power stretches a long history of deep federal government involvement with the industry. From its inception, the private nuclear power industry in the United States was promoted, subsidized, and insulated heavily from political and economic shocks by the federal government. Well into its third decade, the industry and its governmental regulators collaborated to make management of the "peaceful atom" the work of a largely invisible and unassailable subgovernment whose components included congressional committees responsible for nuclear power policy, the federal regulatory agency responsible for controlling the nuclear power industry, the trade associations representing the manufacturers of the technology, and the scientists in institutions, public and private, working on the program.

Washington Creates an Industry

Peaceful atomic power was first promoted by the Eisenhower administration to demonstrate to the world that the United States was concerned with more than the military uses of nuclear power and to inhibit the global spread of nuclear materials. The White House relied on the Atomic Energy Commission (AEC), already created to regulate existing civilian uses of atomic energy, and the congressional Joint Committee on Atomic Energy (JCAE) to convince private U.S. utilities to collaborate in developing nuclear reactors to generate electric power. To soften resistance from the largely unenthusiastic private utilities the federal government assured the industry of massive federal research and development funds to commercialize the new technology, gave a waiver on initial costs of expensive nuclear fuel, and offered many other concessions. Later, Washington also would pass the Price-Anderson Act (1957) limiting the insurance liability of a nuclear utility to $540 million for any single reactor accident and ensuring that the industry would be able to obtain needed insurance. Through direct and indirect support and subsidies the federal government by the early 1980s had invested by very conservative estimates between $12 billion and $15 billion in the nuclear power industry. It had an enormous political and economic stake in the industry's viability from its inception.[11]

The government's primary advocates for civilian nuclear power, the AEC and the JCAE, pursued this mission with evangelical intensity. Although created as a legislative watchdog to ensure the AEC's objectivity and competence in regulating the emerging nuclear industry, the joint committee became the principal advocate, guardian, and booster for the nuclear program. "The Joint Committee itself originated many of the ideas [for the program] from the start and directed the AEC to develop the appropriate technology and sell it to the public," writes Peter Metzger. "The public had nowhere to go in order to reject an idea but to its author, an unlikely place to get a fair hearing." [12] The AEC was charged by Congress with both regulating and promoting the new industry—an incompatible combination. The five AEC commissioners and their staffs created the very model of a mission-oriented agency, relegating regulatory responsibilities to promotional ones. Eventually, these conflicting roles led to the dissolution of this dual mandate but not to the end of the problem it had created.

The new industry, nurtured with benevolent regulation, seemed vigorous. By the time the first prototype atomic reactor to generate commercial electric power began operation at Shippingsport, Pennsylvania, in 1957, orders from private utilities for reactors had reached a level that seemed to ensure the industry's growth. Until the 1970s all but a handful of scientists, economists, and public officials associated with the new technology seemed, in the language of economist Irvin Bupp, so "intoxicated" by the new technology that grave technical and economic flaws already apparent to a few critical observers were largely ignored.[13] When problems could not be ignored they were usually suppressed from public view or debate and the critics discredited by Washington's aggressive defense of the industry. The rates at which new nuclear utilities were being built and additional ones planned by the nation's private utilities mounted through the 1960s. This development crested in 1975 with 56 plants built, 69 more under construction, and an additional 111 planned. By then the problems that would affect nuclear power in the 1980s no longer could be ignored or suppressed.

The Problems of the Peaceful Atom

The 1978 nuclear reactor accident at Three Mile Island (TMI) near Harrisburg, Pennsylvania, was the most politically damaging event in the industry's brief history. It capped a decade of gathering misfortunes for civilian nuclear power. The industry had been in serious trouble long before the TMI incident forced national attention upon the industry's safety problems and regulatory failures. Serious technical and economic ills, apparent by the early 1970s, became increasingly evident as the decade progressed. TMI was a catalytic event in the political history of U.S. civilian nuclear power, strongly altering public consciousness about the nuclear power industry, increasing the credibility of industry critics and strengthening their political influence. By the mid-1980s statistics about nuclear power read like the industry's obituary. If the Nuclear Dream was not dead, it was dying, as even spokesmen for the industry privately admitted.

The nuclear power industry's existing condition is writ large in the data of Table 7-2, which lists the number of U.S. commercial reactors built, being built, and licensed over the last decade. After 1975 an unarrested decline began in the number of reactors both under construc-

Table 7-2   U.S. Nuclear Reactors Built, Being Built, or Planned, 1973-1981

Year[1]	Built[2]	Being built[3]	Planned[4]	Total
1973	42	56	116	214
1974	53	63	117	233
1975	56	69	111	236
1976	63	71	101	235
1977	67	80	74	221
1978	70	90	47	207
1979	70	91	27	188
1980	70	82	11	163
1981	73	78	11	162

[1] Data are as of December 31 of the year indicated, except for 1981, which are as of September 30.
[2] Includes reactors licensed to operate and licensed for low-power or zero-power testing.
[3] Includes reactors that have had construction permits granted.
[4] Includes reactors under construction permit review and those that have been ordered or announced.

Source: Council on Environmental Quality, *Environmental Quality 1981* (Washington, D.C.: Government Printing Office, 1982), 226.

tion and planned. In 1972 industry experts were predicting that by the year 2000 the United States would be generating 1,200 million megawatts of electricity from nuclear reactors; by the early 1980s they were predicting little more than 100 million megawatts.[14] Many of the problems contributing to the industry's malaise are directly related to environmental policy.

Economic Ills. The costs of constructing and maintaining commercial nuclear power plants have become so high within the last decade that investment capital is scarce and costly. Many planned facilities no longer seem economically manageable; others under construction may never be completed in light of their mounting costs and dubious prospects. Construction costs for a moderate-sized, 1,000-megawatt plant rose more than 250 percent between 1971 and 1978, and some industry projections suggested a 400 percent rise before the end of the 1980s.[15] Utilities began to retrench. Thirty-five planned facilities were scrapped between 1978 and 1980; no new reactor orders have been placed with U.S. manufacturers since 1978. Utilities with multibillion-dollar nuclear plants under construction are cancelling further work or considering it, often with severe economic penalties. The largest bond default in U.S. utility history occurred when the Washington Public Power Supply System, after cancelling further construction on two nuclear reactors in 1982, was forced in 1983 to default on payments for $2.25 billion in bonds.

Among the factors accounting for these economic ills are several related to concern for public safety and environmental protection. One is the continually lengthening time required for a facility to secure the many governmental licenses required for its operation; these licenses are usually required to ensure that facilities have met governmental safety standards for man and the environment. Currently, surmounting all these regulatory hurdles for a new power plant requires between four years and eight years and may involve almost a hundred different federal, state, and local governmental permits. Industry officials also complain of the costs imposed during plant construction by the regulatory "ratcheting" of the Nuclear Regulatory Commission (NRC)—its habit of requiring facilities to make new safety modifications or other expensive changes in design or process retroactively. Additional costs have been imposed upon many utilities by protracted litigation involving environmental groups and others challenging various aspects of plant design and operation. Such litigation in the late 1970s, for instance, cost owners of the nuclear facility under construction at Seabrook, New Hampshire, more

230

than $15 million monthly while the court battles continued. Industry spokesmen often assert that litigation and other methods to delay the construction of planned facilities are a deliberate harassment by environmental and antinuclear organizations intended to drive the facilities to bankruptcy.

The industry's regulators and environmental critics, however, cannot be blamed for all the industry's major economic problems. Operating plants have rarely performed at design levels; the average facility has been "down" about a third of its total operating time due to routine maintenance or technical problems. Also, the industry, like all utilities, faces an unanticipated drop in the rate of demand for new electric power, and as a result many planned or operating facilities lack the markets for which they were originally designed. Rising interest rates in the late 1970s and early 1980s made investment capital far more expensive than many utilities had expected only a few years earlier.

Technical Problems. The industry also has to contend with a multitude of design and operating problems, many only recently revealed. Spokesmen for the industry correctly argue that its historic safety record, not withstanding TMI, is excellent and that technical problems are often exaggerated unreasonably by critics. However, these revelations of technical problems suggest serious deficiencies in the basic design and operation of the plants, and frequent carelessness or incompetence in plant management. These problems, whatever their "real" importance, have worked against the industry politically. Substantial doubts about plant safety have been raised among the public and public officials while the industry's credibility has been undermined. Experts brought into disputes over technical problems rarely reach a consensus on plant safety to put doubt at rest. Continuing revelations of design errors, operating mistakes, and other technical problems have given fresh encouragement to organized opponents of nuclear power.

Several technical problems are particularly damaging to the industry. First, materials and design standards for many nuclear power plants currently operating or under construction fail to meet essential safety requirements. Existing materials fail to perform as expected, or mistakes are made in the specification or construction of facilities. So often have revelations of this sort occurred in recent years that the problems no longer can be considered isolated. Proponents of the industry must now defend themselves against the following kinds of discovery:

An NRC investigation shows that California's Pacific Gas and Electric Company inadvertently had switched some blueprints for several reactors under construction at its Diablo Canyon site. The reactors and their housing consequently had been constructed with inaccurate calculations of their resistance to seismic stress, a critical issue since the facility was located in an active earthquake zone. "It is a first-rate screw-up," said one NRC commissioner at the time.[16]

The NRC announced that at least 13 operating nuclear reactors had serious problems with growing brittleness in the metals of the reactor pressure vessel; this brittleness was increasing much faster than had been expected when the reactors were built.

The NRC's director of operations announced that "serious quality assurance breakdowns with broad repercussions" had been found in nuclear plants located in Indiana, Michigan, Ohio, and Texas. This meant that the adequacy of the engineering calculations used to ensure that a plant would work as planned and that the structure was actually built to these calculations was in question.[17]

Increasingly the competence of nuclear power plant managers and technicians is also questioned. A 1981 report by a subcommittee of the House Government Operations Committee, written after an investigation of numerous nuclear facilities, warned of "serious and wide-spread management failings" and provided evidence. An inspector entered the control room at Commonwealth Edison's reactor near Morris, Illinois, and found two operators asleep; another inspector for Florida Light and Power found a reactor at one site operating at full power with no one in control. The committee was particularly unsettled by the inexperienced operator who mistakenly opened a valve at the TVA's newly licensed Sequoyah plant near Chattanooga, Tennessee, and endangered the reactor by discharging 110,000 gallons of water from the primary cooling system. "He became aware that he may have caused a problem," a subsequent report noted, "when he met people evacuating the containment structure as he left the building."[18] Investigations into the management of the TMI nuclear facility after the 1978 accident suggested widespread technical deficiency in staff training—half the senior operators had flunked their federal skill exams—that critics charge is characteristic of most nuclear facilities.

Spokesmen for the nuclear power industry assert that managerial incompetence is relatively rare when all facilities are considered. However, any uncertainty about nuclear technology, when raised to the level of a public debate, tends to assume ominous implications once public and official confidence in the industry has weakened. For example, when large cracks were discovered by NRC inspectors in the cooling pipes of 13 nuclear reactors in late 1982, measurements were taken to determine which pipes were damaged so severely that they had to be replaced. Shortly thereafter, the NRC's Advisory Committee on Reactor Safeguards asserted that the method used to measure the depth of these cracks was so unreliable that results could be accepted "only as a matter of faith." Even though the reliability of the measurements was a matter of continuing expert debate, raising the issue only increased pressure on the NRC to shut down the affected reactors. Technical controversies all seem to work against the industry.

Softening Public Support. In the aftermath of TMI the American public is more reserved about the continued development of the nuclear power industry, more sensitive to the risks, and more concerned about future safety. The public has not wholly rejected further nuclear power development or the full utilization of existing plants. In a careful appraisal of the public's mood, Mark Schulman observed: "It is clear that in the aftermath of Three Mile Island, public opposition to nuclear power plants has soared, but . . . the public is unwilling to declare a moratorium on new development—the bottom line had not fallen out of public support." [19] But the bottom line is sagging enough to prompt enormous hesitation at all governmental levels about proceeding with earlier plans for "the nuclear tomorrow."

Several opinion trends are significant. Those who favor a moratorium on the further construction of nuclear facilities appear to be a large and growing portion of the population. Less than a year after TMI several major opinion polls indicated that a slight majority of the public favored more nuclear facility construction. By the early 1980s polls conducted by the Roper and Gallup organizations indicated that little more than 30 percent of the public still supported such construction; several polls instead suggested that a majority would approve an immediate moratorium on plant construction. [20] The public also seemed more convinced that nuclear power plants involved significant risks. While support for nuclear power development did rebound slightly following a steep decline immediately after TMI, the proportion of the public approving a nuclear power plant in their own community sharply diminished after TMI and remains below 40 percent in most polls. Yet the public is not resolutely antinuclear. Many referendums intended to prevent further construction of nuclear facilities within individual states have been defeated; some polls still show majorities favoring more nuclear facility construction with adequate safeguards.

The public's future mood is still uncertain. Less doubtful is the political effect of current public sentiments on nuclear power regulation. Doubts and ambivalence about nuclear power, no doubt intensified by TMI, have thrown the nuclear power industry sharply on the defensive, sapping its political strength. It has been easier for public officials to express criticism and doubts about nuclear electric power, more politically safe to urge greater moderation and study before pushing ahead with new development schemes. It is certainly a mood that creates greater boldness and credibility for the antinuclear activists, whose political fortunes seem to prosper with each revelation of the industry's problems. A portent for the peaceful atom may have occurred in late 1983 when Congress voted after more than a decade of bitter debate to deny further funds for the Clinch River Breeder Reactor, ending the nation's major developmental program for the breeder reactor, once expected to be the next great technological leap in the industry's development. Many observers perceived in that vote the beginning of a long requiem for the peaceful atom.

It is against this background of extensive governmental involvement in the development of nuclear electric power and deeply divisive scientific controversies that the current environmental management of nuclear power is best understood. For the environmental issues remain, even if no more nuclear facilities are built. A complete moratorium on future nuclear facility planning would still leave about 75 nuclear power plants operating and an additional 78 under construction. Most experts predict conservatively that at least 120 nuclear plants will be operating by the year 2000. Environmental issues associated with nuclear electric power will continue to be significant in nuclear power regulation for many decades.

Two Environmental Issues

Controversy over nuclear power has raised two issues with major environmental implications. Each involves difficult and controversial problems of defining acceptable levels of risk and creating agreement among experts on the validity of technical data drawn into the disputes. These issues raise additional questions about the ability of political institutions to manage these risks competently.

Is a Catastrophic Accident Possible? The continuing revelations of technical and managerial problems sustain doubts about the safety of reactors and about the ability of plant managers and responsible governments to handle an emergency. Apprehensions about accidents have grown in part from the many recent revelations of deficiencies in plant design and maintenance such as those previously noted. Another cause for concern is evidence, based upon elaborate statistical studies, that potentially catastrophic accidents may occur more frequently than once had been supposed. The NRC's current reluctance to state with conviction that a serious nuclear plant accident is a possibility too remote to cause significant concern—a position it had maintained until the late 1970s—adds weight to arguments by critics of plant safety.

Two particular events suggest that the NRC has more misgivings about plant safety than it had a decade earlier. In 1979 the NRC repudiated conclusions it had endorsed earlier from the so-called Rassmussen Report. In 1976 a scientific commission appointed by the NRC and headed by physicist Norman C. Rassmussen of the Massachusetts Institute of Technology reported to the NRC that a potentially catastrophic reactor accident such as the loss of reactor coolant causing a core meltdown was likely to occur only once in 10 million years of reactor operation, or as probable as a single meteorite striking an individual on earth.[21] In 1979 the NRC failed to endorse this conclusion and appointed another review panel, which subsequently suggested that the conclusion, like some other aspects of the report, was "inscrutable." In 1982 a study of many thousand nuclear plant accidents from 1969 through 1979, conducted for the NRC by Oak Ridge National Laboratories, suggested that an accident as serious as the TMI event, or worse, could be expected every 10 to 15 years and that the probability of a major accident was about 10 times greater than the Rassmussen estimate. The NRC continues to ponder differing estimates of plant safety without endorsing any. In the words of one scientific observer, the effect has been to "drop the bottom line" on plant safety, leaving silence and suspicion.

Many industry critics also are concerned by a widespread lack of preparation by local, state, and federal governments to deal with a reactor emergency. Most local governments have failed to meet federal requirements that they prepare and practice emergency evacuation procedures for populations living close to a nuclear facility in the event of a major reactor accident. By late 1983, for instance, local governments had failed to create such procedures at 37 of the 53 sites where evacuation plans were required. Closely related has been the common lack of preparation to get information and technical advice quickly to the public officials who must make critical decisions about emergency management in case of a plant accident. Although the TMI affair revealed to the NRC grave deficiencies in the institutional planning for nuclear emergencies that the commission pledged to eliminate, the NRC itself has seemed unwilling, or unable, to make the necessary changes quickly. Some critics believe the NRC lacks the will, or capacity, to force such reforms upon an industry with which it traditionally has had close and congenial ties.

The growing uncertainties about the probability of a major reactor accident and the pervasive lack of practical governmental planning to deal with the likely consequences of such an emergency should be a cause for considerable concern among both critics and proponents of the nuclear power industry. The industry and its regulators seem caught in a morass of bureaucratic and political problems, which are stifling many reforms whose necessity was dramatized by the TMI affair. So long as this situation remains, fears about reactor accidents will continue to persist.

The Waste Nobody Wants. No problem has been more politically troublesome to the nuclear power industry and its federal regulators than where—and how—to dispose of the enormous, highly toxic, and growing volume of nuclear wastes in the United States. The unprecedented and largely unanticipated problems of nuclear waste management, first evident in the late 1960s, have been especially difficult to resolve because nuclear waste incites great public fear and its disposal provokes strong conflicts between federal, state, and local governments. Many experts would assert that the comptroller general's conclusion about high-level waste disposal applies to all nuclear waste: "The major obstacle to geological disposal is not the technology, but public and political acceptance of the waste disposal concept and of the localities where the repositories will be located." [22] To understand the political controversies inseparable from nuclear waste, it is helpful to examine briefly the character of these wastes and the reasons for their continued existence.

Nuclear waste today originates from the mining of uranium, the military nuclear weapons program, civilian nuclear power plants, hospitals, educational institutions, and research centers. Current controversies involve four categories of this waste:

> 1. *High-Level Wastes.* Highly radioactive liquids created through the reprocessing of reactor fuels. These wastes are generated by both civilian and military re-

actor programs. Currently, more than 100 million gallons of high-level wastes are stored in temporary containment facilities in the states of Washington, Idaho, South Carolina, and New York.

2. *Transuranic Wastes.* Radioactive byproducts of reactor fuel and military waste processing. Some of these elements remain dangerous for extraordinarily long periods. Plutonium 239, with a half-life of 24,000 years, and Americum with a 7,300-year half-life, are among the transuranics. Other more exotic transuranic elements have a half-life exceeding 200,000 years.

3. *Spent Nuclear Fuel.* About 6,000 metric tons of spent fuel, mostly from civilian reactors, are stored temporarily in "cooling ponds" at reactor sites. By 1995, as more nuclear power plants become operational, this spent fuel is expected to increase to 63,000 metric tons.

4. *Low-Level Wastes.* Any material contaminated by radiation and emitting low levels of radioactivity itself belongs in this category. This includes workers' clothing, tools, equipment, and other items associated with nuclear reactors or nuclear materials. Low-level wastes currently are stored at repositories in South Carolina, New York, and Nevada.

Most of this waste was not expected to exist when nuclear reactor development was planned initially. But a variety of unanticipated problems beginning in the early 1960s have made the waste issue increasingly difficult for both military and civilian nuclear programs. Spent fuel from civilian and military reactors, it was assumed, would be reprocessed; the usable fissionable materials, primarily plutonium, would be recovered for use again as reactor fuel and the remaining high-level waste eventually would be contained and isolated at appropriate disposal sites. Planners, confident that reprocessing would prove economically attractive, expected private industry to process the civilian spent fuel routinely. In the planners' early view, the high-level and transuranic wastes remaining after reprocessing posed a largely technical and readily solvable problem of finding the appropriate containment materials and geographic location for permanent storage. They did not anticipate the failure of civilian fuel reprocessing and the resulting volume of nuclear waste. Nor did they deal realistically with the political difficulties this created.

Commercial reprocessing of spent reactor fuel has been a failure. The one existing commercial reprocessing plant, at West Valley, New York, closed permanently in 1972 after a multitude of economic and safety problems; other planned commercial reprocessing facilities in Illinois and South Carolina never were constructed fully. In 1978 the Carter administration, fearful that widespread fuel reprocessing would lead to a dangerous proliferation of weapons-grade plutonium, ordered a complete halt to all civilian reprocessing. The nuclear power industry unexpectedly was confronted with the problem of finding a satisfactory permanent disposal site for a rapidly accumulating volume of spent fuel.

Most existing and future plants were designed to store temporarily no more than three years' accumulated spent fuel in cooling ponds until the fuel assemblies were reprocessed. Since the early 1970s, however, virtually all spent fuel has been stored in the cooling ponds; space and time are now running out. The United States continues to reprocess its military spent fuel, however, generating most of the current high-level liquid wastes. Although the Reagan administration declared its intention to lift the restrictions on civilian fuel reprocessing, it will be many years before reprocessing, if it occurs, has a significant impact upon the growing volume of spent fuel. The spent fuel assemblies currently multiplying in cooling ponds for the most part will have to be transported to a safe permanent depository.

Until 1982 the federal government had no comprehensive plan for the permanent storage of the nation's nuclear wastes. Washington and the states quarreled for more than a decade over how a permanent waste depository would be designated and which states should be depository sites. The states already accommodating large volumes of high- and low-level wastes were increasingly reluctant to accept more. Other states fought vigorously against any federal policies that might designate them as waste depositories.

Washington encouraged this continental game of Not In My Back Yard by technical and political bungling during its early efforts to find a permanent depository. In the early 1970s the AEC insisted, over the objections of state political leaders and scientists, that it would study salt vaults near Lyons, Kansas, as a repository. The AEC abandoned the plan after evidence was presented that it had not correctly assessed the probable safety of the site. In the late 1970s the Energy Department, acting upon a congressional directive, informed New Mexico that it intended to develop a site near Carlsbad for the permanent deposit of high-level wastes over the state's objections and despite President Carter's earlier pledge to respect state sentiments on the matter. New Mexico officials forced the federal government to negotiate further on the issue, but Washington never relinquished its final authority to determine the location of the site. Such episodes created a legacy of distrust that continues to affect state attitudes.[23]

The controversy over disposal of nuclear waste also is complicated by technical disputes over the safety of specific geologic sites and the techniques used to encapsulate the waste materials. Some high-level and transuranic wastes remain dangerous for thousands, sometimes many hundreds of thousands, of years; a "safe" disposal strategy must appear to offer secure isolation of radioactive substances for periods so long that all judgments about safety are estimates. Almost all federal proposals to designate specific sites for waste disposal have been challenged on the grounds that the sites are not sufficiently secure geologically or that the specific technology used to stabilize the waste materials is suspect.

In 1982 Congress passed the Nuclear Policy Act (Public Law 97-425) establishing a national policy for nuclear waste disposal. The act, to be examined later, postponed some bitterly controversial decisions for a few years and at the same time created a process Washington hoped would win state support for the eventual choices of a permanent disposal site. In the mid-1980s, however, new conflict between Washington and the states erupted over the transportation of these wastes. Nuclear power plants attempting to move spent fuel rods to other sites for temporary disposal and federal efforts to relocate existing wastes are generating a rising volume of nuclear wastes in transportation. The federal government's relocation of spent fuel rods from the West Valley, New York, site involved 30 truckloads of fuel rods sent to Illinois, 114 truckloads to Wisconsin, and hundreds of truckloads elsewhere. Illinois expected about 200 tons of spent fuel to be transported through its borders in 1984. The volume of nuclear waste being transported has prompted some state and local governments to attempt a ban on all such transportation within their jurisdictions, while others have insisted upon setting regulatory standards for such shipments. Although cities have largely failed in both efforts, several states including Ohio and Illinois have pledged to take legal action to prevent such shipments until they are satisfied that Washington has given appropriate regard to their concerns. In the meantime the issue is one more simmering controversy in a struggle unlikely to cool very soon.

The Political Thicket

Few events have shaped more decisively the character of civilian nuclear power development in the United States than the thorough politicizing of nuclear power issues in the last 20 years. Virtually every major technical, economic, and institutional issue involved in the civilian nuclear program has become a source of political conflict among organized public and private institutions. Disputes over the safety of nuclear facilities and the proper management of nuclear wastes have become thoroughly intermingled with disputes over the integrity and competence of governmental agencies responsible for nuclear regulation. Private interests, the states, and federal agencies—indeed, all organized groups with a stake in nuclear power development—have attempted to exploit the political process to their advantage. Political controversy tends to polarize technical disagreements; scientific uncertainties and disagreements perpetuate political cleavages. This is evident in managing the environmental risks of nuclear power.

Politicizing the civilian nuclear power program has its benefits. Decisions no longer are made by a small, cloistered, technocratic and political elite to whom the public and its officials routinely defer. Important scientific and political controversies can be exposed to the public, and in the process the public and its officials may be gradually educated into a more enlightened understanding of the benefits and risks of civilian nuclear power. But politicization also makes difficult a deliberate and fair appraisal of issues. It also delays and complicates decisions that need to be made as quickly as possible. It makes it difficult for public officials, agencies, and private interests to separate their own self-interest from the public interest when policy conflicts must be resolved.

Many of these political dimensions to nuclear policy will be evident as we examine three elements that currently influence the resolution of the environmental issues we have examined.

The Controversial NRC. "The NRC is structurally incapable of calling the tough shots on a consistent basis," complained Rep. Edward J. Markey of Massachusetts, whose House subcommittee oversaw the agency's activities. "Although it may do sporadically good work, it doesn't consistently produce the kind of criticism of the industry that would build public confidence." [24] Critics of the nuclear power industry almost ritually indict the NRC for its regulatory failures. But even its friends recognize a problem. It was an NRC commissioner newly appointed by President Reagan, a pronuclear spokesman for a pronuclear administration, who publicly complained shortly after assuming office about the "surprising lack of professionalism in the construction and preparation ... of nuclear facilities" and "lapses of many kinds—in design analysis resulting in built-in design errors, in poor construction practices, in falsified documents. ..." [25] It was a litany of industry practices the NRC is supposed to prevent.

The NRC's regulatory deficiencies arise, in large part, from the political circumstances of its origin and the outlook of its professional staff. The NRC was created in 1974 when Congress abolished the AEC and vested its regulatory authority in the new NRC. This act was a congressional effort to eliminate a serious problem: the AEC, responsible for both regulating and promoting the nuclear power industry, had subordinated its regulatory duties to promoting and defending the industry. But Congress could not readily dissolve the strong, congenial professional and institutional relationships linking former AEC staff to the nuclear power industry nor could it eliminate the impulse to promote and protect the industry so deeply rooted in the AEC's history. Successive NRC commissioners and their staffs often tried to regulate without prejudice and sometimes succeeded. But institutional history and professional experience largely prevailed against regulatory rigor. By the mid-1980s the NRC seemed unable to remedy apparently widespread deficiencies in the design and operation of the nation's civilian nuclear facilities.

The most serious regulatory failures involved carelessness in enforcing proper safety standards for the design of nuclear power plants, lax inspection of operating facilities, inadequate supervision of plant managers and technicians, and protectiveness toward the industry when major problems were uncovered. Among the many incidents that stirred widespread official and public concern about the NRC's competence were the following:

> The NRC provided draft reports on quality control inspection of California's Diablo Canyon facility to its operators before congressional committees were given the information. The NRC earlier had certified the safety of one facility reactor on the basis of the wrong blueprints.
>
> In 1982 the Justice Department criticized the NRC for its reluctance to refer to the department cases involving important matters such as the failure of facility operators to meet safety and construction standards, particularly when criminal actions might be involved.
>
> The U.S. Nuclear Safety Oversight Committee, appointed by President Carter, released a letter broadly critical of what it called the "business-as-usual" attitude at the NRC despite the need for major reforms in industry regulation revealed by investigation of the TMI accident.[26]

The agency increasingly has been criticized for its lack of aggressiveness in prosecuting regulatory violations. By 1983 the problem was recognized widely within the agency. An internal study of the agency's

241

own investigative practices led to a recommendation that the NRC needed an inspector general to goad it into enforcing its own rules more aggressively. This fusillade of criticism, while sustaining controversy over the safety of nuclear reactors, emboldens antinuclear activists and diminishes the credibility of scientists defending the agency's technical determinations. It also frustrates the agency's attempts to aid the nuclear power industry by casting such large doubts over the integrity of the industry's most reliable bureaucratic ally.

State and Local Problems. State and local governments across the United States are increasingly reluctant to cooperate in the continuing promotion of nuclear power facilities and to accept the economic or legal responsibilities for facility safety and waste management. One symptom of this disenchantment is the moratorium on the licensing of new nuclear reactors that was in effect in six states in 1984 (California, Maryland, Oregon, Montana, Connecticut, Maine, and Wisconsin); in several instances, the moratorium has been extended until the federal government certifies the existence of a safe permanent depository for nuclear waste.

Many local governments also refused to cooperate in creating evacuation plans for populations that might be threatened by a nuclear facility accident—plans required by the NRC for most operating or planned nuclear facilities in the aftermath of TMI. Some local governments have asserted that they lack sufficient resources and training to meet the federal requirements. Others, in the view of industry promoters, used the emergency planning requirement to extort from Washington or utility owners various economic concessions in return for their cooperation. The commissioners of St. Lucie County, Florida, for example, asked Washington to pay for constructing a bridge, installing sirens, setting up a communications center, and creating other emergency arrangements needed to comply with evacuation planning. Antinuclear activists have skillfully exploited this requirement for local government planning to oppose and disrupt the construction of new nuclear facilities. By persuading local governments not to collaborate in this planning or to auction their cooperation at a steep price, opponents of nuclear utilities have often imposed enormously costly and time-consuming delays on new plant construction.

The nuclear waste problem has exacerbated state and local misgivings about peaceful atomic power. The full force of the state backlash against nuclear waste in fact may be several years away. The Nuclear Waste Management Act of 1982 requires the secretary of energy to study five potential sites for high-level waste repositories and to recommend three of these to the president by January 1985; the president may then select one site as the nation's first permanent high-level repository. The act also mandates that the secretary study five additional sites, three of which were not among the earlier sites selected, and recommend to the president three sites from which he may select one as the second national high-level waste depository. The first and second sites must be designated no later than 1987 and 1990, respectively. The states are ostensibly protected in the act by requirements for extensive federal consultation with the states before any sites are designated and by provisions permitting a state to veto its designation as a waste depository; this veto can be overridden only by a concurrent majority in both congressional chambers.

There is little existing evidence that states likely to be selected as potential waste depositories—Nevada, Utah, New Mexico, Louisiana, North Dakota, and Wyoming are among them—are inclined to become nuclear waste dumps without a fight. Spokesmen for these states are quick to note that all the states under consideration by the Energy Department, with the exception of Louisiana, are west of the Mississippi River, while most of the nation's nuclear facilities are east of it. Congressional representatives of these states have been scrambling to write into legislation restrictions that would keep nuclear waste out of their constituencies. Few of these states, however, are blessed with large congressional delegations or voting populations. In a confrontation with Washington over waste site selection, those states most poorly defended politically are likely to be most at risk of designation as a waste depository. It is quite plausible that ultimately Washington will solve the waste problem only by imposing its will upon protesting states. Even this, however, could take years as the conflict rumbles through the federal courts and any other political arena to which the states resort in their efforts to thwart federal action.

A Pronuclear President. The mounting difficulties burdening the nuclear power industry might be sounding a requiem were it not for the Reagan administration's determination to keep the industry alive. The president and his energy spokesmen support further development of the existing generation of nuclear reactors and continued federal funding of breeder reactor research, the next generation of nuclear technology in the opinion of its proponents. The president had not promoted nuclear power with the vigor his early statements had promised; nonetheless, the administration's energy policies clearly tilted in a nuclear direction.

Funding for federal energy conservation programs was virtually eliminated under Reagan, but federal support for civilian nuclear research and development programs rose slightly. The Reagan White House continued to promote the Clinch River Breeder Reactor over increasing congressional opposition. So long as Reagan remained in the White House, promoters of nuclear power could still hope, in the face of gathering misfortunes, that their time of troubles would end.

Black Gold

Every American president since 1973 has tried to dam the flow of imported oil into the United States with a wall of coal. Coal is the nation's most plentiful fossil fuel; it is inevitable that Washington's energy planners should repeatedly attempt to substitute abundant domestic coal for expensive and insecure imported oil. Economic and environmental problems, however, continue to inhibit a massive national conversion to coal combustion. The Reagan administration, convinced that excessive environmental regulation impedes coal utilization, has been determined to promote more coal production and less environmental regulation. This has alarmed and aroused environmentalists who fear an environmentally catastrophic new coal boom. The resulting confrontation has created Washington's bitterest environmental conflicts since the Environmental Era began.

The Saudi Arabia of Coal

Coal represents about 90 percent of the remaining U.S. hydrocarbon reserves; there is so much that the coal industry has reminded Americans that they have the equivalent of Saudi petroleum reserves in coal. This coal rests in three geologic reserves: Appalachia's wooded hills and hollows sprawling across parts of seven southeastern states, the midwestern plains, and the western plains and grasslands.

In the mid-1980s coal provided little more than 18 percent of U.S. energy consumption. Afflicted since the 1950s with declining employment, chronic labor violence, and production problems, the industry was tied to the nation's electric power companies and metallurgical industry, which consumed respectively 85 percent and 13 percent of annual coal production, for its fortunes. Because more than eight in every ten tons of mined coal in the United States are transported by rail, many railroads had become heavily dependent upon coal production for revenue.

Every recent administration has proposed massive new coal utilization to relieve the United States of its dependency on imported petroleum. The Nixon and Ford administrations' largely fanciful "Project Independence" promised that the United States could become almost independent of imported petroleum by 1980 through reliance on coal and conservation. President Carter, ignoring the chimera of "energy independence," still proposed in his 1977 energy plan to diminish U.S. dependence on petroleum through a 66-percent increase in domestic coal combustion within a decade and the creation of a massive new synthetic fuels industry based on coal feedstocks. The Reagan administration announced its intention to sell new coal mining leases in western public lands containing 5 billion tons of coal as a means of encouraging more production. The coal industry, sensing a possible reversal of its fortunes, was quick to proclaim coal the "great black hope of America" and to shift its political weight behind new White House coal initiatives.

There were several plausible reasons for coal's continuing attraction to energy planners despite related economic and environmental problems.[27] According to some estimates, accelerated coal combustion might displace as much as 2.5 million barrels of imported petroleum consumed by the United States daily. A coal boom might bring 100,000 new workers to Appalachia, reviving its stagnant economy, and perhaps 50,000 more workers to the West; coal-related income in the West and Great Plains might rise by $850 million to $1 billion. Large "mine-mouth" electric generating plants, located adjacent to coal seams to reduce transportation costs, could provide dependable, secure electric power for the growing West and Midwest. The Carter energy plan might have increased railroad coal loadings by 350 percent between 1978 and 1985. Coal was secure energy, unmenaced by Middle Eastern politics and unpredictable world petroleum markets. Coal could glitter as gold if only the new coal boom could be made environmentally and economically tolerable.

Can Surface Mining Be Regulated?

The most significant adverse environmental impacts associated with coal utilization are created by surface mining and combustion. Many of the problems associated with coal combustion have been examined in chapter 3 on air pollution. The regulation of surface mining has been no less contentious.

Surface Mining. Virtually all coal mined west of the Mississippi River and half produced in Appalachia is surface mined. Surface mining has rapidly replaced underground mining because it is cheaper, more efficient, more profitable, and less labor intensive. Unless rigorously regulated, however, surface mining is environmentally catastrophic. More than 1.5 million acres of American land have been disturbed by coal surface mining; more than a million of these acres remain a wrecked and ravaged waste, long abandoned by its creators. More than 1,000 additional acres are disturbed each week by surface mining, and more than 30 states have been scarred by unreclaimed surface mines.

In Appalachia surface miners roamed the hills virtually uncontrolled for decades; the evidence is written in thousands of sterile acres, acidified streams and rivers, decapitated hills, and slopes scarred by abandoned mine highwalls. In western prairies and grasslands, unregulated surface mining left thousands of barren, furrowed acres buried under spoil banks so hostile to revegetation they seemed like moonscapes to observers. After decades of resistance, the mining industry has come to recognize the necessity for the environmental regulation of surface mining, but vigorous controversy continues over the manner of this regulation and its effectiveness.

The Surface Mining Control and Reclamation Act. President Carter, fulfilling a promise made during his election campaign, signed the Surface Mining Control and Reclamation Act of 1977 (SMCRA) and thereby created the first federal surface mining regulatory program.[28] The act, strongly promoted by environmentalists against fierce resistance from the mining industry and two vetoes by President Gerald R. Ford, was intended to control the environmental ravages of surface mining by restoring surface-mined land to productivity whenever possible. The major features include:

1. Environmental performance standards with which all surface miners were to comply in order to operate. Standards were to be established to regulate the removal, storage, and redistribution of topsoil; siting and erosion control; drainage and protection of water quality; and many other matters affecting environmental quality.

2. Requirements that mined land be returned, insofar as possible, to its original contours and to a use equal or superior to that before mining commenced.

3. Special performance and reclamation standards for mining on alluvial valley floors in arid and semiarid areas, on prime farmland, and on steep slopes.

4. Enforcement of the act through a mining permit program administered

jointly by the federal government and the states, according to federal regulations.

5. Protection of land unsuitable for mining from any mine activity.

6. Creation of a special fund, financed from a tax on existing surface mining, to reclaim "orphan" mine sites.

7. Creation of an agency, currently the Office of Surface Mining Reclamation and Enforcement within the Interior Department, to enforce the act.

The Reagan Onslaught. Few federal regulations were more directly and consistently attacked by the Reagan administration than those arising out of the SMCRA. To the Reagan reformers, the act epitomized the excesses of federal authority, the red tape and confusion, and the enormous costs inflicted upon regulated interests. Administration spokesmen alleged that the act inhibited the production of coal at a time when the nation needed it.

Under Secretary of the Interior James G.Watt, pervasive alterations were made in the administrative structure set up to enforce SMCRA, which the Reagan administration maintained made the act's implementation more efficient and cost-effective. The economic and regulatory problems associated with the act will be examined in the final chapter. Environmental critics, however, charged that objections to the act's allegedly excessive costs were an administration pretext; the administration, they argued, wanted to frustrate the act's enforcement and thus to alter the intention of Congress without actually changing the wording of the law itself. This subversion of congressional intent, argued environmentalists, was being achieved largely by administrative means: technical and legal staffs were radically cut, funding was greatly reduced, and the responsibility for enforcement increasingly was thrust upon states largely unprepared for the greater responsibilities.

Within the first 18 months of the Reagan administration, the field offices of the Office of Surface Mining Reclamation and Enforcement had declined to 20 from 37 and its 5 regional offices in effect were abolished. The political chill settling into OSME was evident when personnel at the Denver office were notified abruptly that they could resign, retire, be "terminated," or move to Caspar, Wyoming. The number of full-time federal OSME inspectors had diminished from 115 to 69 by 1983. Estimates suggest that Secretary Watt's office may have rewritten more than 90 percent of the regulations originally formulated by the Interior Department under President Carter—an ominous statistic to environmentalists alert to the importance of regulations in determining the actual impact of laws.[29]

Enforcement of the act was further weakened by the Reagan administration's determination to vest in the states increasing responsibility for the task. Many states, suffering the effects of a prolonged recession upon revenues, did not have the money or personnel to increase investigations or to initiate more litigation under the act. The radical reduction of federal technical assistance from OSME's regional and local offices denied the states irreplaceable resources. Environmentalists increasingly resorted to litigation to force federal initiative in enforcing the act. U.S. District Court Judge Barrington D. Parker, in his reprimand of Interior for flouting the enforcement provisions of the SMCRA, suggested the impact of these administrative changes. Citing Interior's "three year disregard for the statute and regulations," Parker ordered the secretary to enforce 1,700 outstanding cease-and-desist orders against coal miners violating the law and to collect $44 million in back penalties. Environmentalists also sued Interior for allegedly approving implementation plans too permissive of environmental damage in several states.

Despite judicial prodding, implementation of SMCRA proceeds at a halting pace under the Reagan administration. The administrative alterations engineered by the Reagan leadership have effectively weakened the legal and technical resources of both federal and state agencies responsible for implementing the act; regulations flowing from Washington and the states since 1980 suggest a continued relaxation of the strict regulatory stance toward surface mining that characterized the Carter administration. Among state agencies responsible for enforcing SMCRA, there is a broadly shared perception that Washington has neither the will nor the means to enforce the act aggressively. Under these circumstances, environmentalists must rely upon litigation, pressure through Congress, or pressure on state enforcement agencies to produce better implementation. These are strategies demanding in time and money; they do not attack directly the structural changes and alterations in personnel within Interior that have contributed most substantially to SMCRA's ongoing debilitation. Indeed, the administrative changes achieved in Interior may remain among the most durable, and environmentally costly, of all the administration's regulatory reforms.

The Restoration Gamble. Obscured in the controversy over SMCRA's enforcement has been an issue even more important to the future of surface mining: Is restoration of mined lands in the manner contemplated by the act achievable? Technical studies suggest that the capacity of mining companies to restore mined land to conditions equal or superior to their original condition is likely to be site specific—that is, dependent upon the particular biological and geological character of each mining site. Western mining sites are often ecologically fragile; relatively limited varieties of sustainable vegetation and scarce rainfall make ecological regeneration of the land difficult. With only limited experience in the restoration of western mine sites, most experts are reluctant to predict that mine sites can be restored to ecological vitality even with good intentions, generous funding, and high-quality technical resources.

The prospects for restoration are less forbidding in Appalachia where an abundance of precipitation, richer soil, and a greater diversity of native flora and fauna are available. Nonetheless, many experts believe that disruption of subsurface hydrology and the drainage of acids and salts from the mines' spoil heaps may not be controlled easily even when surface revegetation is achieved. Thus, restoration remains a gamble with nature. If restoration proves difficult, confronting public officials with the prospect that a major portion of all surface-mined land may remain virtually sterile for centuries, a further national controversy may erupt over the continuance of surface mining.

The Coal Leasing Controversy

The fate of the public lands has become deeply implicated in current controversies over coal policy. The protection of the public domain—more than 1 billion acres of national parks, national forests, wilderness areas, grasslands, and other open space owned by the federal government—is deeply etched into the history and ideology of the environmental movement. The nation's first great conservation movement was inspired by a fierce determination among its leaders to create and preserve for all future American generations an inheritance of open space, with all its natural endowments, unspoiled by economic exploitation. This land ethic, still pervading the movement, has become almost a secular religion to many organizations.

Unlike its immediate predecessors, the Reagan administration was committed to an ambitious program that would greatly expand the sale of federal leases for coal exploration and mining on federal lands.[30] This placed all other disputes about coal use into the broad and highly volatile context of arguments over the proper use of the public domain. Environmentalists saw the new coal policy as an attack on the sanctity of the public domain, and the response was ferocious. "If Watt messes with the wilderness system," growled the executive director of the Wilderness Society, "he will find it is like sticking his hand in a Cuisinart." Spokesmen for the administration treated such sentiment as further evidence that environmentalists were ideologically rigid, insensitive to the nation's economic needs, and selfishly determined to lock up the public lands for the exclusive benefit of a conservationist minority.

The Reagan administration was committed to selling mining leases, primarily in the West, to land containing more than 5 billion tons of coal; several hundred thousand acres of public domain, including some wholly undeveloped wilderness areas, were involved. The Wilderness Act, passed in 1964, permitted Washington to issue until 1984 leases for coal exploration and extraction in wilderness areas, provided such leasings were "compatible with the preservation of the wilderness environment." Under traditional "multiple-use" doctrines, many nonwilderness areas already were open to mining and other economic activities provided such uses did not preclude recreation or conservation activities on the same land. Acting principally through the secretary of the interior, the administration in its first three years attempted to accelerate the issuance of new federal coal leasing, which had practically ceased since the Nixon administration. During this period Interior produced the largest single lease sale in its history: 16,500 acres in the Powder River Basin of Montana and Wyoming, which the administration hoped would be a portent of even larger sales to come.

This new leasing embroiled Watt not only in predictable controversy with the environmental movement but also in acrimonious disputes with Congress over Interior's legal obligations to the legislative branch. Environmentalists argued, in general, that the new leasing was environmentally reckless and economically unjustified. Foreign and domestic demand for coal was decreasing, noted the critics; the steel industry and public utilities were revising their projections downward for coal use in the mid-1980s. Furthermore, mining companies seldom developed their existing federal leases. Grave concern was expressed for the ability of the states—who increasingly assumed responsibility for strip mine regulation—to control adequately any new mining activity on public lands. Environmentalists were angered especially by Interior's aggressive efforts to sell leases in wilderness areas, which they contended were a unique and irreplaceable public trust to be protected against economic exploitation whenever possible.

Institutional rivalries and party politics nourished repeated conflicts between Interior and Congress. In the Democratic-controlled House of Representatives, committees with authority over Interior's leasing programs repeatedly criticized and in several instances prevented the sale of mining leases in wilderness areas and other public domain. The committees alleged the department had exceeded its authority in authorizing the sale of many leases without first consulting Congress. Democrats in both Houses diligently sought opportunities to embarrass the administration and to wrest some political advantage from the conduct of the leasing program. The Interior Subcommittee of the House Appropriations Committee, for instance, accused Interior of a "giveaway" in selling leases to 23,000 acres of land containing 1.6 billion tons of coal in the Powder River Basin. Interior had offered the coal at an arbitrary price half the current market value. Shell Oil, as a result, had acquired for $29.5 million a tract whose current market value was approximately $52.2 million.

Interior also ran into trouble in the Republican-controlled Senate. A bipartisan coalition of Democratic and Republican environmentalists, together with other senators jealous of congressional prerogatives, forced the secretary to withdraw several large tracts from leasing because he allegedly had exceeded his delegated authorities under the Wilderness Act and other legislation related to leasing programs.

Nonetheless, Interior's leadership remained publicly unapologetic about its ambitions for the public domain and ostensibly determined to press for more future leasing. The Reagan administration had succeeded in issuing more coal leases than any of its predecessors for 30 years. Whether it would, in fact, press its program with the promised vigor would be determined after the 1984 presidential elections. As the administration became absorbed with the elections, environmental programs likely to arouse strong controversy were temporarily put in abeyance lest they jeopardize the president's reelection. But the leasing dispute would erupt again should the Reagan administration return to Washington or should another administration adopt similar views about the public lands.

The Environmental Implications of Energy Policy

Coal combustion and civilian nuclear power are two examples of the implicit and inevitable association between environmental quality and patterns of energy development. The United States is currently following a path of energy development that will make vast, and possibly irreversible, changes in the nation's environment. The continuing growth of coal utilization will accelerate the spread of surface mining, along with all its environmental risks, across Appalachia and the American West. Industrial and utility coal combustion will perpetuate problems of air pollution, acid rain, and possibly the "Greenhouse Effect" through the decade. Even if civilian nuclear power should fail to develop beyond facilities currently operating or under construction, the risks of accidents and the institutional difficulties of managing plant emergencies will remain significant well into the next decade at least. It should be evident that serious technical, administrative, and political difficulties exist in the enforcement of legislation intended to protect the nation from the most environmentally malignant impacts of these technologies. The current status of the SMCRA and the Nuclear Waste Act, in particular, serve as a reminder that the severe ecological risks of inadequately regulated coal and nuclear power development remain.

Equally important are the environmental implications of current energy policy for the future. First, the United States today has no explicit, comprehensive program of energy conservation, nor does it have any governmental commitment to promoting the development and proliferation of energy conserving technologies beyond what may be accomplished through the deregulation of energy prices. This implies that energy development throughout the remainder of the decade is likely to place growing stress upon environmental quality and nonrenewable resources such as fossil fuels. Second, the continuing U.S. dependence upon nonrenewable energy resources, along with the adverse environmental impacts often associated with these resources, is slowly but resolutely moving the United States into a position where it may have to contemplate a severe energy-environment trade-off should a new energy crisis emerge. Public opinion polls have long suggested that environmental quality is most politically vulnerable to an energy crisis. Should the public and its officials feel they must choose between more energy or continuing environmental protection, there seems to exist a strong disposition to opt for energy development. Continued reliance upon environmentally threatening energy sources leaves U.S. policy makers with few options but environmentally dangerous ones in the face of another energy crisis.

Finally, it should be apparent from discussions of coal and nuclear power development that many of the environmental risks associated with these energy sources are created or exacerbated by failure of institutional management or design. Stated somewhat differently, the problems of dealing with evacuation of communities during a reactor failure or finding a safe and publicly acceptable repository for nuclear waste illustrate the failure of policy makers to anticipate the institutional arrangements essential to ensuring the safety of energy technologies. An essential aspect in planning the future development of energy technologies through government, whether it be synfuels technologies, nuclear fusion, or something else, should be careful and prolonged consideration of the institutional arrangements essential to ensure the technologies' safety—a sort of institutional risk assessment that raises tough and realistic questions about the impact of technologies on governmental institutions and their capacities to manage such technologies environmentally.

Notes

1. Council on Environmental Quality (CEQ), *Environmental Quality 1980* (Washington, D.C.: Government Printing Office, 1981), chapter 6.
2. CEQ, *Environmental Quality 1981*, 246, 220-221.
3. See *Roper Index*, January 1982, 17.
4. Daniel Yankelovich, "The Failure of Consensus," in *Uncertain Power*, ed. Dorothy Zinberg (New York: Pergamon Press, 1983), 29-36.
5. Robert Stobaugh and Daniel Yergin, eds., *Energy Future* (New York: Random House, 1979), 240.
6. Joel Darmstadter, Hans H. Landsberg, and Herbert C. Morton, *Energy Today and Tomorrow* (Englewood Cliffs, N.J.: Prentice-Hall, 1983), 21-23, 115-117.
7. Rochelle L. Stanfield, "Lights Out in the Year 2000?—It Depends on Whose Forecast You Believe," *National Journal*, April 14, 1984, 710.
8. Conservation Foundation, *State of the Environment 1982* (Washington, D.C.: Conservation Foundation, 1983), 402.
9. Robert Stobaugh and Daniel Yergin, eds., *Energy Future*, 3d ed. (New York: Vintage Books, 1983), 288.
10. Ibid., 173.
11. These estimates, probably very conservative, are quoted in U.S. General Accounting Office, "Nuclear Power Costs and Subsidies," Report No. EMD-79-52 (June 12, 1979). The history of nuclear power development is carefully traced in Steven L. Del Sesto, *Science, Politics and Controversy* (Boulder, Colo.: Westview Press, 1979).
12. Peter Metzger, *The Atomic Establishment* (New York: Simon and Schuster, 1972), 20.
13. Irvin C. Bupp and Jean-Claude Derian, *The Failed Promise of Nuclear Power* (New York: Basic Books, 1978), chapter 5.

14. Congressional Quarterly, *Energy Policy*, 2d ed. (Washington, D.C.: Congressional Quarterly, 1981), 80.
15. *New York Times*, March 8, 1981.
16. *New York Times*, October 1, 2, 3, 1981.
17. *New York Times*, November 21, 1981.
18. *New York Times*, June 14, 1981.
19. Mark Schulman, "The Impact of Three Mile Island," *Public Opinion*, June/July 1979, 7.
20. *Gainesville Sun*, November 24, 1981.
21. On the history of the Rassmussen Report, see Nuclear Regulatory Commission, *Statement on Risk Assessment and the Reactor Safety Study Report (WASH 1400)* (Washington, D.C.: Government Printing Office, 1979); and Daniel F. Ford, *A History of Federal Nuclear Safety Assessment: From WASH 740 through the Reactor Safety Study* (Cambridge, Mass.: Union of Concerned Scientists, 1977).
22. U.S. General Accounting Office, "Is Spent Fuel or Waste from Reprocessed Spent Fuel Simpler to Dispose Of?" Report No. EMD-81-78 (June 12, 1981), iii-iv.
23. The history of these controversies is traced in Walter A. Rosenbaum, "Nuclear Waste and Federalism," in *Public Lands and Natural Resources in an Age of Changing Federalism*, ed. John Francis and Richard Ganzel (New York: Greenwood Press, 1984).
24. *New York Times*, October 16, 1983.
25. *New York Times*, December 12, 1981.
26. *New York Times*, November 11, 1980.
27. On the benefits of coal development generally, see Walter A. Rosenbaum, *Coal and Crisis* (New York: Praeger Publishers, 1978), chapter 2.
28. Public Law 91-57. On the regulatory problems associated with the law, see U.S. Congress, Office of Technology Assessment, *The Direct Use of Coal* (Washington, D.C.: Government Printing Office, 1978), chapters 5 and 7.
29. These and other changes in the program are summarized in the Conservation Foundation, *State of the Environment 1982*, 403-410. Estimates of the number of regulations rewritten are found in *New York Times*, November 5, 1983.
30. The issues are summarized usefully in Paul J. Culhane, "Sagebrush Rebels in Office: Jim Watt's Land and Water Policies," in *Environmental Policy in the 1980s*, ed. Norman J. Vig and Michael E. Kraft (Washington, D.C.: CQ Press, 1984), 293-318.

What I want to speak for is ... the wilderness idea. ... Being an intangible and spiritual resource, it will seem mystical to the practical-minded—but then anything that cannot be moved by a bulldozer is likely to seem mystical to them.

—Wallace Stegner

These are magnificent mountains. ... But how is a mining company operating a pit on the other side of this ridge going to hurt all this? ... We just have to have copper.

—A mining engineer discussing copper reserves in Glacier Peak Wilderness.[1]

Our 700 Million Acres: The Battle for the Public Lands

In 1976, the bicentennial year of the Republic, the government of the United States officially ended after almost two centuries its policy of conveying the public lands to private control. During that time more than 1.1 billion acres of land, an expanse larger than western Europe, had been surrendered to the states, to farmers and trappers, railroads, veterans, loggers and miners, canal builders—to any interest with the political strength to make a persuasive claim on the public lands to Congress. It was the American land, whose abundance of natural resources constituted one of the greatest geographic inheritances of any civilization, that shaped American character more decisively than any other aspect of the nation's environment. Though vastly reduced, the public domain remains an enormous physical expanse embracing within its continental sprawl, often accidentally, some of the nation's most economically and ecologically significant resources, a biological and physical reserve still largely unexploited. The struggle to determine how this last great legacy shall be used constitutes, in large part, the substance of the political struggle over the public lands.

Once most of the land was public domain. Over the last two centuries the federal government has owned almost four of every five acres on the continental United States. This land, held in trust for the people of the nation, is governed by Congress, in whom the Constitution vests the power "to dispose and make all needful Rules and Regulations respecting the Territory or other Property belonging to the United States." [2] Until the turn of this century, Congress had been concerned primarily to divest itself rapidly of the lands, turning them over to the states or to private interests in huge grants at bargain-basement prices. Only belatedly did Congress, powerfully pressured by the new American conservation movement, awaken to the necessity of preserving the remaining natural resources on the public domain before they were wholly lost. By this time most of the remaining public lands lay west of the Mississippi River; much was wilderness too remote and inaccessible to be easily exploited or grasslands and rangelands seemingly devoid of economic attraction.

The Public Domain

Today the federal government owns approximately 715 million acres of land, about a third of the total U.S. land area. Many western states are largely public domain: more than half of Alaska, Nevada, Idaho, Oregon, Utah, and Wyoming are federally owned; the public lands constitute more than a third of Arizona, California, Colorado, and New Mexico. Much of this land, originally ceded to the western states when they joined the Union, was rejected as useless for timbering, grazing, or farming; some was held in trust for Indian tribes by the federal government. Only later, well into this century, did exploration reveal that vast energy and mineral resources might reside under the tribal reservations, wilderness, timber, and grasslands remaining in the public domain. The economic value of the public lands was increased greatly by a 1953 Supreme Court ruling vesting control of 1.1 billion acres of submerged Outer Continental Shelf (OCS) land, an area generally beginning three miles off the U.S. coast, in the federal government. Thus by accident and design that third of the nation, together with its spacious offshore lands, now controlled by Washington has become a public trust of potentially huge economic value.

An Unanticipated Bounty

The actual magnitude of mineral, timber, and energy reserves on the public domain remains uncertain, for many areas, including much of the gigantic Alaskan wilderness, have yet to be explored. Estimates of resources on more accessible lands also can be controversial. However, commonly cited figures suggest the reasons why the public lands have assumed such importance to major economic interests in the United States:

Perhaps one third of the nation's remaining oil and gas reserves, 40 percent of its coal reserves, and 80 percent of its shale oil may be on public domain.

About 60 percent of low-sulfur U.S. coal resides on federal lands west of the Mississippi River.

About 56 percent of undiscovered U.S. petroleum reserves and 47 percent of natural gas reserves may be found on federal OCS lands.

Nearly a third of the nation's forests remain untimbered on federal wilderness land or national forest areas.[3]

Beyond those resources upon which a price can be placed, the public domain contains both incalculable natural treasures whose worth has become evident to generations—Yosemite, Yellowstone, Grand Canyon, and the other national parks—and nameless wild and free places, the wilderness that the naturalist Aldo Leopold has called "the raw material out of which man has hammered the artifact called civilization" and to which, he reminds us, we need often return, in fact and imagination, as to a sanctuary.[4] Indeed, much of what remains undisturbed on the American earth, still available to this generation in something like its original condition, can be found on this continent only in federal wilderness areas. Whether wilderness is or should be a thing beyond price and beyond exploitation remains among the most bitterly controversial of all environmental issues.

Diversity Within the Public Domain

The public domain has been divided by Congress into different units committed to different uses and administered by different executive agencies. The most important of these uses are the following:

U.S. National Wilderness Preservation System: Created by Congress in 1964, the National Wilderness Preservation System currently includes 79.8 million acres of land, including more than 50 million acres of Alaskan wilderness added in 1979. By legislative mandate wilderness lands are to be set aside forever as undeveloped areas.

National Park System: Begun more than a century ago with the creation of Yellowstone National Park, the system currently constitutes 37 parks and 257 national monuments, historic sites, recreational areas, near-wilderness, seashores, and lakeshores, altogether embracing more than 77 million acres. Closed to mining, timbering, grazing, and most other economic uses, the system is to be available to the public for recreational purposes.

National Wildlife Refuge System: The system currently includes almost 89 million acres, two-thirds in Alaska but distributed among all 50 states. The 413 refuges are to provide habitat to migratory waterfowl and mammals, fish and waterfowl hatcheries, research stations, and related facilities.

National Forests: Since 1897 Congress has reserved large forested areas of the public domain and has authorized the purchase of additional timberlands to create a forest reserve, to furnish continuous timber supplies for the nation, and to protect mountain watersheds. Forestlands are to be managed by a "multiple-use" formula that requires a balance of recreation, timber, grazing, and conservation activities. Currently exceeding 190 million acres, national forests are found principally in the Far West, the Southeast, and Alaska.

National Rangelands: The largest portion of the public domain, located primarily in the West and Alaska, is made up of grassland and prairieland, desert, scrub forest, and other open space collectively known as "rangelands." Although often barren, a substantial portion of the 328 million acres of rangeland is suitable for grazing; permits are issued to ranchers for this purpose by federal agencies.[5]

Such a classification implies an orderly definition of the uses for the public domain and a supporting political consensus, which do not exist. Behind the facade of congressionally assigned uses stretches a political terrain strewn with conflicts of historic proportions over which lands shall be placed in different categories, which uses shall prevail among competing demands on the land, how much economic exploitation should be permitted in the public domain, and how large the public domain should be. A major source of these conflicts is the congressionally mandated doctrine of multiple use, or balanced use, for much of the public domain. In this chapter we shall examine the ecological and political context in which multiple-use conflicts arise and the participants drawn into the struggles. These conflicts characteristically pit federal resource management agencies, state and local governments, commodity producers and users, and environmentalists against each other over issues that long predate the modern Environmental Era.

Multiple-Use Conflicts

Disputes over multiple use of the public domain customarily evolve in roughly similar political settings. Conflict focuses upon land administered by one of the federal resource agencies, usually the Interior Department's Bureau of Land Management (BLM) or the Agriculture Department's U.S. Forest Service, charged with the stewardship of millions of acres of the public domain under a multiple-use mandate. Struggling to interpret an ambiguous congressional mandate for land management, the agency will commonly find among the parties in conflict over its interpretation of multiple use the states within whose jurisdictions the land resides, the various private economic interests with a stake in the decision, congressional committees with jurisdiction over the agency's programs, and perhaps the White House. Especially within the last two decades, environmental interests have been important and predictable participants. Sometimes the issues are resolved—that is, if they are resolved—only by congressional reformulation of land-use policy.

The Land-Use Agencies

Management of the public domain is vested principally in four federal agencies whose collective jurisdiction, more than a million square miles, exceeds the size of Mexico. As Table 8-1 indicates, the Forest Service, the National Park Service, the BLM, and the Fish and Wildlife Service control about 90 percent of all the land currently in the public domain. The Forest Service and the BLM control by far the largest portion of this collective jurisdiction. Unlike the National Park Service and the Fish and Wildlife Service, Congress requires that the BLM and the Forest Service administer their huge public trusts under the doctrine of multiple use. The two agencies come to this task with strikingly different political histories and territorial responsibilities.

The Forest Service. Created as part of the Agriculture Department in 1905, the service is one of the proudest and most enduring monuments to America's first great conservation movement. Founded by Gifford Pinchot, one of the nation's greatest conservationists, the service has a long and distinguished history of forest management. Widely recognized and publicly respected, the service has been adept at cultivating a favorable public image—who is not familiar with Smokey the Bear and other service symbols of forest preservation?—and vigorous congressional support. The service's jurisdiction includes most of the land, including some grasslands, within the U.S. Forest System. With more than 30,000 employees and a budget exceeding $1.5 billion, the Forest Service historically has possessed a strong sense of mission and high professional standards. "While the Forest Service has frequently been at the center of political maelstroms," writes political scientist Paul Culhane, "it has also been regarded as one of the most professional, best managed agencies in the federal government." [6] Operating through a highly decentralized system of forest administration, local forest rangers are vested with great discretion in interpreting how multiple-use principles will apply to specific forests within their jurisdiction.

The Bureau of Land Management. The BLM manages more than 300 million acres of public domain and leases another 200 million acres in national forests and private lands but remains obscure outside the West. The bureau has struggled to establish standards of professionalism and conservation that would free it from its own long history of indifference to conservation values and from unflattering comparisons with the Forest Service.

The BLM was created in 1946 when President Harry S Truman combined Interior's old Grazing Service and General Land Office to form the new bureau with the largest land jurisdiction of any federal agency. Starting with responsibility for managing federal grasslands and grazing lands, the bureau gradually added to its jurisdiction other lands with mineral resources and, more recently, 78 million acres of Alaskan lands, including many large wilderness areas. The BLM thus has inherited a great diversity of lands with different dominant uses: the Alaskan wilderness, more than 2.5 million acres of prime Douglas timber in western Oregon, 146.9 million acres of grazing lands. BLM also is responsible for arranging the leases for mineral exploration on all public domain and the OCS.

Lacking the prestige of the Forest Service and burdened with a long history of deference to the ranching and mining interests who form a major portion of its constituency, the BLM has struggled to create greater professionalism, more sensitivity to conservation, and more aggressive enforcement of land-use regulations within its jurisdiction. Throughout its history it also has suffered chronic understaffing and underfunding—its budget and staff are less than a third of the Forest Service's despite its greater jurisdiction. And the BLM has never enjoyed the relative insulation from top departmental management that the Forest Service has experienced. This, to many environmentalists, is one of its chronic problems. According to resource expert James Baker, "The multiple-use concept suffers at the BLM because management decisions are influenced by top policy personnel appointed by the administration in power, who inherently focus on one single use, such as mining, and ignore or give short shrift to such other legitimate uses as wildlife and recreation." [7]

These agencies work in a political milieu whose character is shaped by the ambiguous, and sometimes inconsistent, requirements of multiple-use land management; by pressures from the private interests seeking

Table 8-1 Federal Ownership of U.S. Land: by Agency, 1980

Agency	Acres
Department of Agriculture	190,630,798
Forest Service	*190,228,321*
Department of Commerce	55,971
National Oceanic and Atmospheric Administration	*51,381*
Department of Defense	30,327,218
Air Force	*8,276,237*
Army	*10,657,875*
Corps of Engineers	*8,234,484*
Navy	*3,158,622*
Department of Energy	1,575,135
Environmental Protection Agency	274
Federal Communications Commission	2,573
General Services Administration	15,549
Department of Health and Human Services	4,314
Department of Housing and Urban Development	267
Department of the Interior	491,351,124
Fish and Wildlife Service	*84,732,313*
Geological Survey	*1,696*
Bureau of Indian Affairs	*780,987*
Bureau of Land Management	*328,665,859*
Bureau of Mines	*13,058*
National Park Service	*70,541,366*
Water and Power Resources Service	*6,615,818*
Department of Justice	30,016
Department of Labor	4,632
National Aeronautics and Space Administration	133,892
National Science Foundation	3,574
U.S. Postal Service	6,199
Department of State	120,483
Tennessee Valley Authority	988,872
Department of Transportation	188,782
Federal Aviation Administration	*58,837*
Federal Railroad Administration	*38,008*
U.S. Coast Guard	*88,945*
Treasury Department	2,475
Veterans Administration	25,394
Other Federal agencies	9,993
Total Federal	715,477,535

Includes changes due to the Alaska National Interests Lands Conservation Act.

Source: Council on Environmental Quality, *Environmental Quality 1980* (Washington, D.C.: Government Printing Office, 1981), 216.

access to resources on land within agency jurisdictions; by conflicts with environmentalists over the appropriate balance between environmental protection and resource use—both of which the agencies are expected to promote; by frequent conflicts between the president and Congress over their respective authority over the agencies; and by state governments, particularly in the West, determined to press upon the agencies, Congress, and the White House the states' claims for preference in policy making. All these conflicts were exacerbated in the 1980s by the White House's determination to force major changes in existing understandings about such issues.

An Ambiguous Mandate

In carrying out their assigned tasks, managers in these agencies often must walk an administrative tightrope fashioned from the inconsistencies and vagaries of their legislatively defined missions. Three different federal statutes charge the BLM and Forest Service to administer the lands in their trust by multiple-use principles. The most elaborate definition of the doctrine, ripe with the ambiguities that create so many problems in its implementation, is found in section 531 of the Multiple Use-Sustained Yield Act (1960):

> 'Multiple use' means: the management of all the various renewable surface resources of the national forest so that they are utilized in the combination that will best meet the needs of the American people; making the most judicious use of the land for some or all of these resources or related services over areas large enough to provide sufficient latitude for periodic adjustments in use to conform to changing needs and conditions; that some land will be used for less than all of the resources; and harmonious and coordinated management of the various resources, each with the other, without impairment of the productivity of the land, with consideration being given to the relative values of the various resources, and not necessarily the combination of uses that will give the greatest dollar return or the greatest unit output.[8]

The intent of this complicated mandate is to make sure that in land management "any use should be carried out to minimize interference with other uses of the same area and, if possible, to complement those other uses."[9] But it provides to agency managers scant information concerning how these differing values are to be defined and balanced when differing claims upon land use must be resolved. Since almost 60 percent of all public lands are held by federal agencies under some form of multiple-use law, such problems are commonplace and conflict over their resolution predictable. The BLM, for instance, has wrestled for years with managing desert areas east and north of Los Angeles to the satisfaction of both conservationists and racing enthusiasts. Each year the BLM processes more than 100 applications for motorcycle races, some annual events with as many as 3,000 competitors. Conservationists have argued that the races permanently scar the land, alter the native ecological balances, and create noise and other disruptions for other recreationists.[10] In trying to reduce the impact of such racing, the BLM must determine the proper balance between recreation and conservation values in terms of these specific desert lands; any decision becomes controversial.

The agencies frequently discover that multiple use also leads to a conflicting mandate. The Forest Service is expected to protect the national forests from excessive timbering but at the same time to assist state and private forest owners in obtaining access to federal forests. Wildlife refuges are supposed to protect and preserve the ecologically viable habitation for endangered species but also to provide grazing, hunting, and perhaps mining opportunities to private interests. And so forth.

But the multiple-use doctrine also gives both agencies, and particularly the local resource managers who must often translate the doctrine into operational terms, a means of managing the conflicting interest pressures upon the land. Multiple use requires a balancing of uses, and concern for a variety of claims upon the land, without ensuring any one dominance—a formula that leaves resource managers with the opportunity to balance and negotiate among interests claiming use of public resources. It also promises constant pressure upon the agencies to create or alter interpretations of multiple use by whatever interests feel existing interpretations discriminate against their claims upon the land.

State and Regional Interests

State governments, particularly in the West, historically have been deeply concerned with federal land-use policies and for more than a century have pressed Washington for greater control over public lands within their boundaries. Since the public domain constitutes so large a portion of many western states, decisions made in Washington affecting land use can have an enormous economic, political, and social impact upon the western governments. The states have a direct economic stake in multiple-use management. Approximately 20 percent of Forest Service receipts for timber sales are returned to local governments in lieu of property taxes on federal lands. More than a third of the BLM's annual receipts for mining royalties and other uses of its land also is returned to the states. There are also large political concerns. Generally, the western states have long believed that they have been denied a properly important voice in decisions affecting their lands; they often perceive themselves to be governed by a remote and unresponsive bureaucracy insensitive to their special concerns. In particular, the western states want a larger voice in determining grazing rights, in setting conditions for mineral exploration, in establishing timbering quotas, and in deciding how revenues from resource use on the public domain will be allocated. Many states, such as Utah, have insisted that the federal government ought to divest itself of much land within the state borders, turning the land and all its resources over to the states. By the 1980s the western determination to assert greater state and regional control over federal lands had assumed a political identity as the "Sagebrush Rebellion" for which the Reagan administration, with deep western political roots, professed considerable support.

Conflict between Washington and the states over land use has been exacerbated by the Energy Crisis. Even before the 1973 oil embargo, the states had fought bitterly and unsuccessfully with Washington to control the energy resources immediately off their shores in the OCS. By the late 1970s many western political leaders shared Colorado governor Richard D. Lamm's "growing feeling of regional paranoia" because they suspected the western lands might be reduced to an "energy colony" through exploitation by the more populous, politically powerful, and energy-hungry states in the Northeast and Sun Belt. Animating this fear is a realization that conditions for coal, oil, and natural gas exploration in the West are largely determined in Washington. At the same time, western states want to know that they will receive a substantial royalty for any mineral resources extracted from federal lands within their jurisdiction. In the opinion of many northeastern states, the royalties have become too substantial. These states, as major consumers of western coal, have complained of excessive severance taxes. By the mid-1980s the severance taxes going to western states for coal and other energy resources will exceed $9 billion annually; to one spokesman for northeastern and midwestern states, the western energy states were becoming "a United Arab Emirates of Western states which will have all the resources." So long as the federal government continues to push aggressively for greater energy exploration and production on the public lands, the states will continue to press with equal determination for greater influence, if not control, over decisions about such activities within their own borders.[11]

State and regional interests, in short, constitute one of the organizational givens in the policy arena where federal land-use decisions are fashioned. They represent the continual problem of reconciling national land-use needs and policies with local considerations, of balancing one set of public interests against another.

Private Resource Users

Interests using resources on the public domain, or ambitious to be among the elect, are important participants in the process of making public land-use policy. Each of the major federal land-use agencies has its "clientele," that coalition of organized groups with a major economic or ideological stake in the agency's programs. Generally, resource users want to expand their access to resources on the public domain, to use the resource as cheaply as possible, to protect the continuing availability of renewable resources, and to maintain or enhance their influence within the agencies making decisions about resources strategic to them. Thus, ranchers, sheepmen, and cattlemen customarily participate actively in the political struggles over BLM rangeland regulations; individual timber companies, such as Weyerhaeuser and Crown Zellerbach, and timber trade associations, such as the National Forest Products Association, are involved in Forest Service determinations about allowable timber harvests; Peabody Coal and Climax Coal, two of the largest coal-mining companies, will be found with the spokesmen for the National Coal Association actively attempting to influence the BLM or the Fish and Wildlife Service in writing regulations for coal leasing on land within their agency jurisdictions.

This intimate and historic involvement of clientele in land agency politics often has been criticized sharply, first by the earlier conservation movement and currently by environmentalists. Critics have asserted that agencies are easily "captured" by the clientele, who then promote resource exploitation at the sacrifice of balanced use and, particularly, with little regard for environmental values. Often environmental and conservation groups constitute practically the only politically active and effective force for balanced use within the private pressure group system. Conservationists once dismissed the BLM as the "Bureau of Livestock and

Mining"; environmentalists routinely have sued the BLM in the 1980s for allegedly failing to enforce surface mining regulations on coal lessees in New Mexico and Wyoming. The Forest Service's exemplary reputation has been no shield from accusations that it sanctions "clear cutting" and other timber practices abhorrent to environmentalists because the service allegedly has come to define its mission largely as timber production in response to commercial timber company demands. Agency administrators, however, often have a legislative mandate to promote resource use within their jurisdictions, and consequently some community of interest with resource users is inevitable. And, as we have often observed, the right of access by affected private groups to those administrators making decisions affecting such groups is regarded as fundamental principle in American politics. Thus, both tradition and law make the continued involvement of resource users in agency decisions inevitable and their self-interested pressures upon the agency a continual threat to the concept of balanced use.

Congress and the Public Domain

Congress ultimately decides how the public domain shall be used. Although it cautiously shares some of this authority with the president, Congress traditionally has been a jealous and vigilant guardian of its prerogatives to decide finally how the states, federal land management agencies, private resource users, and others shall use the lands it holds in trust for the people of the United States. This authority flows from Article IV of the Constitution and from numerous Supreme Court decisions affirming the primacy of legislative authority in determining the character of the federal lands. Recent Supreme Court decisions have compelled Congress to share with the president the power to withdraw public lands from private use, but Congress has been quick to challenge presidents and their executive agencies when it felt they were usurping a legislative prerogative in land management.

As in other policy areas, congressional control over the public domain is exercised through the committees and subcommittees in each chamber with jurisdiction over federal land management agencies. However, while Congress vigorously defends its authority to define agency programs, it has also left the agencies with enormous discretion, as we have seen, in deciding how lands within their jurisdictions will be used; the many multiple-use laws enacted in the last several decades leave to local land managers great latitude in establishing the character of specific land uses. These agencies, as a result, operate in a politically risky milieu, where discretion is always subject to congressional challenge. When the presidency and Congress are controlled by the same party, conflicts between the two branches over agency decisions are seldom prolonged or serious. But the situation becomes ripe for conflict when differing parties control the White House and one, or both, congressional chambers. Then agency managers, exercising what they believe to be their discretionary authority on behalf of the president's program, may find themselves and their agency under congressional attack. Many of the most publicized conflicts over the Reagan administration's land-use policies erupted as battles between the secretary of the interior and Democratic-controlled House committees with jurisdiction over the department's land programs. Feeding the conflict were partisan disagreement over which programs the department should implement and traditional disputes over the limits of executive discretion.

In the last several decades Congress has demonstrated an increasing concern for environmental values by enacting legislation requiring federal land management agencies to give conservation greater importance in land-use decisions. The Wilderness Act of 1964, an early manifestation of this growing ecological sensibility, designated by statute for the first time more than 9 million acres of public lands as wilderness and provided for additional future designations. Later, the National Environmental Policy Act of 1970 (NEPA) required federal land management agencies, among many other executive agencies, to create Environmental Impact Statements (EISs) in which the environmental consequences of land-use decisions had to be identified and considered in decisions affecting the public domain. Several major multiple-use laws passed in the 1970s, to be examined later, explicitly required the relevant federal agencies to incorporate ecological protection among the uses to be protected on the affected public domain. This concern for environmental value demonstrated in good part the rising political strength of environmental groups in the legislative process. Congress, particularly the House of Representatives, came to be the principal institutional bastion within the federal government from which environmentalists mounted their attack on President Ronald Reagan's land-use policies at Interior.

The Environmental Movement and the Public Lands

Environmentalists always have given the management of public lands a high priority. Both the National Park Service and the Forest

Service were created at the turn of the century in response to vigorous promotion by the great American conservation movement, the ideological and political predecessor of the existing environmental movement. Historic legal and political battles had been waged by the Sierra Club, the Audubon Society, and other environmental groups against ecologically reckless projects promoted by federal water resource agencies long before the Environmental Era was named. In the 1970s environmentalists achieved a number of legislative and judicial victories that vastly expanded their influence in federal land management activities and compelled even the ecologically primitive BLM to develop, at least fitfully, an environmental conscience.

Among the most important of these achievements was passage of NEPA. As defined by the Council on Environmental Quality (CEQ), which is responsible for its implementation, NEPA required that EISs be prepared by federal land management agencies for major land-use decisions affecting the environment—in effect, for most major land management planning. Draft statements had to be circulated for public review and comment prior to completion; agency officials were obligated to give the statements careful consideration in all relevant decisions.

In practical terms, the EISs became an early warning system for environmental groups, alerting them to the implications of numerous agency policies whose importance might otherwise have been ignored. Environmentalists thus had opportunity to organize a political strategy for influencing land management decisions. Further, the statements often forced agencies, such as the BLM, to give greater attention to the ecological impacts of their management practices. Not least important, the EIS was a legally enforceable procedure; environmental groups skillfully exploited many opportunities to use the federal courts to delay or frustrate agency decisions they opposed by challenging the adequacy of impact statements.

Federal courts, often with the explicit approval of Congress, greatly expanded the environmentalists' "standing to sue" federal agencies for alleged failures to give environmental values sufficient attention in land-use planning. This greatly liberalized standing often enabled environmental interests to compel federal agencies to give them a voice in agency proceedings. Critics charged, sometimes justifiably, that environmentalists were seizing upon these new strategies primarily to disrupt administrative procedures and thereby to harass their opponents even when their case lacked merit. But the environmental activities inspired by enlarged standing, as well as the impact statement procedures, quite often resulted in valuable ecological improvements in federal land management and greater federal attention to the balanced use of land, to which many agency managers had previously given little more than lip service.

Finally, congressional attempts to encourage greater public involvement in the making of land management decisions by the Forest Service, Park Service, and BLM also provided environmentalists with effective strategies for influencing federal policies, particularly at the local level where so many land-use decisions were made. Indeed, environmental groups have perceived correctly that generous provision for public involvement in federal land-use planning has been among the most effective structural means of giving them access and influence in the administrative process generally. For this reason, they have been acutely concerned about the enforcement of these participation provisions in federal land law and convinced that any attempts to narrow such opportunities, by law or administrative manipulation, were covert attacks upon their political base.

The many institutional interests, organized groups, agency programs, and conflicting philosophies of land use involved in managing the public domain mean that conflict and disagreement over policy are inevitable. The 1980s have been characterized by unusually open and bitter conflict over management of the public domain triggered by the Reagan administration's vigorous attempts to change land policies in a manner that angered and alarmed conservationist and environmental groups across the nation. At issue were fiercely held and strongly felt convictions on both sides.

Energy and Public Lands

The Reagan administration began the 1980s with a determination to open the public lands to energy and mineral exploration and to transfer tracts of the public lands to state and private control on a scale unmatched by any other administration in this century. The responsibility for achieving these ambitious objectives was largely vested in James G. Watt, the administration's secretary of the interior, whose agency controlled the largest portion of the public domain. The administration's aggressive and unapologetic determination to turn much of the public land and its resources over to private use was based on a conviction that too many resources, particularly coal, gas, and petroleum, had been locked up on the public domain. "I want to open as much land as I can," Watt remarked in explaining a philosophy that would prevail long after he left the department. "The basic difference between this Administration and liberals is that we are market-oriented, people-oriented. We are trying to bring our abundant acres into the market so that the market will decide their value."

The Reagan Land Program

What opening up the public lands meant to the Reagan administration became evident between 1981 and 1983 in a series of proposals to alter profoundly the character of vast tracts within the public domain. Among the most disturbing to environmentalists were:

> The Interior Department's proposed leasing of exploration rights to more than 11 billion tons of coal on federal rangeland, timberland, and wilderness areas in New Mexico, southwest Utah, Montana, and North Dakota. This plan, opening more coal to exploration than Washington had done in the previous decade, would affect several hundred thousand acres of previously undeveloped open land.

> The department's proposal to open for gas and petroleum exploration by 1987 about 1 billion acres of the OCS, virtually all the offshore lands within federal jurisdiction, including 41 lease sales—16 off the Alaskan coast—that would likely result in exploration before the end of 1984.

> A plan to sell to state and private bidders 35 million acres of public land, an area roughly equal in size to Iowa. This property, including abandoned military bases, urban land and parks, and a great diversity of other tracts not included within any of the major federal land-use programs, would have amounted to the largest transfer of public lands to private control in the century. The Reagan administration anticipated receiving $1.3 billion from sales the first year and then $4 billion annually for an indefinite period.

> A proposal to permit the Forest Service to open wilderness areas within the national forests to mineral and energy exploration before 1984, when such lands had to be placed beyond exploration in the U.S. Wilderness System.[12]

The scale of these proposals appalled environmentalists; so did the administration's untroubled conviction that resource use, especially energy production, should have a higher priority than any other value on most federal land, including many wilderness areas.

The Department in the Middle

The Interior Department was inevitably the focus of controversy over energy exploration on the public domain. More than 200 billion tons of coal, perhaps a fourth of the nation's coal reserves, lie below western lands under the department's jurisdiction. Since passage of the Mineral Leasing Act of 1920, the interior secretary has had the discretionary authority to sell leases and to establish conditions for private mineral and energy exploration on the public lands. Such leases, to be sold at "fair market value," must be "diligently developed" into mining operations within a decade; both federal and state governments charge royalties for coal production within their boundaries. Until the 1980s, however, the department promoted coal and other resource exploration on its lands rather indifferently, and during the 1970s leasing was virtually suspended while the department, Congress, and the White House struggled to fashion a comprehensive leasing program. One finally emerged in the late 1970s but soon was challenged by the Reagan administration's new coal programs.

The change in coal leasing philosophy under the Reagan administration was immediate and dramatic. In 1981 alone, Interior leased more than 400 times the acreage for coal exploration than it had the previous year. Proponents of a greatly accelerated leasing program asserted that the nation needed the energy resources lying unused on the public domain, that federal regulations could protect the lands from the ravages of surface mining, and that the economic productivity created by private use of the energy resources would generate more jobs and greater prosperity. Many of the department's political leadership would have said a hearty, if perhaps private, "amen" to the summary conclusion on the subject by the president of the American Mining Congress: "Our society is built on the stuff that comes out of the hole in the ground and if we don't unplug the red tape stuffing the hole, this country is going to be in one hell of a mess." [13]

The department's announced intentions to accelerate the sale of leases for oil and gas exploration on the OCS and its interest in leasing when legally possible even wilderness areas for exploration convinced environmental groups and congressional opponents of the Reagan programs that a massive public campaign to counteract the new policies was imperative. Congress became the institutional weapon.

The Congressional-Environmental Connection

"The probability of our developing any meaningful dialogue with this Administration is low indeed," lamented Russell Peterson, the politically seasoned president of the National Audubon Society, after talking with White House officials less than a year after the president's inauguration. Most environmentalists agreed.[14] Environmental interests, turning to Congress as the institutional check upon the president's land programs, were able to exploit constitutional and partisan rivalries to advantage. Constitutional checks and balances became one lever with which to move the executive branch, for the issue quickened again the institutional rivalries at the heart of the constitutional system. The White House programs aroused among many legislators, particularly in the House and Senate committees with oversight of Interior's programs, a conviction that the department, with White House encouragement, was abusing its delegated authority and subverting the legislative intent of Congress in its handling of the new energy leasing programs. Especially in the House, Democrats on the oversight committees sought opportunities to challenge and embarrass the White House through attack on the land programs.

In the battle over land policy, the House Interior Committee became the most aggressive congressional opponent of the White House. The committee's attack upon the new leasing programs generally was based on the assertion that the interior secretary lacked authority to initiate these new leases without congressional approval or consultation and, more generally, that the secretary's delegated authority in law had been interpreted too broadly. Rather than create a legal and political confrontation over their respective powers, the secretary often agreed, with much protestation, to consult more closely with the committee—in effect, to back down on some of his announced lease promotions. In this manner, the Interior Committee was able to prevent oil and gas leasing in BLM wilderness areas in Montana, New Mexico, and California. The proposal to permit oil and gas exploration in Los Padres National Forest, including parts of California's starkly beautiful Big Sur coastland, stirred California's whole congressional delegation into a rare show of unanimity. Committees in both chambers were also able to put off reorganization plans for Interior's Office of Surface Mining, which congressional critics believed were intended to weaken surface mine regulation.

Congressional opposition to Reagan's public land programs generally was most effective when the administration had to draw upon discretionary authority clouded by ambiguity and unbuttressed by tradition. Effective opposition also required that Congress and environmentalists be able to perceive when administrative actions by the department or the White House amounted to major land-use decisions—administrative language manipulated by skilled practitioners can shroud the intent of an act in a fog of obscurity. Such circumstances did not always prevail; many land-use policies were implemented, as we shall shortly note, in spite of the congressional-environmental nexus.

State and Regional Opposition

Despite Sagebrush Rebellion rhetoric, the states are often guilty of doublethink about resources on the public domain, as the controversy over land policy in the 1980s illustrates. Anxious to reap the economic advantages of greater resource use on lands within their domain—more royalties, more severance taxes, greater industrial development, and the like—the states are equally determined not to pay calamitous ecological and economic costs for rapid resource exploitation. Washington's new public land policies often aroused not enthusiasm but hostility among the western states. They wanted resource development *and* environmental protection.

Conflict between the federal government and the states was focused most sharply on Washington's proposal for accelerated leasing of exploration rights to oil and gas on the OCS. In 1978 Congress had passed the Outer Continental Shelf Amendments to increase greatly the environmental safeguards required for OCS exploration; to this end, extensive federal consultation with the states was required prior to any lease sales off their shores. Washington's announced intention to sell 32 oil lease tracts off the central California coast sent California to the federal courts seeking an injunction to prevent the leasing; citing federal failure to consult with the state under terms of the 1978 legislation, the court issued the injunction and the Interior Department subsequently withdrew most of the disputed tracts from auction.

Responding to pressure from California state officials, including the new Republican governor, most environmental groups, and most of the state's congressional delegation, Congress in 1982 and 1983 further restricted lease sales off the northern and central California coast by denying appropriations to implement the leasing. In 1984 Congress further banned leasing in several OCS basins off Florida and Massachusetts. Thus, the OCS states had succeeded in substantially reducing, at least temporarily, the scope of offshore energy exploration through a combination of legal and political strategies. Environmentalists, however, were uneasy about the future, for substantial OCS leasing was still permitted, and the administration seemed determined to press ahead on its OCS development plans whenever it was not massively challenged.

The Continuing Conflict

Watt's resignation as interior secretary in October 1983 did not end the conflict over land policies initiated by the Reagan administration, nor did it diminish the administration's determination to open up the public domain to further energy exploration.

Through the use of existing budgetary authority, established discretionary freedom, and "a thousand small changes," the secretary had managed in the face of formidable opposition to move federal policy strongly toward more resource development on public lands. Interior had accelerated the sale of leasing rights on OCS lands, including the largest leasing sale in history: 78 energy companies had bid $3.5 billion to explore about 3.2 million acres of OCS territory off the Louisiana and Alabama coasts. The BLM had issued more than 38,000 leases, covering about 95 million acres, for energy exploration on its territory—about twice the total of the Carter administration. Interior's Office of Surface Mining Reclamation and Enforcement had been severely depleted of personnel and much of its regulatory responsibility entrusted to the uncertain will and capacity of the states to implement. The BLM had succeeded in opening more than 400,000 acres of recreational areas for mineral exploration, mining, and drilling, including Glen Canyon (Utah) and Lake Meade (Nevada and Arizona). While Watt's successor, William P. Clark, created less public stir than his predecessor, new leaders of the department were likely to pursue the same objectives in land policy as long as the Reagan administration remained in office.

Pressure to develop resources on the public domain persists. In 1984 more than 1,000 applications for oil and gas exploration rights in wilderness areas and perhaps 50,000 other kinds of mineral claims on wilderness remain pending. The pressure is not confined to energy and minerals, as the national forests have become another arena in which the resource struggle persists.

The Fate of the Forests

More than one in every ten acres on the public domain could be used for commercial timber production. This land, about 89 million acres, lies mostly within the jurisdiction of the Agriculture Department's Forest

Service. Since the end of World War II, pressure has been unremitting on the Forest Service to increase the size of the annual timber harvest from national forests to satisfy the nation's growing demand for wood products. Recently, there has been increased pressure to open many undisturbed "old-growth" timber stands and wilderness areas to commercial logging. Against this economic pressure, the Forest Service is required not only to enforce the doctrine of multiple use, which forbids the service from allowing timber cutting to preclude other forest uses, but it also must manage timber cutting to ensure a "sustained yield" from any forest reserve used for commercial timbering. Congress has left to the service the difficult and politically contentious responsibility for defining how much timber cutting is compatible with multiple use and sustained yield.

The struggle over competing timber uses is fought in the arcane language of forest economics—"non-declining, even-flow" formulas, "allowable cuts," and "allowable-cut effects"—but the larger interests and issues at stake are apparent. The struggle represents a collision between preservationist and developmental priorities for timber, between competing definitions of the nation's economic needs, and between differing definitions of the Forest Service's mission. It is a struggle likely to intensify throughout the 1980s.

A Disputed Treasure in Timber

About half of the nation's softwood sawtimber reserves and a very substantial portion of its remaining hardwoods grow today in the national forests. The Pacific Coast region, particularly the timbered hills and lowlands of the Pacific Northwest, contains the largest of these timber stands within the public domain; the Pacific Coast area contains almost half the pine, spruce, fir, and other softwoods in the national forests. These timber reserves, more than three times the size of all the private commercial forests in the United States and currently worth more than $20 billion, will increase in value throughout the 1980s.

Although timber cutting was permitted in the national forests from their inception, the demand for commercial timber in the forests assumed major proportions only after World War II. In the early 1940s the service sold about 1.5 billion board feet of timber a year; by 1973 the cut exceeded 12.3 billion board feet. Driven by the nation's ravenous postwar desire for new housing, the demand for wood products rose steadily in the three decades following 1945. Private timber companies, approaching the limits of their own production, began to look increasingly to the national forests as an untapped timber reserve. This demand, if wholly satisfied, would likely result in a doubling of the annual timber harvest from the national forests in keeping with the industry's estimates that the U.S. demand for wood products would double before the turn of the century.

Pressure to expand the allowable timber cut has been particularly intense in the Pacific Northwest. Many of the Douglas fir forests in Oregon and Washington are old-growth stands, virgin forests never touched by a logger's saw, growing in a continuity of development many centuries old. These forests are among the most ecologically diverse and historically unique of all timber stands in North America, reminders of a continent once largely timbered with a profusion of species greater than all of Europe's. Many virgin forests, together with other less spectacular timberlands, are on Forest Service lands still classified, or eligible for classification, as "wilderness." To many environmentalists and to organized preservation groups such as the Sierra Club and the Wilderness Society, these lands are the living expression of the preservationist ethic, the values of the movement made visible. They are, in political terms, "gut issues."

Multiple Use and Sustained Yield

Since Congress has chosen not to specify how it expects the foresters to define multiple use or sustained yield in specific jurisdictions, the service has been left with enormous discretion in translating these formulas into practice. Like the multiple-use doctrine, the congressional definition of sustained yield is open to diverse interpretations, as section 531 of the Multiple Use-Sustained Yield Act suggests:

> Sustained yield ... means the achievement and maintenance in perpetuity of a high-level annual or regular periodic output of the various renewable resources of the national forests without impairment of the productivity of the land.

Both these doctrines become particularly important to the commercial timber industry because they provide the basis for the service's determination of the allowable cut in a given timber reserve—the amount of timber that can be removed from a particular resource area in a given chronological period. The service has interpreted sustained yield to require a non-declining, even-flow policy, which limits the timber cut in a given area to a constant, or increasing, rate—but never a declining one.

In effect, this severely limits the cutting of old-growth forests, particularly in the Pacific Northwest, to the ire of the timber industry, local communities, and some forest economists who believe a larger cut in old-growth timber is more economically efficient and compatible with multiple-use doctrines. Environmentalists, however, generally support protection of old-growth forests and advocate further restrictions on the allowable cut elsewhere.[15]

In response to pressure from the timber industry and the Reagan administration's own preferences, the Forest Service has planned to increase the timber harvest to 12.5 billion board feet in 1985 and higher by the end of the next decade. This expansion, contend Forest Service professionals, is consistent with the statutory mandate to maintain a sustained yield. But the timber industry wants more production. With its own reserves rapidly depleting, the industry contends that only a timber harvest from the national forests significantly above the currently· projected levels will provide enough wood for the U.S. economy in the next three decades. The Carter administration, responding to the rising costs of new housing, had ordered the service to depart "in a limited and temporary way" from its general sustained-yield principles and to open up some wilderness areas not specifically included in the Wilderness System for timber harvesting. The Reagan administration has been more sympathetic to the viewpoint of the National Forest Products Association, the timber industry's principal representative, that the service should permanently modify its sustained-yield practices to permit greater timber cuts without violating the balanced-use principle. In keeping with this production bias, the Reagan administration's budgets significantly increased spending for Forest Service activities closely associated with timber production, such as new forest road construction.

The Forest Service asserts that it can meet the higher timber production levels demanded by the Reagan administration and the timber industry only by cutting deeply into the Pacific Northwest old-growth timber, including many of the nation's remaining virgin forests. While the towering stands of old Douglas fir and associated species within these forests provide incomparable vistas and sustain a great diversity of plant and animal life, they are not particularly productive from an economic viewpoint. About a quarter of the trees will rot once they mature. Most of these forests have already matured and most timber has ceased to grow; they cover highly productive land upon which second- and third-growth timber would flourish and would produce much greater income over the next century than could be realized from the forests' current use. Professional foresters associated with the commercial timber industry have asserted that protecting most of the old-growth forests from commercial cutting largely prevents decaying old forests from being converted to more productive young stands. Moreover, note the service's critics, higher timber cuts do not mean an end to all, or even most, of the old-growth stands but a selective cutting in some and the conversion of others to second-growth production.

Environmentalists have asserted that intensive logging in the old-growth forests, with the building of logging roads and disruptive soil practices sure to attend it, will greatly reduce the forests' ability to conserve water and prevent soil erosion, which violates the principle of balanced use. Spokesmen for environmental organizations have also contended that much of the old-growth timber is found where soil is poor—at high elevations and on steep slopes—and exposure to weathering will cause rapid erosion after logging begins. Environmentalists have also argued that these forests support a unique ecosystem with a great variety of important plants and animals; such forests, they maintain, cannot be replaced. Finally, environmentalists have generally challenged the presumption that a major increase in the timber harvest would significantly decrease the cost of housing. In any case, there are many acceptable substitutes for wood in the U.S. economy that can be had without sacrificing virgin forest, they note.

Currently, the struggles tend to occur on a forest-by-forest basis, as the service proposes the required long-range plans for each forest and then files the necessary EISs. Environmentalists customarily challenge the overall adequacy of the impact statements and their specific timber production goals. The struggle over timber use spills into the related issue of wilderness designation, where the Forest Service also exercises discretionary authority.

How Much Wilderness Is Enough?

A substantial portion of the 62 million undeveloped acres under the jurisdiction of the Forest Service, the "roadless regions," could become part of the National Wilderness System, thereby forever excluded from timbering. A large portion of this roadless area is currently eligible for assignment to timber production. Timber producers, environmentalists, the Forest Service, and Congress have disagreed for more than a decade over how much of this roadless area should be designated for multiple use—in effect, opened to timbering, mineral exploring, and other nonrecreational and nonconservation uses. Perhaps as much as a third of the whole national forest system, including many old-growth stands, are in these roadless areas.

Environmentalists have been apprehensive that any multiple-use designation for large undeveloped tracts will be an invitation not only to aggressive timbering but to oil, natural gas, and coal exploring. They predict that energy industries, upon locating energy reserves, will seek exceptions to environmental regulations. Air pollution from electric power plants and energy refining operations adjacent to public lands with energy reserves will result, predict environmentalists, and the quality of the lands will be irreversibly degraded. They would prefer that most of the roadless areas under the Forest Service's jurisdiction be included in the National Wilderness System.

With some justification, environmentalists also allege that the service's strong commitment to its traditional multiple-use doctrine makes it reluctant to turn large tracts of roadless areas over to a single dominant use, such as wilderness preservation. It is this conviction that led environmentalists to criticize the manner in which the service conducted its first major inventory of roadless areas within its jurisdiction in the early 1970s.

Nonetheless, the Multiple Use-Sustained Yield Act requires the Forest Service to include wilderness protection among other multiple uses of land within its jurisdiction; the National Forest Management Act (1976) also requires it to draw up a master plan for the use of land under its jurisdiction that includes consideration of wilderness designation. Thus, the service was given both ample authority and explicit responsibility to recommend to Congress additional roadless areas for inclusion in the Wilderness System; while Congress alone possesses the authority to assign land to the system formally, the service's recommendations often influence the decisions. The White House, however, has often proposed its own plans for the roadless areas, sometimes at variance with Forest Service initiatives.

Both the Carter and Reagan administrations have offered proposals to Congress for allocating the roadless areas between wilderness and multiple-use categories; both proposals departed in significant ways from the Forest Service's own proposals. The Carter administration's plan, the more conservative, would have allocated about 10 million acres to wilderness and reserved another 10 million for further study. The Reagan administration, committed to increasing the size of territory open to timbering and energy exploring, rejected the Carter proposal and ordered a new one still in preparation. Congress, however, has often chosen to go its own way on such matters, departing from both the White House's and the Forest Service's recommendations.

RARE I and RARE II

The three-sided debate within the federal government over the use of roadless areas—dividing Congress, the Forest Service, and the White House, together with their allied interest groups, into competing coalitions—is a reminder of how pervasively the constitutional dispersion of authority affects resource planning in Washington. It also illustrates how administrative discretion can be challenged and thwarted by skilled interest groups using the Congress, and even the chief executive, against the professional administrators of an agency.

Twice in the 1970s the Forest Service invested enormous time and money in comprehensive surveys of its roadless areas in an effort to provide Congress with a plan for their future development. The first Roadless Area Review and Evaluation (RARE I) recommended in 1976 about 12 million acres from a total of 56 million for wilderness classification. This study was shelved after environmentalists challenged the plan in the federal courts on grounds that the service had not prepared adequate impact statements and had failed to include sufficient public involvement in the plan's preparation.

The Carter administration, attempting to open more public domain to timbering in response to pleas from the commercial timber industry, ordered a second study. RARE II, completed in 1978, recommended more area for wilderness designation (about 16 million acres) but also left more area open to multiple use than had RARE I. RARE II provoked opposition from environmentalists, who still believed too many multiple use tracts had been proposed, and from the states of California, Oregon, and Washington, which opposed the exclusion of various roadless areas within their boundaries from wilderness designation. Litigation initiated by environmentalists and the state of California kept RARE II in limbo until the end of the Carter administration. President Reagan subsequently ordered the service to begin yet another study, this time under guidelines intended to maximize opportunities to designate forest areas for multiple use.

During this whole period Congress continued to designate portions of roadless areas for inclusion in the Wilderness System and to order other areas to be reserved for further study, while leaving still other tracts open to multiple use. Congress was planning roadless area development on an ad hoc basis, allocating tracts in response to changing political pressures and circumstances in the context of RARE I and RARE II. As often happens in environmental affairs, Congress had become the final arbiter among the contentious White House, environmental, administrative, and private interest factions with a stake in RARE I and RARE II and a determination to change some recommendations to their own advantage.

Areas in Oregon and California not proposed for wilderness designation under RARE II were so designated by congressional committees. Some tracts originally proposed for wilderness were opened to multiple use. Generally, environmentalists felt that Congress was a more hospitable arena in which to fight for their vision of roadless area development than either the Reagan White House or the Forest Service operating under White House directives.

The Uncertain Future

Conflict over roadless area management continues into the mid-1980s, leaving perhaps half the undeveloped areas under Forest Service jurisdiction in limbo, awaiting final assignment to either the wilderness or multiple-use category. The Reagan administration is committed to expanding the multiple-use areas managed by the Forest Service for timbering and for energy exploration. Although studies by the U.S. Geological Survey suggest roadless areas in the 11 western states, excluding Texas and Oklahoma, are likely to contain relatively small amounts of undiscovered petroleum and natural gas, some tracts may be sufficiently rich in energy reserves to attract massive development should they be opened to multiple use. Others, not only old-growth timber, could be heavily cut for commercial wood products. The wilderness struggle, therefore, is likely to persist well into the 1980s and 1990s and remain intense so long as the need for new energy resources and increased timber harvests are considered credible claims upon the public domain.

The Politics of Resource Conflicts

The struggles over energy exploration, mining, and timbering on the public lands reveal a durable structure to the political conflicts over the use of public resources in the United States. The pattern tends to be repeated because it grows from political realities inherent in the U.S. governmental system.

First, at the center of the conflict, is a federal executive agency guarding the resource as a public trust and wrestling with an ambiguous mandate for its management. Most often this agency will be part of the Interior Department, or the Forest Service. The mandates will be vague because Congress must rely upon the professional administrator to make expert resource decisions—hence the generality of the mandates—and ambiguous because Congress often shrinks from choosing between conflicting claims on resources. Thus, multiple-use prescriptions for forest or range management appear to offer something to recreationists, conservationists, and resource developers without really settling competing claims. The administrative managers for the public resource inevitably will find their professional decisions politicized as conflicting interests seek to influence technical decisions to their advantage. And technical decisions themselves can often be made and justified in different scientifically defensible ways. All this means that resource administrators sometimes can exercise their professional judgment in the service of their own group and political loyalties. In all these ways, the resource management agency finds itself at the center of political conflicts over the public domain.

Second, both the White House and Congress will become partisan advocates of resource management policy, attempting to influence administrative decisions relevant to resource management and responding to pressure from organized interests with a stake in resource management. We have observed in timber, wilderness, and energy development policies the predictable tendency of Congress to intervene in administrative management planning in order to protect interests particularly important to legislators. So, too, both presidents Jimmy Carter and Ronald Reagan, as indeed every president before them for a half century, have directed the Interior Department and the Forest Service to pursue specific objectives in resource management compatible with their ideological biases and political commitments. Indeed, Congress and the White House often compete in attempting to influence administrative determinations affecting the public domain. And the president, despite the illusory title of chief executive, has no guarantee of success in the struggle.

Third, the plurality of organized interests involved in resource decisions means that Congress, the White House, and the administrative agencies all are enmeshed in a process of coalition building with organized groups during resource policy making. These organized interests, moreover, involve not only private interests but also the states within which the public domain resides and for whom the use of the resources on the domain has significant economic and political consequences.

Finally, policy struggles quite often are waged in the technical language of resource economics and scientific management. Perhaps more than most environmental issues, public resource management is an arcane business to most Americans, particularly those living where few public lands exist. In such circumstances specialized private groups, such as environmentalists and resource users, tend to operate almost invisibly to the public; the outcome of policy struggles depends particularly upon their own organizational resources, technical expertise, and political adeptness in the administrative infighting and legal wrangling that often characterize resource policy making. It is a political arena, more particularly, where organized environmental groups often constitute practically the only expression of viewpoints not associated with resource users or administrators.

Notes

1. Quoted in John McPhee, *Encounters with the Archdruid* (New York: Farrar, Straus & Giroux, 1971), 17.
2. Article IV, Section 3, Clause 2, of the U.S. Constitution.
3. Congressional Quarterly, *The Battle for Natural Resources* (Washington, D.C.: Congressional Quarterly, 1983), chapter 1.
4. Aldo Leopold, *A Sand County Almanac* (New York: Oxford University Press, 1949), 222.
5. A useful survey of the public lands may be found in U.S. Department of the Interior, Bureau of Land Management, *Managing the Nation's Public Lands* (Washington, D.C.: Government Printing Office, 1983).
6. Paul J. Culhane, *Public Land Politics* (Baltimore: Johns Hopkins University Press, 1981), 60.
7. James Baker, "The Frustrations of FLPMA," *Wilderness*, vol. 47, no. 163 (Winter 1983): 13.
8. On the impact of sustained use upon the Forest Service, see Culhane, *Public Land Politics*, chapter 2.
9. Ibid., 126.

10. Council on Environmental Quality, *Environmental Quality 1979* (Washington, D.C.: Government Printing Office, 1980), 309.
11. Quoted in *New York Times*, June 27, 1981.
12. *The Battle for Natural Resources*, chapters 4 and 5.
13. *New York Times*, July 2, 1982.
14. Ibid.
15. Culhane, *Public Land Politics*, chapter 2.

America woke up in the 1970s to the realization that its life-sustaining resources were endangered. The challenge for the 1980s is to avoid going back to sleep.

—S. David Freeman, former commissioner,
U.S. Nuclear Regulatory Commission

An Agenda 9
for the 1980s

Among the most significant environmental controversies of the 1980s are those concerning the fundamental design and purpose of the public agencies responsible for environmental management. Such issues transcend specific policies and programs; they address the character of the public agencies creating and implementing environmental policies and the basic premises upon which the agencies act.

These issues have assumed importance in the 1980s partially because the decade began with an administration ideologically hostile to the premises of many environmental policies enacted in the last 20 years. The subsequent attack on these policies and the agencies responsible for their implementation created a sharp public controversy over the fundamentals of environmental policy and a climate of critical appraisal unmatched since the Environmental Era was proclaimed more than a decade ago. Many of these issues, however, have been debated in more subdued fashion since the early 1970s. The controversy will persist, for it springs from enduring differences of belief concerning the importance of environmental issues, the proper role of government in society, and the capacity of American political institutions to innovate. Other issues arise less from antagonistic confrontations between environmentalists and their critics than from experience with new policies and encounters with new environmental problems that seem to require institutional innovation; the problem is how best to innovate. In this final chapter we shall examine several of the major institutional issues likely to be important throughout the decade.

Is Regulation Too Costly?

Among the most persistent controversies pervading every domain of environmental regulation is conflict over the underlying institutional and philosophical structure of current regulatory programs. Spokesmen for the business sector, state and local governments, and other regulated interests have commonly joined many economists in advocating: (1) fundamental changes in the criteria by which environmental standards and technological controls on pollution emissions are determined; and (2) sweeping alterations in the methods used to secure compliance with environmental regulations. More than controversies over specific laws or programs, they involve the basic structure of regulation itself.

The Cost-Benefit Debate

A common complaint about almost all environmental regulations written by Congress since 1970 is that the mandated procedures for setting environmental standards and emission controls are insensitive to costs. "Cost-oblivious" procedures for setting environmental standards, such as those in the Clean Air Act and Occupational Health and Safety Act described earlier, are cited as examples of congressionally ordained disregard for the economic consequences of regulation. Other laws, such as the Resource Conservation and Recovery Act (RCRA), have been criticized for their failure to require specifically that regulatory agencies consider costs among other factors in setting environmental standards. In the view of critics, this mandated indifference to the economic realities of regulation breeds a cost carelessness among regulators that inflicts severely excessive economic penalties upon regulated interests.[1]

The Case for Cost-Benefit Analysis. The economic penalties of cost-oblivious regulation allegedly accrue in several ways. Economists frequently assert that environmental standards or technological controls mandated in this manner often fail to achieve the most cost-effective forms of control or neglect to use capital resources in the most socially effective manner. In the language of economics, the regulations often fail to achieve economic efficiency. Put another way, regulations written without careful regard for costs of compliance often, if not regularly, will produce regulations whose net costs greatly exceed their net benefits. Moreover, regulators often disregard less expensive methods of achieving the same results. In their comprehensive study of "regulatory unreasonableness," political scientists Eugene Bardach and Robert Kagan list many other intangible costs they believe result from economic failures of regulation including the loss of productive efficiency among workers in regulated industries through "the diversion of managers' and engineers' time into planning, negotiating, and monitoring regulatory compliance measures." [2]

When all the regulated sectors of the U.S. economy are considered, so the critics reason, a huge, inflationary diversion of capital from more economically desirable uses results. Bardach and Kagan, for instance, cite Labor Department figures suggesting that emission standards proposed by the Environmental Protection Agency (EPA) for coke ovens might result in a 29 percent drop in worker production in that industry. They also refer to data from the Commerce Department indicating that compliance costs with federal environmental, health, and safety regulations would cost U.S. copper producers $3.5 billion between 1978 and 1987, "resulting in slightly lower production, fewer jobs, increased copper imports, and a substantial increase in price." [3] Moreover, critics frequently allege that excessive regulatory costs will drive some firms out of business or out of the country. Spokesmen for major national business associations, such as the Business Roundtable and the U.S. Chamber of Commerce, have alleged that excessive regulatory costs have depressed the growth rate in the Gross National Product (GNP) significantly.[4]

A solution commonly proposed for the alleged extravagances of regulation is the mandatory use of cost-benefit analysis by agencies writing environmental regulations. The purpose is to provide regulatory officials and regulated interests with an estimate of the net benefits or costs associated with a particular environmental standard. Few of its proponents would assert that cost-benefit data should be the sole consideration in selecting regulatory strategies. But most believe that the routine requirement for such a procedure would make regulators more sensitive to costs of their regulatory decisions and more likely to select regulatory procedures with net benefits, or with the least costs among several alternatives. Many also believe that cost-benefit analysis leads to a better quality of decision making. As Paul Johnson observes, "The value is that it injects rational calculation into a highly emotional subject. . . . It offers you a range of alternatives. Without stringent analysis, nobody knows whether costs imposed by regulatory programs are money well spent." [5] And (although it is often unstated), many who advocate such procedures hope that the publicity given regulatory costs, especially if net benefits appear lacking, will deter agencies from choosing such regulations.

Some Things Are Not for Sale. Environmentalists have been hostile to the routine use of cost-benefit analysis in setting environmental standards. Some regard cost-benefit analysis as a categoric evil, wholly inappropriate to the selection of environmental policies. Others, while recognizing that economic considerations may sometimes merit attention in environmental regulation, believe cost-benefit calculations are easily distorted to protect regulated interests from necessary controls. Most environmentalists regard cost-benefit proposals as nothing less than a covert effort to weaken regulation in whatever context the proposals occur.

Environmentalists assert that cost-benefit analysis often distorts economic reality by exaggerating regulatory costs and underestimating benefits. Regulated interests, the argument continues, often deliberately magnify their compliance costs; it is difficult, in any case, to obtain accurate economic data from them. Further, regulated interests give little attention to the economic "learning curve," which often yields a substantial saving over the full period of regulation as they gain experience and expertise in controlling their pollutants. Benefits from regulation, in contrast, are often underestimated because they are not easily calculated. For instance, how are the health benefits from significantly cleaner air over the next several decades to be calculated? What value is to be placed upon rivers, streams, and lakes made fishable and swimmable again? What is the dollars-and-cents value of an irreplaceable virgin forest conserved for another generation?

Some benefits almost defy monetizing when, for instance, regulations involve the possible saving of lives. An agency may consider regulatory alternatives involving different levels of risk to populations from exposure to hazardous or toxic substances. What is the appropriate value to be placed upon a life saved? A variation of cost-benefit analysis sometimes advocated in such a situation is to compare the costs of regulation with estimates of the lives saved from the different strategies. Such a comparison implicitly requires regulators to decide how much an individual human life is worth. As a practical example, an EPA study of acid rain prevention suggested that stricter controls on air emissions from electric power plants in the Ohio River valley would cost several hundred million dollars. It also would avert an estimated 54,000 additional pollution-related deaths by the year 2000. Comparing lives saved with dollars spent on pollution controls in this instance makes economic sense only if one assigns a dollar value to each life—a politically perilous act sure to seem arbitrary, if not morally repugnant, no matter what value is assigned.

But perhaps the most persuasive reason for resisting cost-benefit analysis, in the environmentalists' view, is that reducing an environmental value such as clean air or water to a monetary figure makes it appear to be just another commodity that can be priced, bought, and sold. "Many environmentalists," explains Steven Kelman, "fear that subjecting decisions about clean air or water to the cost-benefit tests that determine the general run of decisions removes those matters from the realm of specially valued things. . . . The very statement that something is not for sale enhances and protects the thing's value in a number of ways. . . . [It] is a way of showing that a thing is valued for its own sake, whereas selling a thing for money demonstrates that it was valued only instrumentally." [6] Indeed, environmentalists often believe they stand apart from regulated business through a profound ethical disagreement over the intrinsic worth of wild places, uncontaminated air and water, and other environmental amenities that the movement defends. This conviction of moral purpose imparts to the movement much of its passion and persistence. It also elevates arguments over cost-benefit analysis to the level of ethical principles that makes it so difficult for environmentalists to compromise on the issues.

Realities and Rhetoric. Despite the blizzard of econometric data normally accompanying arguments over the costs of regulation, much is unreliable. Regulated businesses, willfully or not, often greatly overestimate the costs of regulation. We have seen that proponents of regulation are sometimes excessively conservative in their own projections of compliance costs. Cost-benefit analysis is so vulnerable to partisan manipulation that it is often discounted significantly by officials even when they are permitted to consider the economics of regulation. And many regulatory decisions are ultimately made on the basis of political, administrative, and other considerations (although the decisions later may be sanctified by economics to impart greater credibility). However, experience with environmental regulation suggests some conclusions about the use and abuse of cost-benefit calculations.

In the aggregate, regulatory costs have had a very modest impact on the American economy. Few firms have been driven from the marketplace by such costs. Major industries generally do not flee from states with tough regulatory standards.[7] Although American business will spend an estimated $550 billion in this decade to satisfy environmental regulations, most studies suggest that such private expenditures have a slight inflationary or depressive impact upon the American economy. Altogether, the United States has been spending about 1.5 percent of its GNP on pollution control in recent years—a figure most economists would not consider particularly burdensome.

But individual regulations or regulatory programs can impose what appear to be excessive costs. All recent administrations have struggled to make regulations economically leaner. President Jimmy Carter, an outspoken environmentalist, nonetheless established in the White House the Regulatory Analysis Review Group in an effort to make environmental programs more economical. Another research group studying enforcement of the new Surface Mining Control and Reclamation Act (SMCRA) at Carter's request concluded that many mining company complaints about the excessive costs of strip mine regulation had "substantial substantive merit." [8] Studies of the Occupational Health and Safety Administration under both Jimmy Carter and Ronald Reagan have identified some regulations seemingly too costly for their benefits.

Often costs are grossly inflated not so much by individual regulations as by the multiplicity and unpredictability of regulatory procedures. Consider, for instance, the experience of the Atlantic City Electric Company. In 1969 its Deepwater, New Jersey, plant boilers were converted from coal to oil to meet federal air quality standards. After the 1973 Arab oil embargo, federal officials requested the utility to switch back to coal, but when petroleum again became plentiful in 1974 the company returned to oil. In 1980 new federal and state air pollution regulations caused the facility to return to coal. "We have jerked the industry back and forth on fuels," admitted an Energy Department official. [9]

All this should clarify at least a few aspects of the cost-benefit controversy. First, there is no substantial evidence that regulatory costs have become so economically excessive that cost-benefit analysis must be routinely imposed on all environmental regulatory programs as a solution. Second, there are doubtless instances—perhaps a significant number— where cost-benefit analysis might suggest better regulatory solutions to environmental protection than would be selected without such analysis. For this reason, such analysis should not be categorically excluded from consideration unless Congress specifically mandates such an exclusion. Third, as we have observed, it matters a great deal who does the calculating. All cost-benefit studies should be open to review and challenge during administrative deliberations; regulatory agencies should be required to consider several different studies, including those from interests at conflict in the proceedings and an impartial party, in reaching decisions based upon economic criteria. Fourth, Congress should explicitly indicate in environmental legislation or in its accompanying legislative history how it expects regulatory agencies to weigh economic criteria alongside other statutory guidelines to be observed in writing regulations to implement such legislation. Finally, regulatory costs might be significantly diminished not by the use of cost-benefit analysis but by the use of economic incentives in securing the compliance of regulated interests with environmental programs.

Using Economic Incentives

In December 1979 the EPA broke with the traditional standards-and-enforcement approach to air pollution by introducing its "bubble policy" for controlling emissions from existing air pollution sources. This policy, to be explained shortly, substituted economic incentives for legal prescriptions and technological directives to secure compliance with environmental regulation. Properly used, such incentives appear to be one available and practical means to reduce the costs of regulations.

Why Change from Standards and Enforcement? While the traditional standards-and-enforcement approach to environmental regulation described in chapters 5 and 6 has much to recommend it, it has at least two important economic flaws.[10] First, it presents regulated interests with few economic incentives to comply rapidly and efficiently with mandated pollution control standards; in the economists' perspective, standards and enforcement lacks an appeal to the economic self-interest of the regulated. Penalties for noncompliance with the law, even severe penalties, often fail to motivate polluters to meet required pollution control deadlines. And we have observed that penalties are often unassessed or severely diminished by negotiation with regulatory agencies. Often penalties can be deferred for years, even decades, by litigation. Some firms find it more profitable to pay penalties and continue in violation of the law than to assume the far steeper costs of controlling their pollutants.

A second problem is that traditional regulatory approaches require the federal government to specify the appropriate technologies and methods of their utilization in practically every instance where pollutants are technologically controlled. Highly complicated and exquisitely detailed specifications that may make poor scientific or economic sense for particular industries or firms oftentimes result. One reason is that neither Congress nor administrators implementing legislation may have sufficient scientific training or experience to make correct judgments about the technologies appropriate for pollution abatement in specific firms or industries. And regulators sometimes lack sufficient information about the economics of firms or industries to know what technological controls are economically efficient—that is, which achieve desired control standards least expensively. In general, suggest Allen V. Kneese and Charles L. Schultze:

> Problems such as environmental control . . . involve extremely complicated economic and social relationships. Policies that may appear straightforward—for example, requiring everyone to reduce pollution by the technologically feasible amount—will often have ramifications or side effects that are quite different from those intended. Second, given the complexity of these relationships, relying on a central regulatory bureaucracy to carry out social policy simply will not work: there are too many actors, too much technical knowledge, too many different circumstances to be grasped by a regulatory agency.[11]

Examples of costly mistakes in specifying technological controls are not hard to find. Instances occurred in the writing of regulations to implement the SMCRA (1977):

> Utah International Inc., a General Electric subsidiary, complained that EPA and the Office of Surface Mining in the Interior Department required that all runoff from areas disturbed by surface mining must pass through a sedimentation pond although other management practices, such as the use of straw dikes and vegetative cover, would achieve substantially the same results. The company had to build at its Trapper Mine near Craig, Colorado, a $335,000 sedimentation pond when alternative methods could have achieved the same results at 10 percent of the cost.[12]

> The Conoco Company complained that Consolidation Coal, a subsidiary, unnecessarily spent $160 million annually to meet engineering standards imposed on surface mines by Washington. The National Academy of Sciences, speaking through its National Research Council, had recommended a different approach.[13]

A Different Approach. Prior to 1980 the EPA's regulations for implementing the Clean Air Act specified that a firm emitting air pollutants from several stacks had to install the prescribed technological control on each stack and achieve essentially the same degree of control for each emission source. Many firms complained of the excessive costs involved. In late 1979 the agency promulgated new regulations permitting the bubble concept to be selectively used. The policy assumes "that an imaginary enclosure is placed over an industrial plant. From this enclosure, or bubble, a maximum allowable level of emissions is permitted. A firm in this bubble would be free to use more cost-effective pollution controls than are usually allowed." [14] A firm with three stacks emitting pollution, for instance, may find it least costly to cut back severely on the emissions from one stack while leaving the others only slightly controlled. So long as the total emissions leaving the imaginary bubble over the plant do not violate air quality standards, the firm is free to decide how best to comply with the law. Advocates of this approach assert that it will result in both a substantial cost saving to the firm and quicker compliance with pollution standards because the firm is free to choose solutions in its own self-interest. [15]

The EPA has expanded this policy to permit the creation of multiplant and multi-industry bubbles. The first experimental bubbles were established for an electric power plant in Narragansett, Rhode Island, and an Armco steel plant in Middletown, Ohio, in the early 1980s. The EPA has predicted that these and other early bubbles will save regulated industries more than $100 million.

There have been some other limited efforts to introduce economic incentives into environmental regulation. In 1977 Congress amended the Clean Air Act to make major violators of air quality standards liable to civil penalties up to $25,000 daily for specific violations. EPA is permitted to set the size of the penalty at least equal to the benefits of noncompliance for the firm, thereby removing the economic incentive to continue polluting. Imposing such "administrative costs" is likely to eliminate noncompliance much more swiftly and less expensively than resorting to the courts for assessing penalties. [16] More complex approaches, including the creation of markets for air pollution entitlements, are also being used by the EPA. Further use of performance standards rather than technological standards—specifying to a polluter what pollution must be eliminated while leaving the firm free to decide how to do the job—should also be promoted.

If economic incentives work as predicted, substantial reductions in compliance costs for environmental regulation might well result. Such an approach could significantly reduce the time and complexity of enforcement by eliminating much of the litigation and administrative detail that customarily arise when firms resist administratively mandated technological controls on their pollutants.

Economic incentives, however, can not and should not be applied in all enforcement contexts. Such incentives are sometimes inappropriate or unworkable—controlling hazardous pollutants, for instance, may require a level of technological management firms would be unwilling to create on their own. Further, effectively using economic incentives often assumes regulators have accurate information about the economics of polluting firms; there is opportunity for misrepresentation of such information by polluters and consequently less than the economically feasible levels of pollution control may be tolerated by regulatory agencies.

Environmentalists, accepting the principle of economic incentives but wary of possible abuses by regulated interests, have been ambivalent toward these arrangements. Environmentalists often regard control of pollutants as a duty and freedom from environmental pollution as a right. In contrast, as Kneese and Schultze explain, "the economic approach [to regulation] stresses not rights and duties but incentives. People or firms act in certain ways because their self-interest dictates doing so. . . . Changes in social behavior can be accomplished by modifying the incentives that induce people to act." [17] The idea that government should make pollution abatement economically acceptable by deferring to the firms' economic self-interest strikes many environmentalists as a moral failure to declare pollution wrong in principle. Many environmentalists also believe that economic incentives fail to compel firms to abate pollution as much as possible and, thus, implicitly acknowledge a right to pollute. Most environmentalists are skeptical that firms will provide administrative agencies with accurate economic data on their operations, providing instead information best serving their own economic interest. Perhaps many fear that economic incentives will be the beginning of a progression toward pollution taxes, which substitute a tax on pollutants for traditional regulatory approaches to pollution abatement—an approach most environmentalists abhor as the final, and worst, stage in the use of economic logic for environmental regulation.

Economic incentives will remain controversial and experimental for some time. But there appear to be enough circumstances when their use is compatible with vigorous environmental regulation to justify their continued study and use.

Reforming the EPA

In September 1979 the EPA enacted a regulation requiring inspection and correction for those uses of asbestos posing an unreasonable health risk in schools. The responsibility to issue this regulation was clear: both the Toxic Substances Control Act (TSCA) and later the Asbestos School Hazard Detection and Control Act mandated it. The EPA never requested from Congress the money to implement the regulations despite requests from several states for help. Instead a voluntary program was promoted. After the asbestos industry appealed to the Reagan administration's Commission on Regulatory Relief, the EPA put the asbestos regulation in an administrative limbo. Instances of this regulatory short-circuiting were frequent in the early 1980s, largely because no administration since the creation of EPA was more determined to politicize the agency's programs than Reagan's. The Reagan experience demonstrated both the EPA's vulnerability to political manipulation and the abuses of public trust that could result. The experience provides a strong argument for making the EPA a truly independent regulatory commission rather than the hybrid executive agency it has become.

The Reagan experience throws into sharp relief some of the worst impacts upon sound environmental management that result when a highly partisan leadership manages the EPA in ideological and political conformity with White House interests. Partisanship is common to most agency managers regardless of party; some members of any administration doubtless carry it to excess. But the extent to which EPA's leadership carried partisanship in managing the agency's affairs and the resulting perversion of its mission strongly suggest that the EPA is too vulnerable to this sort of leadership and that the temptations to partisan abuse of office are too great.

How Decisions Were Politicized

In at least three respects, the politicizing of the EPA under the Reagan administration illustrated an undesirable invasion of partisan politics into environmental administration. First, sensitive technical issues often were resolved at high agency levels by explicit political criteria subordinating science to political calculation. Sometimes scientific issues were suppressed or their investigation delayed for political purposes. Second, political influence was manifest more insidiously in the tendency of many technical personnel to avoid even raising issues or revealing data that were perceived to be politically unpalatable to the agency's leadership. Subsequent investigation revealed the politicizing of technical decisions in the following ways:

> Decisions concerning when to award grants from Superfund to cleanup hazardous waste sites and what techniques to use were often based upon the decisions' calculated effects upon state elections or upon businesses giving financial support to the president.

> High officials in EPA permitted the Dow Chemical Company to review a draft agency report on Dow's responsibility for dioxin contamination of surface waters near Midland, Michigan. The company also was permitted to suggest alterations in the report's language.

> EPA employees permitted representatives of the formaldehyde industry to review and comment upon technical studies concerning the hazardousness of the chemical in private meetings from which other interests were excluded.

Finally, through the use of various administrative devices such as budgeting, personnel hiring and firing, and discretionary authority to delay or hasten action of specific programs, the agency's leadership deliberately failed to carry out programs mandated by Congress. Failures to carry out legislated responsibilities because of ideological objections were often difficult for the public or Congress to discover because the agency's leadership did not explicitly challenge these congressional mandates. A more subtle procedure by which the administration moved broadly against the intent of many environmental laws was to require the EPA, among other executive agencies, to introduce a version of cost-benefit calculation into regulation writing. The president's Executive Order 12291 issued early in 1981 required agencies to the extent permitted by law to follow criteria for regulations that would make them "refrain from action unless potential benefits outweigh potential costs to society" and "choose regulatory objectives that maximize net benefits to society."

While the language carefully avoided ordering formal cost-benefit analysis for environmental regulations, it encouraged the EPA to introduce such logic whenever it was not explicitly prevented—an act that often ran counter to the intent, if not the language, of many programs entrusted to the EPA. Many environmentalists perceived Executive Order 12291 as a signal to the EPA that it could risk defying the will of Congress without any White House censure.

Until the political furor leading to the resignation of EPA's administrator Anne Burford in 1983, the agency had virtually eliminated its programs for public involvement in the implementation of TSCA and RCRA despite agency regulations and congressional mandates requiring such programs.[18] Severe reductions in the EPA's research budget, an activity essential to acquiring the data to support regulation of hazardous substances required by law, sharply reduced its capacity to fill its responsibilities under TSCA and RCRA also. The agency reduced the budget and staff of its enforcement division and thereby seriously impaired enforcement of the Clean Air Act and the Water Pollution Control Act Amendments.

Evidence from later congressional investigations suggests that these administrative acts were ideologically and politically motivated, the manifestation of the administration's determination to have "regulatory relief" from major environmental programs even when Congress would not change the law formally. Masked through the language and complexity of administrative procedure, however, such an attack upon the law from those responsible for implementing could continue unnoticed for long periods. The burden of discovering and proving the intent of such acts rested upon environmental groups, congressional committees, and others.

There were other adverse consequences to this highly partisan management. Many of the agency's seasoned professional staff were dismissed or resigned because they found the disruption of programs intolerable. EPA's credibility, damaged by the political controversy surrounding scientific programs and the unpredictability of internal policies, diminished. Regulated interests, heartened by the agency's new political climate, were encouraged to resist regulation with renewed vigor. Staff morale sank as many among the professional staff perceived EPA's leadership to be at war with the agency's own mission.

Why had it been possible to politicize the agency's leadership and administrative processes so thoroughly in so short a time? Two major reasons were the accessibility of the agency to the so-called administrative presidency and the tradition of political executives in managerial positions within EPA and other executive agencies.

The Administrative Presidency

The Reagan administration came to office with a strong belief in what Richard Nathan has called the administrative presidency, the belief "that management tasks can and should be performed by partisans." [19] In the EPA, as in other executive agencies, this translated into the appointment to upper- and middle-management positions of individuals whose first and most important qualifications were a strong commitment to the president's program of "regulatory relief" and to other ideological principles compatible with the president's platform. Indeed, as we observed in chapter two, the president was willing to designate as EPA's first administrator in his term an individual with no standing among environmental interests—who in fact was identified with organizations hostile to major EPA programs—so long as ideological loyalties were acceptable. Using this authority to appoint political executives, like all his predecessors for a half century, President Reagan populated the EPA's more sensitive managerial positions with loyalists who saw their primary responsibility as carrying out the president's own program rather than the agency's mission.

The president further extended the sweep of partisan influence in EPA and other administrative agencies through the frequent use of the Office of Management and Budget (OMB) to change the congressional intent of regulations. The OMB, created to assist presidents in preparing and administering their budgets and in overseeing the work of executive agencies, was intended to be a staff agency. OMB's traditional responsibilities included the review of agency regulations and other decisions to ensure compatibility with the budget and White House administrative directives. The OMB was not intended to be an executive "line agency" with substantive policy-making responsibilities or a party in private deliberations with regulatory officials intended to influence rule making. The elaborate procedures for rule making required of administrative agencies are intended to prevent such *ex parte* conversations.

Under the Reagan administration, however, OMB enforced presidential directives, such as Executive Order 12291, which in the guise of executive management actually attempted to influence regulatory agencies to change substantive policy. This OMB activity became pressure upon the EPA to make major substantive changes in regulations that appeared to contradict the legislative intent of Congress. In several respects, this seemed an improper role for the OMB in the regulatory arena. Negotiations between OMB and EPA over the substance of regulations often became, in effect, a process of informal rule making without the procedural safeguards and public visibility normally required. It also appeared to jeopardize, if not to eliminate, the independence in making regulatory policy, which Congress intended for the EPA to possess. So widely did the OMB exercise this sort of influence through the executive branch that the Congressional Research Service (CRS) characterized the OMB under Reagan as a "formal, comprehensive, centralized and substantively oriented system of control of informal rule making that is without precedent." In the language of the CRS, the OMB had become an informal new entry point for those interested in influencing the outcome of particular agency rulings with "no explicit safeguards to protect the integrity of the process in the interest of the public against secret, undisclosed and unreviewed contacts." [20]

What was attempted at EPA was best described by Secretary of the Interior James Watt before he fell victim to his own ideological excesses. Speaking to the Western Governors' Conference, he observed that there was no need to write into law all the major changes they wanted to make in his department's policies because "I am already accomplishing the goals through administrative action." [21] It was this logic—the determination to change substantive regulatory policies in EPA through administrative devices without congressional approval and often in contradiction to congressional intent—that guided the administrative presidency in the EPA.

Reform

The EPA, the nation's largest regulatory agency in budget and personnel, remains formally and informally open to White House influence in a manner unlike most other regulatory agencies within the executive branch. So long as this condition exists, the agency will remain vulnerable to the kind of partisan disruption and subversion of its mission evident in the Reagan administration. While congressional oversight might frustrate this sort of agency manipulation, as it did in the early 1980s, congressional vigilance is an uncertain bulwark against future repetitions of the Reagan experience. Congress may have neither the time nor motivation to exercise its oversight aggressively, especially if the same party controls both congressional chambers and the White House. Nor can environmentalists or other organized groups protective of the EPA's mission depend upon having enough access to agency activities to identify and disclose White House abuses.

Several structural changes would seem to offer more enduring and dependable constraints upon partisan abuses. First, the EPA should be made far more independent of direct White House manipulation by changing the administrator's term to a five- or seven-year renewable tenure, an arrangement making it far more difficult for presidents to change leadership quickly and expediently to suit their own disposition. Second, most of the EPA's current middle- and upper-management positions populated by political executives should be transformed into permanent civil service positions to be filled by people recruited on the basis of professional competence. Third, the agency should have a permanent inspector general with the capacity to initiate appropriate administrative or legal action against internal abuses of authority. Fourth, the EPA's technical decision making should be subject to mandatory five-year review by an external scientific panel whose mission would be to evaluate both the quality of technical information and the freedom from political interference that the agency strives for in its scientific decision making.

Such changes clearly would place the EPA in a position more closely resembling the status of other federal regulatory agencies. These changes inevitably would involve risks and would remove the EPA from what sometimes might be a beneficial responsiveness to White House interests. More specifically, reforming the EPA as suggested would make it far more difficult for a president, bearing what he believes to be a public mandate for change, to impose changes. From this perspective, the changes might even seem to make the EPA a less responsible agency because it would be more insulated from the influence of electoral majorities and public opinion expressed through the president's own program.

Further, there is always a risk that the agency may be captured or undesirably biased toward some set of interests—congressional, private, or otherwise—without a countervailing source of remedy in the presidential office. In short, insulating the EPA from abuses of presidential administrative authority can also mean shielding it from the necessary discipline of presidential authority.

Political realities confirm that risks will be involved in changing the status of EPA; dire predictions about the consequences can not be dismissed as unthinkable. Balanced against such risks, however, should be consideration of the problems that arose and that are likely to arise again if efforts are not made to change the status of EPA within the executive establishment.

For those committed to promoting the agency's broad mission of environmental protection and enhancement, the risks of reform often seem worth the taking when the alternatives already experienced are considered.

Technology's Institutional Risks

Many of the nation's current environmental problems arise directly from the government's failure to anticipate the legal and institutional arrangements needed to control the new technologies and the products of those technologies, which it has been promoting resolutely. The private sector is often guilty of a similar disregard for the long-term management of risks from its own technological innovations. The result has been the emergence of technological crisis—in the guise of a Three Mile Island or Love Canal incident—created or exacerbated by the absence of legal or institutional controls on technology failures. Many of the essential controls on publicly or privately promoted technologies that seemed lacking in the throes of a crisis could be anticipated. Many controls were deliberately ignored or prematurely dismissed in the early enthusiasm of technology development. In short, the ecological risks often associated with technological development arise not only from the physical and biological consequences of technologies but also from failures to provide adequately for their social management. One practical consequence should be greater governmental attention to what can be called institutional risk assessment in technology development, a procedure promising substantial environmental benefits.

Technology and Institutional Risks

As a people fiercely committed to technological innovation, Americans always have been gamblers with the future. In the United States, technological innovation has been driven by an implicit assumption that the legal, economic, and governmental resources will be available to protect society from the worst impacts of attractive technologies. It was assumed that social or scientific engineering always would be equal to the challenge of technological change. One consequence of this faith in social innovation has been the tendency for public and private institutions to create technological innovation first and worry about the social management of the technology later. Another was to define the risks of technological innovation primarily in scientific or economic terms rather than to assess the ability of social institutions to manage the technologies satisfactorily. This confidence in the social manageability of new technologies often has inhibited public institutions from planning prudent strategies for eliminating or reducing the ecological dangers often inherent in technology development.

Two kinds of institutional risk, in particular, have had major ecological importance for the United States during the last half century. First, technologies have been developed in both private and public sectors without explicit and operational contingency plans for dealing with possible technological crises. Second, public and private institutions have lacked the financial, technical, and legal resources appropriate to deal with technology problems. Such failures of institutional planning can be attributed partially to the reluctance of both public and private promoters of technology to discuss candidly the full risks lest they encourage too much opposition. The neglect of institutional planning for technology development partially reflects the absence of law or tradition requiring such deliberation. And, in the case of federally funded projects, the zeal of mission-oriented agencies to produce results in their own bureaucratic interest doubtless blunts the instinct to examine the long-term consequences of failure. In any event, perhaps some of the adverse impacts of new technologies could not have been anticipated in advance of their development. Yet experience suggests that failures in institutional planning are more likely to result from a lack of will to anticipate problems.

The Lesson of the Peaceful Atom

Perhaps the clearest illustration of institutional risk in technology development is provided by the history of commercial nuclear power in the United States. Many problems in reactor safety can be traced directly to flawed institutional arrangements for managing plant accidents. Both the federal government and the private nuclear power industry share responsibility for these failures of institutional planning and also for the related nuclear waste problems. It has become evident that neither Washington nor the private promoters of nuclear power were prepared to plan realistically for the possible financial, legal, or scientific problems in the technology. In their passion to promote the peaceful atom, private and public sponsors were loath to admit even the wisdom of exploring tentatively the institutional arrangements needed for major system failures. This aversion to institutional risk analysis has resulted in managerial crises at almost every significant stage of the commercial nuclear fuel cycle:

> *Reactor Safety:* The nation's most publicized nuclear technology failure, the crisis at Three Mile Island beginning on March 28, 1979, was described by both major commissions investigating the incident as primarily a failure in institutional management. The Rogovin Commission, appointed by the Nuclear

Regulatory Commission (NRC) to investigate the incident, was the most explicit: "The principal deficiencies in commercial reactor safety today are not hardware problems, they are management problems, ... problems that cannot be solved by the addition of a few pipes or valves ... or, for that matter, by a resident federal inspector." [22] In light of the Rogovin Commission's emphasis upon institutional management as a problem generic to the commercial nuclear power industry, it is significant that prior to 1978 the NRC's major studies of reactor safety did not consider failures of institutional management among the several hundred "human errors" whose relevance to reactor accidents it investigated.

Nuclear Fuel Reprocessing: The nation's only commercial nuclear fuel reprocessing plant, the showpiece technology at West Valley, New York, intended to demonstrate the feasibility of commercializing nuclear fuel reprocessing, failed economically in 1971 and closed permanently in 1976. Abandoned at West Valley were more than a half million gallons of high-level liquid radioactive waste, two solid radioactive waste burial grounds, a spent nuclear fuel storage facility, and a contaminated fuel reprocessing plant. The West Valley facilities could safely contain the high-level wastes for less than 40 years; no permanent depository for such waste currently exists. Further, as late as 1982, Washington and New York state continued to quarrel over which should accept the financial and technical responsibility for the site's cleanup. The terms of the original contract between Washington and New York state, signed when the facility was begun in 1962, "bear no relationship to the facts as they exist today [because] ... the parties contemplated a successful venture and did not specifically address ... their respective liabilities for the radically different situation which exists in West Valley today." [23]

Nuclear Facility Disposal: Although the average commercial nuclear power facility has a planned operating life of only 50 years, no comprehensive federal program exists providing the money, legal authority, and technical resources needed to ensure that the plants are safely closed, or decommissioned. In fact, the United States currently lacks an integrated program for the decommissioning of any nuclear facility, including temporary waste sites. Warned the U.S. General Accounting Office, "Unless a national policy is developed to provide for unified and effective decommissioning actions and a lead agency is designated to monitor implementation of that policy, the impact will be, at worst, potential hazards to the public's health and safety." [24] The practical problems of planning the decommissioning of a single plant are suggested by the current status of funding arrangements. While the satisfactory decommissioning of even a small plant may exceed $100 million, no public or private agencies have currently established any trust funds or other revenue allocations for the retirement of a single facility.

A Continuing Need

While the U.S. experience with commercial nuclear power development provides the most persuasive example of poor institutional planning in technology development, other examples abound. Appalachia has become the nation's showcase of institutional failure in strip mine management. The region's hills and hollows, littered by more than 250,000 acres of orphan spoil banks, were devastated between 1950 and 1977 by local, state, and federal governmental reluctance to investigate the long-term ecological and economic costs of the technology's unregulated operation. The Carter administration's ambitious program to promote a commercial synfuels industry in the United States initially gave virtually no attention to governmental problems involved in managing the enormous volume of highly toxic sludges likely to arise from the industry; nor did it consider the capacities of local and state governments to regulate such a complex new technology.

To be sure, the record is mixed. Appalachia became the bitter lesson leading to the SMCRA passed in 1977. Love Canal produced Superfund, and regulation of the toxic sludge associated with the production of synfuels may well occur. But the time lag between the development of institutional failures in technology management and the governmental efforts to remedy them is often great; the economic, ecological, and health risks involved in such long delays is often substantial. Moreover, often a solution to a technological crisis that is formulated in the midst of the crisis itself is haphazard and expedient, lacking technical finesse, economic efficiency, and comprehensiveness.

Some Solutions

U.S. District Judge David Bazelon, a jurist experienced and perceptive in technology issues, has remarked that a major task in governmental risk assessment of new technologies is "to face the hard questions created by a lack of knowledge." [25] How can federal agencies or the private institutions they support be compelled to face the hard questions about possible technology failures and to plan realistically for prospective crises or emergencies? A conservative approach would be to encourage the White House, federal departments, and regulatory agencies to interpret a number of existing requirements for risk assessment in technology development to include institutional assessment in technology-related programs. The statutory language of TSCA, the Outer Continental Shelf Lands Act, the Occupational Safety and Health Act, and several other federal laws would seem to permit institutional risk analysis under broadly defined risk assessment requirements already incumbent upon implementing agencies. Even President Reagan's Executive Order 12291 urges federal agencies to use a "regulatory impact analysis" in deciding whether to adopt new regulations or to revise older ones; this analysis is to include an "evaluation of effects that cannot be quantified in monetary terms" —language sufficiently ambiguous to permit institutional impact analysis in the regulatory process for technology development.

A more incisive but difficult approach would be for the president or Congress to issue a mandate that institutional risk assessment be conducted regularly and uniformly in all federal agencies responsible for the creation, development, or regulation of new technologies. This mandate would demand uniform procedures for assessment, similar to requirements for "environmental impact statements" filed by federal agencies under the National Environmental Policy Act (NEPA) of 1970.[26] A variety of other possible strategies for encouraging institutional risk assessment have been explored as well. In the end, the most serious obstacle to the development of better institutional impact assessment for federally managed technologies remains political feasibility. Given the enormous political costs, there is unlikely to be a political push or a public clamor for such assessment in the absence of some arresting crisis pointing to the need for better institutional planning of government-funded technologies.

Restoring a Global Perspective

During the 1980s the United States has gradually abandoned its once strong and dependable commitment to a variety of international environmental programs whose vitality is essential for the nation's own ecological welfare. Indifference, if not hostility, toward international strategies of environmental management has become pervasive in federal environmental planning. This retreat from global environmentalism reflects less hostility than indifference from the Reagan White House, less a comprehensive strategy than a series of ad hoc decisions by administration officials lacking any sense of urgency about the international environment. The result, however, has been a major policy change. "The generally negative appearance of the Reagan administration toward international environmental cooperation was extraordinary," observes Lynton Caldwell, "not only for its frequent reversal of well-established positions, but equally for its erratic character and the lack of any significant advantage to be gained thereby for the nation or the administration." [27]

A Pervasive Attitude

Few national or international environmental programs under the administrative direction of the Reagan administration have survived without some significant cutbacks in funding, personnel, or priority since 1980. This pervasive decline in international programs can be attributed to several factors. One is the president's own lack of information or interest in most environmental issues. Another is the Reagan administration's general belief that global environmental problems, like national ones, usually can be attacked more effectively through reliance upon market forces and private enterprise rather than through elaborate national or international governmental arrangements. In this spirit, spokesmen for the administration exhorted delegates to the second United Nations' Conference on the World Environment meeting in 1982 to "take advantage of national corrective measures that can work through market forces, if governments allow them to operate" and to "place more reliance on private enterprise." The administration also nourished a strong distrust of most international organizations, which it perceived to be dominated by Third World or Marxist nations hostile to the United States and surviving upon large infusions of U.S. economic support. Many environmentalists also asserted that the administration opposed many international environmental programs, such as restrictions on the export of hazardous substances, because they interfere with the free conduct of American business abroad.

This attitude departed significantly from the general trend of international environmental policy during the 1970s and particularly from the strong international environmentalism of the Carter administration. Evidence of the changes appeared early in the Reagan years. The administration proposed to reduce U.S. support for the United Nations' Environmental Program by more than 70 percent, although Congress later restored a substantial portion of the eliminated funding. The international activities of the Council on Environmental Quality (CEQ) were virtually eliminated by other administration budget cutbacks. The administration also proposed to eliminate funding for the World Heritage Convention to protect areas of unique natural importance and did eliminate U.S. support for the United Nations' Man and the Biosphere Program. Perhaps most symbolic to environmentalists, the United States failed to sign the third United Nations' Law of the Sea Conference agreement largely because the United States objected to international control of deep sea mining. Administration spokesmen also made known their strong disapproval of the *Global 2000 Report* on world environmental trends produced under the Carter administration by the CEQ, the State Department, and other federal agencies. While the report's warning of imminent and severe global environmental problems had been debated by experts, the administration generally encouraged the critics and lent its own resources to refuting the conclusions. Among the international programs falling under the pall of indifference, those dealing with acid precipitation and the export of hazardous substances were particularly notable because they addressed environmental issues of immediate importance to the United States itself.

Acid Precipitation

No international environmental issue generated more pressure for action upon the Reagan administration than did acid precipitation. Studies by the National Academy of Sciences, a federal interagency task force, and by the White House's own staff, all released in the early 1980s, urged immediate federal action to reduce national sulfur oxide and nitrogen oxide emissions contributing to the problem. Under the Carter administration, the EPA had taken an official position that national coal-combustion emissions were the major source of the problem and should be reduced. On the eve of Ronald Reagan's election victory, the United States had signed a memorandum of agreement with the Canadian government pledging both nations to take measures reducing pollution from coal burning facilities in both countries—actions considered extremely urgent by the Canadians.

During its first three-and-a-half years in office, however, the Reagan administration steadfastly resisted any proposals to place controls on industrial or utility stack emissions. This was evident early in the administration's opposition to the Clean Air Act Amendments intended to strengthen such controls and later in its 1982 reduction of EPA funding for acid precipitation research. The administration, arguing that the scientific evidence pointing to the causes and sources of acid precipitation was still inconclusive, yielded only slightly when confronted with new scientific reports, growing Canadian ire, and increased congressional pressure for more incisive action.

In late 1983 EPA's newly appointed administrator William Ruckelshaus proposed to the president and his advisers an experimental program requiring the reduction of sulfur and nitrogen oxide emissions from selected industries and utilities in four to six midwestern states—a program estimated to cost between $1.5 billion and $2.5 billion and to re-move about 3 million tons of sulfur oxide emissions yearly. Although small in comparison with the estimated costs of a comprehensive acid precipitation control program, the White House considered the proposal prohibitively expensive and premature. Instead, the administration pro-posed to double federal funding for research and monitoring on acid precipitation, asserting that scientific data were still insufficient to justify a regulatory program. Environmentalists widely regarded the acid precipitation proposal as a test of Ruckelshaus's ability to move the administration toward more environmentally constructive programs and his failure as proof that the administration was still resolutely hostile to environmental values. Many saw in the acid precipitation issue a portent of more angry confrontations with the White House if Reagan were elected to a second term.

Controlling Trade in Hazardous Substances

As one of his last public acts, President Carter issued on January 15, 1981, Executive Order 12264, restricting the export of dangerous or toxic substances and requiring the vendors to notify receiving nations of the risks associated with specific hazardous products. One of President Reagan's first public actions, less than a month later, was to rescind that executive order. Carter's action was the culmination of more than two years' consultation between his administration, Congress, and a special interagency task force studying the export problem. Though belated, his executive order represented a strongly held conviction that the export of hazardous substances constituted a major international problem. The rapidity with which Carter's action was repudiated was the first of many indications that the Reagan administration held very different opinions.

International trade in hazardous substances has become a domestic issue because current federal law permits domestic firms to ship freely abroad a great variety of hazardous or toxic substances whose use has been suspended or cancelled within the United States. Accurate data on the volume of these shipments are elusive, but fragmentary evidence suggests that large quantities are often involved. Although most domestic uses of DDT have been banned since 1972, for example, an estimated 40 million pounds of the pesticide are still exported annually. Other heavily controlled pesticides widely exported from the United States include aldrin, endrin, chlordane, heptachlor, and strobane. The sometimes tragic consequences of this export trade are suggested by the CEQ:

The powerful and hazardous pesticide Leptophos was manufactured (quite legally) for export only, with no requirements for U.S. approval or notice to importing countries that the product was not approved for use in the United States. . . . Illness in a number of farmers as well as death of more than 1,000 animals in Egypt were attributed to the use of Leptophos there between 1971 and 1976. Workers in the Leptophos manufacturing plant in Bayport, Texas, became seriously ill after exposure to the chemicals in the pesticide, and manufacture was eventually stopped. Meanwhile, Leptophos had been exported to more than 30 countries.[28]

The export of hazardous substances often ends with their return as residues on imported food destined for the U.S. consumer. A minuscule portion of imported food is routinely inspected in the United States for hazardous contaminants—the Food and Drug Administration inspects less than 1 percent of the imports within its jurisdiction. Thus, exported pesticides are almost destined to return to their makers in one form or another. Almost half the green coffee beans imported into the United States from South America, Asia, and Africa, for instance, have been found to contain illegally high residues of carcinogenic pesticides such as DDT, BHC, dieldrin, and heptachlor. No accurate data exist concerning the volume of these imported hazards or the extent of public exposure to them, but fragmentary evidence suggest the magnitude of exposure is significant.

While Congress has attempted in recent years to strengthen controls on the export of these hazardous substances, no uniform federal policy exists. In particular, studies of the export problem under the Carter administration suggested that a need exists for more uniform notification by the United States to governments of importing countries that hazardous products are being shipped to them, for uniform labelling of hazardous exports, and for some restriction or ban on especially dangerous materials destined to populations particularly vulnerable to harm from them. Currently, the patchwork of federal regulations affecting hazardous exports creates a variety of loopholes through which dangerous substances may pass.

TSCA permits the EPA to regulate substances intended for export in cases where the substance can be shown to constitute "an unreasonable risk of injury to health within the United States or to the environment of the United States," but the law does not define unreasonable risk. Otherwise, TSCA contains no restrictions on substances, mixtures, or articles manufactured for export and so labelled.

> The Federal Insecticide, Fungicide and Rodenticide Act (FIFRA) was amended in 1978 to require that pesticides intended for export must be labelled in a manner similar to those used domestically. Pesticides banned for use in the United States must contain the warning "Not registered for use in the United States of America," and recipients must sign a statement acknowledging such notification. However, FIFRA does not otherwise restrict the export of substances so labelled.

> The Food and Drug Administration is required to approve for export drugs approved for U.S. use without special requirements, even if misbranded or adulterated, provided they are labelled "for export only" and meet the requirements of the foreign government.[29]

These loopholes might be less serious if the recipients were well informed and trained in the proper use of hazardous materials. However, pesticides and other hazardous chemicals are often used improperly by recipients who may not understand or may ignore deliberately proper control procedures. Moreover, many of these substances involve significant human and ecological risks even when "properly" used. Further, the demand for U.S. pesticides abroad is driven by insistent needs in many developing countries to increase food production enormously. Under such production pressures, foreign governments may define the risks and benefits of hazardous substances quite differently than would domestic users; they may tolerate many risks that would be considered intolerable domestically in the interest of rapidly increased agricultural production.

A variety of international organizations including the Organization for Economic Cooperation and Development (OECD), the World Health Organization, and the United Nations' Environmental Program have proposed treaties strengthening labelling requirements for hazardous substances and encouraging the ban on exports of chemicals posing unusually great ecological and health risks. While recognizing the complexity of the issues and the need to permit importing nations to make their own decisions about hazardous imports, virtually all such proposals acknowledge the inadequacy of present U.S. export controls for hazardous materials. It was against this background of concern that the Carter administration's belated effort to strengthen controls evolved.

The Reagan administration's revocation of President Carter's executive order was the first of several measures indicating that it intended to reverse, if possible, the direction of export controls evolving in the latter 1970s. In January 1983 the United States cast the lone dissenting vote in the United Nations' General Assembly on a proposal to create an international treaty regulating global trade in hazardous materials. The

United States has shown a similar aversion to proposals by the OECD, a group of industrialized western nations, to regulate the export of hazardous materials from Europe. The export issue has vanished from the public environmental agenda; the most recent issues of the CEQ's annual report no longer contain any references to hazardous exports. The Reagan administration has taken no significant international initiatives to improve controls on the trade of hazardous materials and shows no inclination to do so. This has been based primarily upon a conviction that it was inappropriate for the United States to force upon other nations its own views regarding what substances should be used by them for domestic purposes. Strengthening this conviction is the administration's continuing belief that most international treaties on chemical exports would be controlled by nations hostile to the interests of the United States.

The Reagan administration's resolute refusal to assume leadership in efforts to control the global proliferation of hazardous chemicals, whatever its motivation, occurs at a time when the global scale of diffusion and danger associated with hazardous substances is just beginning to be documented and the cumulative risks to be fully appreciated. While the regulatory issues are complex and a comprehensive national policy will take considerable time to achieve, opportunities exist to begin to move toward a more prudent national trade policy for hazardous substances. The failure to act amounts to a willful decision to inflict upon succeeding generations yet another chemical plague of global proportions.

Continuity and Change in the 1980s

Looking at the magnitude of the environmental ills the nation faces, it should be obvious that environmental decades are no solution. Restoring the nation's magnificent heritage and preserving it for future generations will require years, if not centuries. It should be abundantly clear that there are no "quick fixes," either institutionally or technologically, that will substitute for decades of committed, patient, and educated governmental efforts at environmental restoration. The 1980s are significant especially because during this decade the nation's environmental commitments will be tested, its capacity to sustain the environmental ethic measured, its ability to innovate in the face of new ecological challenges assessed.

This chapter suggests that this testing of governmental commitments will take several forms. First, it seems apparent that institutional reforms should be made in response to a decade's experience in environmental management. There should be evidence of a governmental learning curve in reform of the EPA to ensure it greater regulatory freedom from the political manipulation that afflicted it in the early 1980s. There also should be greater sensitivity to planning the institutional means of controlling new technologies lest severe environmental risks, such as those experienced with nuclear power, be replicated through new failures of institutional controls. In only its second decade, the environmental movement also must avoid the ideological rigidness and programmatic dogmatism that prevents it from receiving new ideas and profiting from its own critics. One small but significant test of this flexibility is the capacity of environmental advocates to adopt, when possible, economic incentives to encourage private compliance with environmental regulation. In an important sense, these reforms reflect the capacity of government and environmental leaders to learn from experience and mistakes and to maintain a healthy resiliency essential to prudent environmental planning for the future.

This decade also will involve a testing of this nation's global environmental vision, its capacity to see its own environmental problems in the realistic context of a world ecosystem and to take responsible initiatives to control world ecological ills. Unfortunately, we have observed that such global sensitivity—a recognition, in essence, that the ecosystem is after all global—seems to have atrophied in federal governmental planning. This failure to come to terms with the need for sustained global efforts at environmental restoration in which the United States assumes a major role remains one of the most ominous aspects of the 1980s.

There will be no other future than that we fashion for ourselves. Ultimately, environmentalism is a determination to protect this beautiful and defiled world for another generation. It is a faith, yet to be justified, that we can develop collectively an ecological conscience and an environmental ethic. It is the hope from which books such as this are written and upon which our children will depend for a decent world.

Notes

1. The arguments are usefully summarized in Allen V. Kneese and Charles L. Schultze, *Pollution, Prices and Public Policy* (Washington, D.C.: The Brookings Institution, 1975).

2. Eugene Bardach and Robert A. Kagan, *Going by the Book: The Problem of Regulatory Unreasonableness* (Philadelphia: Temple University Press, 1982), 26.
3. Ibid., 28.
4. Lawrence Mosher, "The Clean Air That You're Breathing May Cost Hundreds of Billions of Dollars," *National Journal*, October 10, 1981, 1811-1820.
5. Paul Johnson, "The Perils of Risk Avoidance," *Regulation*, May/June 1980, 17.
6. Stephen Kelman, "Cost-Benefit Analysis: An Ethical Critique," *Regulation*, January/February 1981, 39.
7. One of the few careful studies of this issue may be found in Christopher J. Duerksen, "Industrial Siting: An Environmental Perspective," *Environmental Forum*, vol. 2, no. 7 (November 1983) and vol. 2, no. 8 (December 1983).
8. *New York Times*, January 11, 1981.
9. *New York Times*, November 20, 1980.
10. See Henry M. Peskin, "Environmental Policy and the Distribution of Benefits and Costs," in *Current Issues in U.S. Environmental Policy*, ed. Paul R. Portney (Baltimore: Johns Hopkins University Press, 1978), 144-163.
11. Kneese and Schultze, *Pollution, Prices and Public Policy*, 117.
12. *National Journal*, May 30, 1981.
13. Ibid.
14. U.S. General Accounting Office, "A Market Approach to Air Pollution Control Could Reduce Compliance Costs Without Jeopardizing Clean Air Goals," Report No. PAD-82-15 (March 23, 1982), 16.
15. Jerome W. Milliman, "Can Water Pollution Policy Be Efficient?" *Cato Journal*, vol. 2, no. 1 (Spring 1982): 165-196.
16. See Clean Air Act, section 113(a).
17. Kneese and Schultze, *Pollution, Prices and Public Policy*, 116.
18. Walter A. Rosenbaum, "Public Participation and Hazardous Waste Management," in *The Politics of Hazardous Waste Regulation*, ed. James P. Lester and Ann O'M. Bowman (Durham, N.C.: Duke University Press, 1984), 176-195.
19. Richard P. Nathan, *The Administrative Presidency* (New York: John Wiley and Sons, 1983), chapter 1.
20. Cited in Conservation Foundation, *The State of the Environment 1982* (Washington, D.C.: Conservation Foundation, 1983), 410.
21. *New York Times*, September 12, 1982.
22. Mitchell Rogovin, *Three Mile Island: A Report to the Commission and to the Public*, vol. I (Washington, D.C.: Government Printing Office, 1980), 89.
23. U.S. General Accounting Office, *Status of Efforts to Clean Up the Shut-Down Western New York Nuclear Service Center*, Report No. EMD 80-69 (June 6, 1980), 15.
24. U.S. General Accounting Office, *Cleaning Up Nuclear Facilities—An Aggressive and Unified Federal Program Is Needed*, Report No. GAO/EMD-82-40 (May 25, 1982), ii.
25. D. L. Bazelon, "Risk and Responsibility," *Science*, July 20, 1979, 279.
26. Walter A. Rosenbaum, "Hidden Risks in Risk Assessment: The Problem of Technology's Institutional Impacts," in *The Politics of Risk Assessment*, ed. Susan Hadden (New York: Kennicat Press, 1984).

27. Lynton K. Caldwell, "The World Environment: Reversing U.S. Policy Commitments," in *Environmental Policy in the 1980s*, ed. Norman J. Vig and Michael E. Kraft (Washington, D.C.: CQ Press, 1984), 320.
28. Council on Environmental Quality (CEQ), *Environmental Quality 1979* (Washington, D.C.: Government Printing Office, 1980), 240.
29. Ibid., 240-245.

Suggested Readings

Bardach, Eugene, and Robert A. Kagan, eds. *Social Regulation: Strategies for Reform.* New Brunswick, N.J.: Transaction Books, 1982.

Bupp, Irvin C., and Jean-Claude Derian. *The Failed Promise of Nuclear Power.* New York: Basic Books, 1981.

Congressional Quarterly, *The Battle for Natural Resources.* Washington, D.C.: Congressional Quarterly, 1983.

Congressional Quarterly, *Environment and Health.* Washington, D.C.: Congressional Quarterly, 1981.

Council on Environmental Quality. *Environmental Quality.* Washington, D.C.: Government Printing Office, issued annually.

Culhane, Paul J. *Public Land Politics: Interest Group Influence on the Forest Service and the Bureau of Land Management.* Washington, D.C.: Johns Hopkins University Press, 1981.

Darmstadter, Joel, Hans H. Landsberg, and Herbert C. Morton. *Energy Today and Tomorrow.* Englewood Cliffs, N.J.: Prentice-Hall, 1983.

Doniger, David D. *The Law and Policy of Toxic Substances Control.* Baltimore: Johns Hopkins University Press, 1978.

Dunlap, Thomas R. *DDT: Scientists, Citizens and Public Policy.* Princeton, N.J.: Princeton University Press, 1981.

Kneese, Allen V., and Charles L. Schultze. *Pollution, Prices and Public Policy.* Washington, D.C.: Brookings Institution, 1980.

Lowrence, William W. *Of Acceptable Risk.* Los Altos, Calif.: William Kaufmann, 1976.

Portney, Paul R., ed. *Current Issues in U.S. Environmental Policy.* Baltimore: Johns Hopkins University Press, 1980.

Schell, Jonathan. *The Fate of the Earth.* New York: Knopf, 1982.

Stobaugh, Robert, and Daniel Yergin. *Energy Future,* 3d ed. New York: Vintage Books, 1983.

Vig, Norman J., and Michael Kraft. *Environmental Policy in the 1980s.* Washington, D.C.: CQ Press, 1984.

Index